NORBERT ELIAS'S LOST RESEARCH

Rethinking Classical Sociology

Series Editor: David Chalcraft, University of Sheffield, UK

This series is designed to capture, reflect and promote the major changes that are occurring in the burgeoning field of classical sociology. The series publishes monographs, texts and reference volumes that critically engage with the established figures in classical sociology as well as encouraging examination of thinkers and texts from within the ever-widening canon of classical sociology. Engagement derives from theoretical and substantive advances within sociology and involves critical dialogue between contemporary and classical positions. The series reflects new interests and concerns including feminist perspectives, linguistic and cultural turns, the history of the discipline, the biographical and cultural milieux of texts, authors and interpreters, and the interfaces between the sociological imagination and other discourses including science, anthropology, history, theology and literature.

The series offers fresh readings and insights that will ensure the continued relevance of the classical sociological imagination in contemporary work and maintain the highest standards of scholarship and enquiry in this developing area of research.

Also in the series:

Affectivity and the Social Bond
Transcendence, Economy and Violence in French Social Theory
Tiina Arppe
ISBN 978-1-4094-3182-4

The Social Thought of Talcott Parsons
Methodology and American Ethos
Uta Gerhardt
ISBN 978-1-4094-2767-4

Transatlantic Voyages and Sociology
The Migration and Development of Ideas
Edited by Cherry Schrecker
ISBN 978-0-7546-7617-1

For more information on this series, please visit www.ashgate.com

Norbert Elias's Lost Research
Revisiting the Young Worker Project

JOHN GOODWIN and HENRIETTA O'CONNOR
University of Leicester, UK

Routledge
Taylor & Francis Group

LONDON AND NEW YORK

First published 2015 by Ashgate Publishing

2 Park Square, Milton Park, Abingdon, Oxfordshire OX14 4RN
52 Vanderbilt Avenue, New York, NY 10017

Routledge is an imprint of the Taylor & Francis Group, an informa business

First issued in paperback 2020

British Library Cataloguing in Publication Data
A catalogue record for this book is available from the British Library

The Library of Congress has cataloged the printed edition as follows:
Goodwin, John, 1970–
  Norbert Elias's lost research : revisiting the young worker project / by John Goodwin and Henrietta O'Connor.
     pages cm. – (Rethinking classical sociology)
  Includes bibliographical references and index.
  ISBN 978-1-4094-0466-8 (hardback)
1. Elias, Norbert, 1897–1990. 2. Youth – Employment
– Great Britain – Longitudinal studies. 3. Dropouts – Employment – Great Britain –
Longitudinal studies. 4. Dropouts – Great Britain – Social conditions – Longitudinal
studies. 5. Working class – Great Britain – Longitudinal studies. 6. Sociology – Research
– Great Britain. I. O'Connor, Henrietta. II. Title.
  HD6276.G7G645 2015
  331.3'470941—dc23

                                                                                    2015008816

ISBN 978-1-4094-0466-8 (hbk)
ISBN 978-0-367-59836-5 (pbk)

Contents

Contents

List of Tables, Figures and Appendices

Tables

Figures

Appendices

About the Authors

John Goodwin is Professor of Sociology at the University of Leicester. He was previously the head of the Centre for Labour Market Studies (2006–2010), and sub-dean (2003–2006) and the first academic director of the College of Social Science (2009–2010) at the University of Leicester. As a sociologist his principal research interests include the broad areas of the sociology of work (especially education to work transitions and gender and work), social science research methods (life histories, work narratives, (auto)biography, the re-use of qualitative secondary analysis and archival data) and the history of sociology. He has considerable expertise in qualitative research methods and he is currently undertaking restudies of the classic community studies *The Established and The Outsiders* (Elias and Scotson 1965) and *Homes in High Flats* (Jephcott 1971). He is currently associate editor of the *Journal of Youth Studies* and an editorial board member of *Education and Training*, and the *European Journal of Industrial Training*. He was previously a member of the editorial boards for *Work Employment and Society* (2002–2005) and *Sociological Research Online* (2008–2010). In 2013 he was made a senior fellow of the Higher Education Academy.

Henrietta O'Connor is Professor of Sociology at the University of Leicester. She has held a number of roles including head of department of the Centre for Labour Market Studies and deputy head of the School of Management. Previously she held posts as sub-dean of graduate studies and director of postgraduate research in the College of Social Science.

Her principal interests include the broad areas of the sociology of work with a focus on transitions, gender and motherhood. She has carried out research and published widely in aspects of transition such as young people's transition from school to work and is currently researching aspects of the graduate labour market.

Henrietta also has expertise in social science research methods; for example, online research methods and the use of virtual interviews. Her current work is based around the secondary analysis of qualitative data, archival research and the use of fieldnotes and marginalia, qualitative longitudinal research and community restudies.

She is an editorial board member of the British Sociological Association journal *Sociology* (2012–2015), and an editorial board member of the *Journal of Youth Studies*. She is chair of the editorial board of *Sociological Research Online*.

Preface

We have been engaged in a restudy of Elias's *Adjustment of Young Workers to Work Situations and Adult Roles* project since 2000, and although we have already written a great deal, this research is very much still ongoing. The reason for this is that Elias's approach to researching young workers, the complex research design constructed (as we shall see) under difficult circumstances, and the sheer wealth of materials surrounding the project means that, in many respects, we have still only scratched the surface. It is always problematic to speculate but given the breadth and depth of materials amassed by the research team, and if the project had been completed, Elias would have written a substantive text that both extended some of the themes he developed in *On the Process of Civilisation* and offered a definitive contribution to understanding the adjustment that young people make during the process of becoming adults. Without wanting to sound clichéd, for us the project has been a genuine 'journey of discovery' with us becoming exposed to a wide range of authors researching youth in the 1960s who have now been forgotten as well as gaining a deeper appreciation of the full majesty of Elias's writings. However, this has not been an 'unaccompanied' journey and we have many to thank – not least the Economic and Social Research Council (grant R000223653), the University of Leicester Research Committee (grant FS14002) and the University of Leicester College of Social Science Research Development Fund (2010 and 2011) for funding our research. We are grateful to the staff at the Deutsches Literaturarchiv, Marbach, and to our friends and colleagues at the Norbert Elias Foundation for allowing us to quote Elias's archived papers. We would also like to thank colleagues at the UK National Archives, the Archives of the London School of Economics, and to Moira Rankin at the University of Glasgow Archives for support in accessing papers on Norbert Elias, Ilya Neustadt and Pearl Jephcott. Special thanks must go to David Ashton, David Field, Eric Dunning, Stephen Mennell, Chris Rojek and Johnny Sung. We are very grateful to Teresa Keil and to the late Richard Brown who were both generous in spirit and in deed. Teresa Keil's archived papers were invaluable in the early stages of the research. We must also thank the past members of the Leicester Sociology Department, who were interviewed at various points throughout the research, the fieldworkers and, not forgetting, the young worker respondents themselves. We must thank and acknowledge our huge debt to Jason Hughes. We have learnt a great deal about Elias from Jason and his unstinting support has been tremendous. We are grateful to Réka Plugor for her help with proofreading the formatting of the tables and to Neil Jordan and Lianne Sherlock of Ashgate for their *considerable* patience. We are also grateful to Amy Jane Barnes for proofreading the text. Any final errors or omissions remain our own.

Unavoidably, given that we have been working on this research for such a long time, this book draws upon some of our earlier writings. In particular: In the Introduction we draw upon debates contained within 'Utilising Data from a Lost Sociological Project: Experiences, Insights, Promises,' *Qualitative Research*, 10(3), June 2010 (DOI: 10.1177/1468794110362875), by SAGE Publications. All rights reserved. ©; Chapters 1 and 2 draw upon material from our paper 'Norbert Elias and the Young Worker Project' and an earlier unpublished version of that paper. The final, definitive version of this paper was published in the *Journal of Youth Studies*, 9(2), May 2006 (DOI: 10.1080/13676260600635623), by Routledge – Taylor and Francis Group, All rights reserved. ©; Chapter 5 is based on our paper 'She Wants To Be Like Her Mum' The final, definitive version of this paper has been published in the *Journal of Education and Work*, 17(1), February 2004 (10.1080/1363908042000174219), by Routledge – Taylor and Francis Group. All rights reserved. ©; Chapter 6 is based on our paper 'Exploring Complex Transitions: Looking Back at the "Golden Age" of Youth Transitions'. The final, definitive version of this paper has been published in *Sociology*, 39(2), April 2005 (DOI: 10.1177/0038038505050535), by SAGE Publications. All rights reserved. ©; Chapter 7 is based on our paper 'Whatever happened to the young workers? Change and Transformation in 40 Years at Work'. The final, definitive version of this paper has been published in the *Journal of Education and Work*, 22(5), 2009, by Routledge – Taylor and Francis Group. All rights reserved.

Introduction

The origins of this book begin with the 're-discovery', some 40 years after collection, of data that had been 'stored' in an attic office. It transpired that the data was from a 'long lost' sociological project – the *Adjustment of Young Workers to Work Situations and Adult Roles* – originally led by Norbert Elias (better known for books, including *The Civilising Process* and *What is Sociology?*), and carried out at the University of Leicester between 1962 and 1964. Following the re-discovery, the authors were funded by the UK Economic and Social Research Council to re-analyse data from the *Adjustment of Young Workers to Work Situations and Adult Roles* research and to create a new study, by tracing members of the original sample with the aim of examining: i) the adjustment these workers made on first entering the labour market in Leicester in the 1960s; ii) the subsequent adjustments they made to changes in the local labour market and associated structure of opportunities in mid-life; and iii) the ways in which they are currently tackling the approach of retirement in the twenty-first century. In so doing the authors would be able to elaborate on this largely unknown aspect of Elias's work, re-consider school to work transitions made in the past and to subsequently find out what happened to those young people interviewed for the *Adjustment of Young Workers to Work Situations and Adult Roles* project in the early 1960s.

In this book we focus mainly on the first two of these aims by offering a unique account of young people's school to work transitions in the 1960s and a discussion of the leading sociologist Norbert Elias's lost research on youth. Although we include two chapters in the volume that deal with the 'what happened to the young workers' aspect of the research, due to the constraints of space, the follow up interviews will be used as the basis for a separate monograph in the future. Instead here we mainly want to tell the story of the *Adjustment of Young Workers* project and present together, for the first time, a detailed account of transitional experiences of youth in the 1960s. In particular we will:

i. Explore a unique and previously unused dataset of over 850 interviews with school leavers who were aged between 15 and 18 in the early 1960s and present data relating to the lives of the young workers, their experiences of school, work, family, consumption and leisure. Using this data we attempt to address such questions as: how far have the lives of young people and their transitions from school to work changed over the last 50 years?; was there a golden age of school to work transitions in the post-war decades when the baby-boom generation were able to leave school and enter full-time employment with ease?; was this a period when young people were shielded from the hardships of unemployment and student debt?; is the representation of life for school leavers in the 1960s more complicated than suggested?

ii. Using this data and other archived materials, this book gives an account of Norbert Elias's *only* foray into large-scale, publicly funded research. For the very first time this book aims to provide a comprehensive account of the *Adjustment of Young Workers to Work Situations and Adult Roles* project by covering all aspects of the research from the development of the research proposal, the selection and management of the research team, the fieldwork, Elias's theoretical work on the data and the ultimate demise of the research project in late 1964. As the *Adjustment of Young Workers to Work Situations and Adult Roles* project remains an obscure and largely unknown aspect of Norbert Elias's work, this text will make a significant contribution to existing Eliasian texts by introducing this project to a wider audience and by exploring and applying Elias's theoretical work to the areas of youth and school to work transitions.

In the remainder of this introductory chapter and before providing an overview of the rest of the book, we provide an account of our 'research journey' and how it came to be that we re-examined the *Adjustment of Young Workers to Work Situations and Adult Roles* project. We also consider the value of such historical data and the benefits of going back to examine past studies for the enhanced understanding. We also outline our general approach to the subsequent restudy.

Our 'Research Journey'

C. Wright Mills (1959) identifies a key location for the generation of research problems as being within the 'personal troubles' and within 'public issues', or more precisely the intersections of biography and history. He writes:

> Know that many personal troubles cannot be solved merely as troubles, but must be understood in terms of public issues – and in terms of the problems of history … Know that the problems of social science, when adequately formulated, must include both troubles and issues, both biography and history, and the range of their intricate relations. (Mills 1959: 226)

Following Mills, in the late 1990s our biographies intersected with the 'troubles and issues' associated with restudying a lost sociological research project. After earlier careers writing on, and around, employment, work and gender (see, for example, Goodwin 1997; 1999; 2002; Goodwin et al. 1999) or Irish migration, parenting and internet-based research methods (see, for example, King and O'Connor 1996; O'Connor and Madge 2001), our 'academic biographies' collided with the biographies of our peers of some 40 years previous and their personal/academic/

research-based troubles and concerns. The collision was all encompassing and we would never have imagined, or predicted, the research journey ahead. When the seemingly discarded interview booklets, from the *Adjustment of Young Workers to Work Situations and Adult Roles* project, were picked up from the floor of an attic office at 103 Princess Road East, Leicester, they changed our research direction and academic biographies forever.

These booklets (see Appendix 1) had followed David Ashton[1] around since the mid-1970s and came to be stored in the attic office of what was to be the first permanent home of the Centre for Labour Market Studies (see Dunning and Hughes 2013). At some point it was clear that the large box, in which the interview schedules were contained, had split and the booklets had variously come to be spread across the floor, the shelving and the unused desks. Their yellow covers so distinctive and so evocative of research from another era marked these interview schedules out from the other papers in the attic office room. It was clear they were 'something different'. The process of re-shelving, arranging and organising the booklets was interspersed with many hours of reading their contents and, gradually, the rich detailed descriptions of young peoples' lives in Leicester, during the early 1960s that they contained, were revealed. The interview booklets comprised vivid and comprehensive descriptions of working lives, of jobs held and companies worked for. They recorded the minutiae of family relationships, leisure pursuits, workplace relationships and education and training experiences and detailed, in many respects, the hopes and concerns of the 1960s' generation of youth. For children of the late 1960s and early 1970s these interview schedules contained much that was familiar. The booklets also contained 'academic clues' – the recognisable handwriting of a previous university lecturer (Teresa Keil[2] supervised Goodwin's undergraduate thesis at Loughborough University), the initials of past members of the Leicester Sociology Department and so forth. Perhaps what was most striking of all were the interviewer notes at the back of the booklets. These contained, as we shall see, detailed accounts of the realities of social research, the problems of undertaking interviews in the field, as well as countless observations (not all positive) the interviewers made in relation to the respondents and their families. In some respects the interviewer notes were the most appealing aspect of the data because of the 'high definition' insights they offered into the realities of the lives of the respondents and their families but also because of the forthright nature in which the interview process is described. For example:

---

1 Professor David Ashton, after brief spells in industry and at the University of Reading, was a lecturer, senior lecturer then professor in the Department of Sociology, University of Leicester from the late 1960s to the late 1980s. He went on to found the Centre for Labour Market Studies at Leicester in the 1990s – a highly successful multidisciplinary research centre focusing on skills, training and employment.

2 E. Teresa Keil worked at the University of Leicester between 1962 and 1964. She later went on to sociology in the Department of Social Sciences, Loughborough University, as well as serving as head of department for social sciences at Loughborough University.

This was an interesting interview to which I have probably not done justice because of the conditions under which it was conducted. The boy and myself sat in the corner of the living room which was occupied by 6 other adults all carrying on conversation with each other and a young baby was being bathed and crying in the centre of the room. A large corner of the room was made into a cage housing a monkey, and a cat and a dog were wandering around. A TV set blared forth all the time. [The respondent], who was pleasant, friendly and eager to tell everything about his working life talked rapidly and I found it difficult both to hear him and at the same time to pick out the important points of his conversation. In consequence I have missed some of the details of his present job … [mother's] comments indicated the control of the father had over the family – i.e. when [respondent] asked his mother if he could be interviewed, "You must ask your father you know he is the boss of this house". [The respondent] isn't allowed to mix with people around here … Several times [the respondent] referred to his love of heights i.e. climbing high ladders in his first job, erecting high wires in his second job. At work his problem is finding a suitable job into which he could be apprenticed and finally become [a] skilled worker. In manner he was extremely polite, well spoken and well dressed and appeared more suitable to being a wine waiter than to doing a manual job. The Home – pre-war, non-parlour Council house packed with well-worn furniture, some of it very battered. Two lines of clean washing strung across room. The baby belonged to married sister, a pale quiet girl who looked very young (age 17).

Immediately, based on the detailed and complex richness of 'everyday life' portrayed in these interview notes, one is transported to that boisterous living room, with the television blaring out, the noise of the adults there, the menagerie of animals (some caged, some free to wander), the patriarchal father and subservient mother, the teenage mother and all this *before* we find out anything of the details relating to the actual respondent's experiences of education, work and the transition to adulthood. The depicted scene could have be taken directly from any one of the British 'kitchen sink' dramas of the 1960s – John Braine's *Room at the Top* (1959); Alan Sillitoe's *Saturday Night, Sunday Morning* (1960); Shelagh Delaney's *A Taste of Honey* (1961); or Lindsay Anderson's *This Sporting Life* (1963) – perhaps. Furthermore, the interviewer comments could be linked directly to the personal information about the respondent, included at the front of the interview schedule, thus conveying everything we could possibly want to know about the respondents – their names, date of birth, the schools they attended, where they lived through to their employment experiences, their family composition, housing transitions and so forth. Needless to say, given the combination of richly detailed interviewer notes and accurate biographical information, underpinned by our initial readings of interviews themselves, these discarded interview booklets contained such material as to stimulate and inspire, not only a strong desire to find out what happened subsequently to the young people who were interviewed in the 1960s but also to find out more about the original research itself and those involved. We wanted to answer such questions such as:

i.   What were the initial aims of the research?
ii. What research questions were being explored?
iii. How was the research funded and organised?
iv. Who was the research team?
v.   Who collected this richly detailed and complex data?
vi. How could the data be re-used?
vii. What could the data tells us about school to work transitions in the 1960s?
viii. Whatever happened to these young people?

Unfortunately, the interview schedules were not accompanied by any additional material, no supporting documentation nor any explanatory notes. There was limited reference made to this research in writings by or about Elias (see Chapter 1; see also Brown 1987; Mennell 1992; Elias 1994). Initial conversations with David Ashton, starting in the mid-1990s, revealed that the original research was linked to Norbert Elias and to Teresa Keil, Richard Brown,[3] Sheila Allen[4] and others,[5] but that it had had not been successful, that it had been conducted under difficult circumstances and that his later involvement – the use of a few of the interview schedules in Ashton and Field (1976) *Young Workers: From School to Work* – had necessitated a clear acknowledgment to the original research team in the book.[6] Such information was even more intriguing and as such added to the basic questions we wished to explore:

---

3   Richard K. Brown (1933–2007) was 'a major figure in postwar British sociology, who was renowned for his studies of work and workers in industrial settings' (Beynon 2007: 1). After studying in Cambridge, Vienna and at the LSE, Richard was employed at Leicester between 1959 and 1966 initially to work on the married women research project (see Chapter 1). He moved to Durham in 1966 and became a professor in 1982, remaining at Durham until his retirement in 1995. Richard was the founder of the prestigious journal *Work, Employment and Society* and president of the British Sociological Association, 1983–1985.

4   Sheila Allen (1930–2009) after studying at the LSE and spells in Sarawak and the prison service, Sheila worked at Birmingham University and then the University of Leicester before moving to the University of Bradford in 1966, where she directed the *Youth and Work: Differential Ethnic Experience* project. She became the first woman professor at Bradford in 1972 and was a pioneer of women's studies (see Afshar 2009 and Reisz 2009).

5   The research was supported by research assistants Colin Tipton (1962–1963), Bryan Green (1963–1964) and Harry Fawcett (1964–1965). Harry Fawcett also appears to have undertaken fieldwork for the research as part of his second year undergraduate studies at Leicester (see Neustadt 21 July 1964).

6   Footnote 4, page 19, of the *Young Workers* book states: 'Some of the interviews on which this book is based were conducted in the mid-1960s. They were part of a research project carried out in Leicester under the direction of N. Elias. The senior author (Ashton)

i.   Why was the research not referred to in writings by or about Elias?
ii. How did the research relate to the broader canon of Eliasian writings?
iii. What where the difficult circumstances surrounding the research?
iv. Given the existence of the interview schedules, why was it that the research was not 'successful'?
v.   How much of the material had been used by Ashton and Field and how many of the interviews remained 'unanalysed'.

In order to answer these questions, a more immediate problem was where to access materials relating to the research? In the end we located materials via two sources. First, as mentioned above, it just so happened that one of the researcher officers on the project was Teresa Keil who had taught Goodwin at Loughborough in the late 1980s. Fortuitously, and quite by coincidence, while planning how we were to tackle the restudy of the *Adjustment of Young Workers to Work Situations and Adult Roles* project, we literally 'bumped into' Teresa Keil at the British Sociological Association Conference in York, England, in April 2000. We explained our intentions for the research, to which Teresa suggested that she had always known that someone would return to the *Adjustment of Young Workers* research and as such, she had retained her own files. However, she also added that she never expected it to be one of her past students. In subsequent correspondence with us, she explained what she had retained and/or copied:

> When I left Leicester I kept only my own files; all others remained in the Department of Sociology. My own files covered Steering Committee minutes, documents prepared by the research team and miscellaneous correspondence. When I met up with Sheila and Richard we paid particular attention to the Steering Committee minutes file and selected items for photocopying. I did copies for myself too ... (Alas, there are no minutes for the very first meeting of the Steering Committee. The ones here were given to me at the first, informal, meetings in Leicester before I joined the project. Richard was in at the beginning but was not able to find his own file). I have also included other items, including drafts, from the research team file (which overlaps with that of the Steering Committee as you can imagine). I have added ... the draft memorandum written by the researchers on the current position of the project at the point when they were leaving the project. (Teresa Keil 28 June 2000)

---

was associated with the later phases of the project and is indebted to Professor Elias for some of his ideas. The research was carried out by Ms E. T. Keil, Ms C. Riddell, Mr C. Tipton, M B. Green and Mr H. Fawcett. These data have been supplemented by work conducted by ourselves and students at the University of Leicester in recent years'. Ashton also includes an acknowledgment to Elias, and Elias's leadership of the young worker project, in his contribution to David Field's (1974) *Social Psychology for Sociologists*. London: Nelson (see Ashton 1974).

This initial documentation provided a clear introduction to the *Adjustment of Young Workers to Work Situations and Adult Roles* research and, although incomplete, provided a useful starting point on which we could begin the 'detective work' of piecing together the genesis of the project in order that we may be begin to answer our questions.

The second source of documentary evidence relating to the *Adjustment of Young Workers to Work Situations and Adult Roles* project was to be found amongst the archived collection of Norbert Elias's papers at the Deutsches Literaturarchiv, Marbach, Germany.[7] From the inventory to the Elias papers, two files were identified that related to the running of the young worker project and the academic issues that underpinned the research and informed its inception. They are *242 – File concerning a research project on 'the Adjustment of Young Workers to Work Situation and Adult Roles'. 1961–1967, 1969, 1971, 1973* and *243 – File concerning a research project 'From School to Work: Social and Educational Determinants of Job Choice', 1966–1969*. Alongside these files are a further 10 folders labelled 'y-worker' containing additional paperwork, draft papers and various other documents relating to Elias's (and his colleagues') interests in the transition from school to work. A review of the Elias papers held at the archive revealed that Elias had retained much of the materials, documentation and correspondence relating to the project himself, spread across folders specifically relating to the project, correspondence with particular named individuals and his archived papers in relation to his time in Ghana. We collected and collated a substantial amount of archived material comprising around seventy individual documents, including letters, memoranda, meeting minutes, reports and other miscellaneous papers spanning 1961–1973.

As a note of caution, we were aware that using materials from such sources was not unproblematic. Inevitably, while comprehensive, the documentation, correspondence and so forth is incomplete. There are issues around which materials were chosen to be archived and retained and which materials became discarded, misplaced or lost during the last forty or so years. Accuracy also has to be a concern given that some of the materials are minutes of meetings and there is a question as to whether those minutes accurately record the discussions of the time. The 'voice' used in correspondence and the 'audiences' for whom correspondence was originally intended also raise issues of accuracy and representation. Yet, despite these concerns, this material was the 'best we had' to reconstruct the project and illuminate this largely unknown aspect of Elias's work. As such, the archived papers of Elias complimented the materials from the Teresa Keil archive and gave us as complete a picture as it was possible to obtain and,

---

7   The authors were fortunate to visit the Deutsches Literaturarchiv, Germany, and view the archive of Elias papers with the aid of a grant from the University of Leicester Research Fund (Grant number FS14002). We would also like to acknowledge the support of the staff at the Deutsches Literaturarchiv and the Norbert Elias Foundation for their assistance in accessing the papers.

when combined together, offered significant insights into the project and Elias's approach to researching young workers. We were also reassured that such an approach was not without precedence. For example, Laub and Sampson (1993: 1) describe in detail their stumbling across 'dusty cartons of data in the basement of the Harvard Law School Library' relating to both original and follow-up data studies of juvenile delinquency carried out by Sheldon and Eleanor Glueck (see, for example, Laub and Sampson 1993; Glueck and Glueck 1930; 1950). They provide an account of how they had to piece together the data, reconstruct the research processes, as well as the historical and context of the research, from archived materials and once again make accessible something seemingly lost or 'inaccessible to the research community' (Laub and Sampson 1993: 45). Indeed, the similarities between Laub and Sampson's resurrection of the Gluecks's past research work and our own attempts to revive the *Adjustment of Young Workers to Work Situations and Adult Roles* project are clear and there are few other studies where this has been attempted.

The Value and Relevance of 'Historical Data'

For some, the sociological, analytical value of 'going back' to restudy a project undertaken in the 1960s would seem questionable. It is a research project from a different time, a different era. Given that between 'then' and 'now' there has been such tremendous, irreversible and 'all encompassing' change, in all aspects of life, what could data from the 1960s possibly tell us beyond what is already known? This is particularly true when one considers the disciplinary areas of youth studies and youth culture where significant emphasis is placed on the contemporary, the current, the 'modern' in order to show how generations of youth are different from their parents or the generations that have gone before. Indeed, as we shall see later in the book (see Chapter 4) this is even more of a problem when one reviews youth employment literature from the period before the mid-1970s, which is treated conceptually and analytically as a period characterised by a homogeneous, mass experience of easily attainable full time employment for 16–25 year olds. This is an accepted 'given' – a 'golden age' against which all subsequent experiences are measured and compared. Yet what Laub and Sampson (2003), alongside Elias (1987), allude to is the limitations of confining or narrowing the sociological gaze to the present – what Elias termed the retreat of sociologists to the present born out of the concern of sociologists to study and then solve 'the short-term problems of their own society' (Elias 1987: 223–4). For Laub and Sampson (2003), focusing our research 'gaze' only on the present lacks scientific sense. They write:

> Critics whose gaze is limited to the present thus suffer in the end from a lack of scientific sense. Because our focus is on within-individual patterns of stability and change, we must rely on longitudinal data that other investigators began collecting many years ago in order to empirically study various life adaptations

over the long term. There is no other way to proceed. (Laub and Sampson 2003: 284–5)

Yet for anyone with an aspiration to develop more processual oriented questions, such as 'how did this come to be?', a focus *only* on the present is limiting for analysis and, as Laub and Sampson suggest, lacks 'scientific sense'. One of the undoubted strengths of having access to extensive historical data is the opportunity to explore continuities, change and transformations over a significantly longer period of time. As such, we have been able to question widely held views about the employment experience of 1960s youth as a homogenous group who were easily able to find employment on leaving school regardless of whether or not they had left school with qualifications. Similarly, the 1960s data has allowed us to re-examine debates around gender and youth transitions. Much of the existing work around historical youth transitions is based very heavily on the experience of boys entering employment and assumptions were made, in the past, that the transitions made by girls were less important and somehow less interesting, as most would simply work to bide time until they married and had children. The data collected allow us to explore girls' transitions and to show how for many young women, the transition to the labour market was equally important to them as to the young men in the study. Furthermore, we can do this; we can examine those 'within-individual' patterns of continuity and/or variability, without being dependent upon the vagaries of the recall or the ability of the respondents to 'reconstruct' the past 40 to 50 years of their lives. As Richard Brown, one of the original research team, suggested:

> As one of the members of the Steering Committee for the DSIR Young Workers project in the early 1960s, I was very pleased to hear ... that you were hoping to carry out a follow up study based around the interviews from that project, as well as analysing the original data ... There are in my view still too few studies which involve re-interviewing respondents about whom information is already available from an earlier project so as to provide a longitudinal – dimension. Partly, of course, this is because only in recent years has much research of this sort become feasible, and it is important therefore to seize every possibility which does occur. In addition to your analysis of the original data, which will be of historical but not just of historical interest, the research should contribute both to our understanding of how in detail the labour market has changed over 35 or more years, and to the effects of labour market and many other social changes on individual work and life histories. (Richard Brown 6 February 2001)

From Cross Sectional to Qualitative Longitudinal Research: Our Approach to Data 'Re-use'

Despite the analytical potential of the data, two of the challenging aspects of revisiting the *Adjustment of Young Workers to Work Situations and Adult Roles* data proved to be in the practical aspects of transforming hand written data, recorded on old interview schedules, into a usable and manageable form and conceptualising our approach to the data itself. For example, were we engaged in a restudy, re-analysis, secondary analysis or a follow-up study? There seemed little beyond Laub and Sampson to define the enterprise in which we were engaged. Our approach was not a simple 'data re-use' project as the data had never been previously used.[8] Our approach could also have been classified as a restudy but, again, as the data had never been used and we were not planning to recreate the original study, our framework for using this data did not fit with the classic understanding of a restudy. We would suggest, as we have done elsewhere (see O'Connor and Goodwin 2010), that the methodological approach we adopted 'best fits' (although not perfectly) with a qualitative longitudinal research (QLR) design. Qualitative longitudinal research is a combination of approaches but 'unlike simple data reuse, involves the generation of new data and the use of the original research questions. The most significant way that QLR differs from both re-use and restudies is that the research is focussed on the same respondents as the original study' (O'Connor and Goodwin 2010: 285). The original *Adjustment of Young Workers to Work Situations and Adult Roles* project was not designed to be longitudinal but our plans to analyse the original data *and* to trace and re-interview the respondents gave this once cross-sectional study a longitudinal element.

In relation to practical concerns, the rediscovery of 854 original transcripts posed the exciting prospect of how to make best use of the data. We approached the task in a number of different ways. First, we created a digital database of the 854 transcripts. This, in itself, was a huge job as each interview consisted of 85 questions plus a significant amount of additional information in the form of profile data, interviewer notes and additional notes. However, having an electronic version of the data proved to be an invaluable first step. It removed our reliance on the paper copies, it reduced the need to grapple with difficult handwriting each time we read a transcript, and it made the database easily searchable and the data analysable. Second, we catalogued all the correspondence and paperwork relating to the project in date order. We also sought out additional papers from a number of different archives and personal contacts known to have links to the original project. Third, we contacted some of the individuals who were involved in the original project and arranged, where possible, to interview them about their recollections of the project. Fourth, given the fact that we, unusually, had access to key biographical data relating to the respondents, we set about tracing as many of the original respondents as possible through mailshots to the last known address, internet searches, the electoral register and media appeals. Realising that the once young workers were now approaching retirement, the original dataset represented an opportunity to create, retrospectively, a longitudinal study spanning the

---

8   In reality only a relatively small number had been used as source material for Ashton and Field's (1976) *Young Workers* – these were identifiable, as the authors had marked the original interview booklets where an interview had been analysed and used for the book.

work-life course of each individual. In the end, we managed to contact over one hundred of the respondents and successfully re-interviewed 100 of them: 90 men and 10 women.

Structure of the Book

The remainder of the book is structured as follows. In Chapter 1 we examine the origins of the *Adjustment of Young Workers to Work Situations and Adult Roles* project and set it within the institutional context of the Leicester Sociology Department of the 1960s. We consider the reasons why the *Adjustment of Young Workers* project has not featured in the boarder canon of Elias's work whilst also considering the reasons why the original project failed. The focus for Chapter 2 will be Elias's theoretical work on the transition to work and adulthood. Elias suggested that the transition from school to work constituted a 'shock' experience and that young people would experience initial difficulties in adjusting to their new role. He suggested that difficulties would emerge in their relationships with older workers, with family and with their new-found income. Elias also identified the causes of shock such as the dissonance between childhood fantasies about work and adult reality of work. For the first time this book presents a critical account of Elias's 'shock' hypothesis and his thoughts on school to work transitions. It is felt that a full exploration of Elias's model is worthwhile as it adds yet a further dimension to the richness and applicability of his other writing. Also, using the archive materials, we piece together the rationale for the original project, the methodological framework used in the research design and the sample selection. The chapter will also provide an overview of the roles of those working on the project, both those on the project steering committee and the research officers who undertook the fieldwork. The chapter also examines the reasons behind the ultimate failure of the project and locates its decline in the conflict of ideas that emerged between Elias and the research officers. In Chapter 3 we examine the extensive interviewer notes that accompanied the original interview booklets. We suggest that while it is highly unusual for any researcher to have access to field notes written by other researchers, the notes themselves provide fascinating contextual information about the young workers, as well as offering insights into the realities of undertaking social science research in the 1960s. There are very few accounts of what it is actually like to undertake research in the field and so we feel this chapter contributes contribution to the history of social science research. The chapter includes a discussion of numerous themes, including the validity of treating interviewer notes as secondary data and the impact of the researchers' own biases and experiences on the data collection in the context of early debates around reflexivity. We reflect on how the respondents' social class and gender as well as their families, their homes and households were viewed by the interviewers. The data presented in this chapter reveals that social research often differs from textbook accounts of the research process. In the middle section of the book, Chapters 4–6, we consider what the *Adjustment of Young Workers to Work Situations and Adult Roles* project has to tell us about the transition to work in the 1960s for this group of workers. Specifically, in Chapter 4, we consider the transition process in more detail, exploring the extent to which past transitions were linear and straightforward or, perhaps, more complex than the 'golden age' caricature, presented in some of the literature, would suggest. We demonstrate that some of the young people interviewed for *Adjustment of Young Workers to Work Situations and Adult Roles* experienced 'complex transitions' of frequent job moves, periods of unemployment and extended transitions, contrary to popular perceptions of the 1960s as being a time of full employment. In Chapter 5 we outline the gendered experience of the transition to work, highlighting the different career choices and eventual career paths of young women and men in the 1960s. The role of the youth employment officer and family and friends was also very significant in the process of securing first time employment and we consider the influence of this on the young people's decisions about work. This chapter also considers how young people acquired the skills needed to do the job they were employed to do. Chapter 6 provides a consideration of the consumption, leisure and lifestyle activities of the young workers. The interview schedule contained a wealth of detail relating to leisure time and patterns of consumption amongst young people in the early 1960s. The chapter also examines how the young workers spent their leisure time and explores their friendships and relationships. The main themes of the chapter, however, prove a useful contrast to Elias's ideas of work as a mechanism via which young people learn the norms and behaviours of the adult world and that a large number of the young workers remained childlike in their out of work leisure pursuits. In Chapters 7 and 8 we bring the story 'up to date' by considering what happened to the young workers generally and the women in the study in more detail. In so doing we highlight the unscripted complex and problematic life stories of this group of once young workers.

Chapter 1

The 'Young Worker Project': Context and Controversies

Introduction

In this chapter we attempt to locate the *Adjustment of Young Workers to Work Situations and Adult Roles* within the institutional context of the Leicester Sociology Department of the late 1950s and early 1960s, the sociology developed there and within Elias's own biography. We return to some of the questions suggested in the Introduction but do so following Elias's own sociological practice that we feel may prove useful here. In particular his orientation towards sociogenetic questions (see, Goodwin and Hughes 2011: 682), such as *how did 'this' come to be?* Specifically, how did it come to be that Elias, along with other members of the Sociology Department applied for public funding to support a large-scale survey of young people's transitions from education to work and adulthood? How did it come to be that the project not only failed to deliver in its initial promise but also came to be ignored/forgotten amidst Elias's other works? To answer the first question requires some understanding of the departmental environment in which the *Adjustment of Young Workers* project was undertaken – an environment that was central to a rapid expansion in teaching and where the primary function of the Department became to be perceived as a training ground for new sociologists. To answer the second question necessitates an exploration of the disputes and academic differences, which impacted upon the smooth running of the research from the outset. To these ends we begin this chapter with a very brief biographical overview of Elias pre-Leicester, before considering his time at Leicester and in Ghana. We consider the 'research culture' within the Department outlining the research that foregrounded the *Adjustment of Young Workers* project. We then consider why the project has not featured significantly in the Elias auto/biographies and explore the possible reasons why the project ultimately failed to deliver on its promise.

Biographical and Institutional Context: Elias, Sociology and Leicester

Elias's biography, and his time in Leicester, have been extensively documented elsewhere (see, for example, Mennell 1992; Elias 1994; Goodwin and Hughes 2011; Dunning and Hughes 2013; Korte 2013), although the period of time he spent as professor of sociology at the University of Ghana, whilst considered by some, has received much less attention (see Goody 2006; Liston and Mennell 2009). However, a review of these biographical sources informs us that Elias was born in 1897 to a Jewish family in the city of Breslau (once part of Germany but now Wroclaw in Poland). Following a classical German education at school, Elias studied medicine and philosophy at the University of Breslau. He abandoned medicine in 1919 graduating instead, in 1924, with a doctorate in philosophy entitled *Idee und Individuum* on the nature of history and the part played in history by individuals and ideas. In 1925, Elias moved to Heidelberg, with Alfred Weber as his *Habilitation* supervisor, and soon began collaborating with Karl Mannheim. In 1930, Elias then moved to the University of Frankfurt to become Mannheim's assistant to the sociological seminar, a role and salary he shared with Hans Gerth (Kettler et al. 2008), completing his *Habilitationsschrift* in 1933. Elias was attached to the Ecole Normale Supérieure, Paris between 1933 and 1935. Despite speaking little English, during 1935 Elias left France for England, where he spent considerable time in the British Museum writing *The Civilising Process* (*Über den Prozess der Zivilisation*). Between 1939 and 1954 he held various short-term and visiting posts at the London School of Economics (LSE), with the support of Morris Ginsberg and Karl Manheim, the University of Hull and Bedford College, where he taught sociology and social psychology. It was not until 1954, when Elias was appointed as a lecturer in sociology at the University College, Leicester, that he secured his first permanent position at a British university. Joly (2011) reflects on why it took so long for Elias to gain an academic post in Britain:

> All in all, it is not very difficult to understand why Elias obtained an academic post only in 1954. For financial reasons, Universities or University Colleges preferred to appoint Assistant Lecturers rather than an experienced candidates like him. What is more, LSE graduates were privileged (Elias was for example beaten in Leicester in 1952 by Joe Banks, who was aged 32). We should also note that he was appointed *after* other Jewish refugees who had been younger when arriving in Britain, and had therefore been able to go on with studying in Britain or to go back to university in Britain. In fact, we then realise how much Elias's age was a disadvantage to him in comparison to younger refugees who were able to gain a degree from the LSE (like Ilya Neustadt) and to older ones who already had a strong institutional position before exile (like Karl Mannheim). (Joly 2011: 6)

As Joly (2011) suggests, Joe Banks was appointed at Leicester before Elias but when Elias joined University College, Leicester, in 1954, it was actually as a replacement for Joe Banks who was then leaving to take up a position at Liverpool. However, it is clear that despite an emerging track record of teaching sociology at Leicester, sociology was still very much in its infancy within the university when Elias arrived. The origins of sociology at Leicester can be traced back to the appointment of Ilya Neustadt[1] as a lecturer in sociology in the Department of Economics in 1949, where Neustadt taught sociology as part of the London External Degree of BSc (Econ) (Marshall 1982: xii). In 1954, a Department of Sociology was established, with Neustadt as the 'senior lecturer in charge'. Neustadt had previously developed a close friendship with Elias during their time at the London School of Economics (where Neustadt had previously worked in the Russian section of the Library) and he was central to bringing Elias to Leicester (see Joly 2011: Goodwin and Hughes 2011). Indeed, it is clear from their personal correspondence that Neustadt was keen for Elias to come to Leicester as early as 1950, with Neustadt regularly corresponding with Elias about sociology at Leicester. After joining the Department, Elias was central to the development and delivery of the first year course, on 'the development and comparative theories of Comte, Marx, Durkheim and Weber' (Dunning and Hughes 2013: 36), as well as supervising master's and PhD theses. Elias also served as acting head of the Sociology Department between 1957–1958 while Neustadt was on secondment in Ghana and was promoted to reader in 1959. Together, their complementary academic and administrative skills, and their close working relationship, meant that Elias and Neustadt presided over a rapid expansion of the Sociology Department.

Elias's contribution to sociology at Leicester was such that he was offered a 'special post' for the 1962/1963 academic year in lieu of his retirement. However, Elias declined this offer and between 1962 and 1964, he went to take up a chair in sociology and serve as the head of the Sociology Department at University College, Ghana. While in Ghana, Elias saw his role primarily to be concerned with 'the building up of a modern Department of Sociology, adapted to the needs of a developing country' (O'Brien 1963: 1), as well as teaching the first year

---

1   Ilya Neustadt (1915–1993) was born near Odessa, Russia. Escaping the pogroms in Russia with his family, he migrated to Romanian Bessarabia. He completed one year of medical training in Bucharest before moving to Belgium where, in 1939, he obtained a doctorate from the Université Liegé entitled 'Le problème de l'organisation internationale en Europe centrale: 1919–1939'. Following the Nazi invasion of Belgium in 1940, Neustadt fled to London, where his 'technical' Romanian nationality prevented his internment as an enemy alien in wartime Britain. After hearing Harold Laski lecture at the London School of Economics, he applied for admission to the LSE to read for an MA in sociology. Morris Ginsberg sponsored Neustadt, both academically and financially. Neustadt was awarded his second PhD, 'Some Aspects of the Social Structure of Belgium', in 1945. Neustadt then worked variously in the Russian section of the LSE Library, as a research assistant for the Town and Country Planning Association and as an evening lecturer, on Russian social and economic institutions, at Goldsmiths College, University of London. His career then ran as follows: lecturer in sociology, Department of Economics, University of Leicester (1949–1954); senior lecturer, Sociology Department, University of Leicester (1954–1962); professor of sociology and head of department, University College Ghana (1957–1958); professor of sociology, Sociology Department, University of Leicester (1962–1981); dean of social sciences, University of Leicester (1962–1965); head of department, Sociology Department, University of Leicester (1959–1980) (for a fuller biography, see Marshall 1982).

course he had originally developed in Leicester (see Elias 1962d). Elias returned to Leicester in 1964 as a research fellow in sociology and remained in, or around, the Department until his move to the University of Bielefeld in 1978 (see, Mennell 1992; Elias 1994: Dunning and Hughes 2013, for fuller biographical accounts).

Foregrounding the 'Young Worker Project'

The Leicester Sociology Department of the late 1950s and early 1960s is widely credited as being one of the most distinctive, significant and innovative departments in the history of British sociology (see Brown 1987; Kilminster 1987; Banks 1989; Mennell 1992; Rojek 2004; Halsey 2003; Turner 2006; Dunning 2006; Goodwin and Hughes 2011). From their early collaborations, neither Neustadt nor Elias wanted to simply repeat the sociology offered elsewhere, such as at the London School of Economics or at Hull.

For example, a past member of the Department pointed to the difference between Leicester and elsewhere:[2]

> ... you asked me a little while ago what sort of sociologist he [Neustadt] was, when he was asked that sort of question himself, and I've heard him several times, 'what sort of sociology do you teach at Leicester' and his answer was always 'good sociology'. (Respondent 1).

The emphasis on the difference between Leicester sociology and the sociologies of other institutions is also captured in the correspondence between Neustadt and Elias. For example:

> I am increasingly impressed by the fact – even though I say so myself of how few people know what sociology is really about: at the moment, again even if I say so myself, I am prepared to except only you, and myself in some ways!! There are, however, I suppose, a few who have an inkling. I am also impressed by the fact how deep anthropological training distorts and simply creates a blockage and deep-rooted inabilities for <u>sociological</u> analysis. At the other side we have the do-gooders and the social investigators and the pop sociologists, and finally, the downright cynics – these, of course, are the most enraging of all. (Neustadt 30 January 1964)

The apparent dissimilarity of Leicester sociology to elsewhere and the idea that only Neustadt and Elias really understood what sociology was *really* about,

---

2   Goodwin and Hughes, as well offering a figurational analysis of the correspondence between Elias and Neustadt (see Goodwin and Hughes 2011) also interviewed past members of the Leicester Sociology Department to gain their insights into the Department of that time and on their experiences of working with both Neustadt and Elias.

may seem to be arrogant and dismissive of sociology more generally. Yet these sentiments embodied the deeply held opinion of Neustadt and Elias that sociology at Leicester *was* different. Of course there were those within the Department with different theoretical, methodological and even philosophical orientations, from Marxists to Parsonian functionalists. Yet the 'good sociology' offered, as variously developed by Elias and, to a lesser extent, Neustadt, was 'historical' and 'comparative' (Banks 1989), 'developmental' and 'empirical' (Brown 1987) or 'developmental' and 'processual' (Dunning 2006b). From their correspondence it is clear that both Neustadt and Elias guarded this approach to sociology very carefully and championed it above all others, reflecting their view that it was how sociology *should* be taught.

This desire to teach sociology in this particular way coincided, to a great extent, with a massive expansion of higher education in the UK following the Robbins report (1962) for the expansion of Higher Education and the attendant increased demand for sociology courses. This, in turn, created a need for more trained sociology lecturers. As Goodwin and Hughes (2011) have argued, the Department at Leicester became uniquely positioned as being primarily a training ground for would be sociologists and providing the sociological labour needed in the expanding British sociology labour market. Ilya Neustadt's ability to 'talent spot' (bringing to Leicester a good number of historians), Elias's direction on curriculum and clear sociological position, Neustadt's 'political nous' and the centrality of both men to the sociological networks of the time (see Joly 2011), were all key to this rapid expansion. Indeed, Brown (1987: 535) argues, the training sociologists received within the Department meant they were equipped with a 'sociology relevant to major problems of the contemporary world – a subject able to provide some real understanding of and purchase on those problems ...'. It is also well recognised by many (see, for example, Dunning 2006), that the staff and students, who were part of the Department at various points between the mid-1950s and late 1970s, include many who went on to make very significant contributions in their own right: such as Martin Albrow, Sheila Allen, David Ashton, Clive Ashworth, Mike Attalides, Joe and Olive Banks, Anthony Barnett, Richard Brown, Chris Bryant, Percy Cohen, Chris Dandeker, Rosemary Deem, John Eldridge, David Field, James Fulcher, Andy Furlong, Mike Gane, Anthony Giddens, Miriam Glucksman, John H. Goldthorpe, Paul Hirst, Sydney Holloway, Keith Hopkins, Earl Hopper, Jennifer Hurstfield, Geoff Ingham, Nick Jewson, Terry Johnson, Teresa Keil, Mike Kelly, Richard Kilminster, Derek Layder, Mary McIntosh, Gavin Mackenzie, Rob Mears, Nicos Mouzelis, Pat Murphy, Chris Rojek, Graeme Salaman, Ken Sheard, Dennis Smith, John Scott, Dominic Strinati, Laurie Taylor, Ken Thompson, Ivan Waddington, Dave Walsh, Rod Watson, Bryan Wilson, Sarah Vickerstaff and Sami Zubaida.

There is little doubt that the robust emphasis on the training of 'would be teachers of sociology' was *the* driver for the expansion at Leicester. The expansion was not driven by or grounded in contributions by members of the Department to research or 'research outputs'. Indeed, it could be argued that the early impetus for the strong learning and teaching focus was a detriment to a stronger and more distinctive contribution to sociological research at that time. It was not really until the mid-1970s that any substantive research began to appear by members of the Department with the research agenda becoming dominated in 1970s and early 1980s by the work of Eric Dunning and others on football hooliganism (see, for example, Dunning 1971; Williams et al. 1984) and Ashton on work (see Ashton and Field 1976). However, the perception of the Department of the 1950s, 1960s and early 1970s as not making any distinctive research contribution are broadly correct. As an ex member of the Department of Sociology suggests:

> In Elias and Neustadt's day the idea of 'salon culture' is crucial because they could talk about these things with the colleagues ... [they] were a small group that respected the discussions and there was no pressure on publishing, there was no pressure on getting research grants, it was just dealing with knowledge. And I think that goes back to the principle thing that I was talking about, they conveyed that love of just knowledge to the student. (Respondent 2)

As this interviewee suggests, there was no pressure for academic staff to publish or obtain research funding departmentally, institutionally or nationally.[3] Where research was being conducted at Leicester it was relatively small scale, isolated and not very successful if judged in terms of publications. For example, there was the (in)famous and very lively Friday seminar series, where colleagues in the Department and some from other institutions presented their ideas and engaged in sociological discussion. The seminars are remembered with equal amounts of fondness and displeasure by members of the Department from that time (see Brown 1987) and were perhaps not always that supportive of those presenting. For example, a seminar presentation based on data from the *Adjustment of Young Workers* project was described as being '... all over the place, and for someone who knew nothing about the research, or very little, it was far from being clear what it was all about. He thinks that he can make up by fast reading and masses of quotations for the absence of incisiveness and focus' (Neustadt 30 January 1964). There was also clear distinction between those established members of the Department presenting, as opposed to those who came from elsewhere. As Neustadt remarks in his correspondence 'We've started the staff seminars, and will also have a few outsiders' (Neustadt 22 October 1962). Here the term 'outsiders' is interesting in the context of Neustadt's earlier quote about who really understands sociology (see above), as it is suggestive not only of those coming from different

---

3   However, it is, perhaps, important to add a slight caveat here. It is tempting to judge the past 'research output' of the Department through the lens of contemporary, national level, research management tools, such as the Research Excellence Framework in the UK (see, for example, Deem 1994). Yet to do so is problematic because given the radically changed landscape of higher education, it is unhelpful to 'retro-fit' the 'research expectations' of the present to the past.

institutions but also those coming from a different sociological orientation. As difficult and as controversial as they may have been, the seminars did provide a focus for sociological discussion and could be seen to represent the basis of a nascent sociological research culture.

Similarly, Elias and Neustadt's links to Ghana were also the basis for sociological research. In his correspondence, Elias makes numerous references to his own research and field trips to places such as Elimina or around the rapidly developing Volta Basin to study 'villages and neighbourhoods'. Field trips that are later referred to in his book *Reflections on a Life* (1994). These experiences of visiting the Ghanaian villages clearly had an early impact on Elias as he writes 'I am trying to get ready as much of the research we have done on the Volta Basin communities … Needless to say I have learned an enormous amount of the structure of African societies and hope to demonstrate in practice the inadequacies of the conventional non-sociological approach' (Elias 13 March 1964). Neustadt also drew upon his earlier experiences in Ghana for talks he gave for the BBC Africa Service in the late 1950s. Additionally Neustadt was involved in research in Ghana during the time of the correspondence. In 1961, the Ford Foundation made a grant of US$55,000 to the National Research Council of Ghana to support a social and economic survey conducted by Neustadt, Walter Birmingham and E.N. Omaboe. This research ultimately led to a two-edition volume entitled *A Study of Contemporary Ghana* (1967). However, the practicalities of contributing to a social survey of Ghana, whilst Neustadt was in Leicester, proved to be very difficult for all concerned with the research. Although the fruits of the Ghana research endeavours were mixed, they were nonetheless important. As Dunning (2002) asserts, regarding Leicester sociology, few 'British Sociology Departments in that period can have boasted comparable competence in teaching about the kinds of societies regarding which anthropologists used, not without justification, to claim a particular expertise' (Dunning 2002: 415). It was an expertise born out of spending time in Ghana, visiting the field, speaking with local residents and making observations (see also Goody 2006; Liston and Mennell 2009).

Perhaps most importantly of all are the references made in the archived materials to more substantive and publicly funded research – *The Employment of Married Women in a Leicester Hosiery Factory*. What became known as the *Married Women Project* in Departmental correspondence was a large-scale empirical project funded by the Human Sciences Committee of the Department of Scientific and Industrial Research. This project had its origins in Pearl Jephcott's *Married Women Working* (1962), an innovative and detailed study of women and work at the Peek Frean biscuit factory in Bermondsey, London. The Richard Titmuss papers at the London School of Economics reveal a collaborative project, led jointly by Ilya Neustadt and Richard Titmuss, undertaken at Leicester with the aim of developing a comparative study of the employment of women in a Leicester factory focusing, in particular, on the N. Corah hosiery factory.

The social science Dept. of the London School of Economics and the Sociology Dept. of the University of Leicester have together been collecting data designed among other things to test the stereotypes in industrial situations ... Ours in Bermondsey at first based itself on the Peek Frean biscuit factory and the later extended into a study of family life in a local community. The Leicester study has so far based itself on the St. Margaret factory of N. Corah & Sons. (Smith 1961: 13)

The aim of the research was to examine the impact of married women's employment in particular factories and to explore stereotypical objections to women's employment – that home ties undermine women's commitment, loyalty and efficiency to work, as well as the general prejudices held by employers about women workers and women part-time workers. The research was also to consider broader themes such as childcare, work life balance, women in management and so forth well before these become the central concern of sociology following the feminist critique of the 1970s and 1980s. The research team – Neustadt, Titmuss, Richard Brown, along with a senior research officer – received £2,025 to cover research work for 15 months from 1 January 1959 to 31 March 1960. An interim report written by Neustadt in July 1959, reports that a written questionnaire was completed by 500 married women working at Corah's and some initial analysis had been completed, that preparatory and informal interviews had been completed and, in addition, the team were in the process of analysing the company's absenteeism and turnover records and so forth. Based on this, Neustadt reported that 'interim results suggest that "concessions" (permission to work up to 1½ hour less than the full hours each day) are a significant factor for the level of absenteeism ...' (Neustadt 1959a: 2). Notwithstanding the apparent good progress being made with the research, Neustadt requested an extension to the grant later in 1959, suggesting that it was not possible to complete the research within the allocated time due to the complexities of the local labour market and the heavy teaching loads of the members of the Department of Sociology who had participated in the research (Neustadt 1959b: 3). Minutes of the Human Sciences Committee meeting held on 22 March 1960, report that 'Professor Glass reported favourably on the work to date' (DSIR 1960: 4–5). As such, and supported by Richard Titmuss, Neustadt was successful in his request for a further grant of £3,961 and an extension of the research for two years from 1 April 1960. However, although a total of £5,986 was awarded and the team took nearly four years to complete the research, conducting a significant amount of fieldwork, the Leicester version of the *Married Women Project* only delivered one substantive paper (see Brown et al. 1964). The married women study was to 'enter the ether' as a substantive piece of fieldwork that ultimately failed to deliver on its promise.

We have a complex set of competing pressures that serves as backdrop to the *Adjustment of Young Workers to Work Situations and Adult Roles* project. Both Elias and Neustadt were leaders of a rapidly expanding Department, a Department that they had tried to steer in a particular way and perhaps counter to the dominant trends in British sociology at that time. They were under incredible pressure to teach, train staff and deliver on the nationally driven expansion of higher education. That the emphasis was placed heavily on teaching, as Neustadt's inaugural lecture 'On Teaching Sociology' reflects, is arguably not a surprise. What research was being undertaken, be it the attempts to foster a fledgling research culture via the research seminars, Elias and Neustadt's explorations in Ghana or the *Married Women Project*, were not wholly successful. It did not appear to be a Department staffed by academics replete with the skills required to drive and complete a major social survey – as the *Married Women Project* had possibly already foretold. The institutional context of the Leicester Sociology Department did not seem suited to this type of research. However, how it came to be that Elias (and Neustadt) was awarded significant research funds for the *Adjustment of Young Workers* project can be linked to the fact that they had *already* been awarded money for survey research. The successful application and subsequent reapplication for money from the Department of Scientific and Industrial Research for the *Married Women Project*, the standing of those involved and their supporters, and the positive interim reports on the research 'to date' *must* have offered some sense of security for Department of Scientific and Industrial Research to award further monies for what was to follow. To the Department of Scientific and Industrial Research, the *Adjustment of Young Workers to Work Situations and Adult Roles* project must have seemed an attractive bet.

Adjustment of Young Workers to Work Situations and Adult Roles Out of View

Elias's writings have been applied to a wide range of concerns reflecting his own desire to explore the breadth of social phenomenon (Van Krieken 1989; Fletcher 1997). Given this desire, Elias's interest in youth transitions is not surprising. Given Szakolczai's (2000) assertion that the main aspects of Elias's life and work are well researched and well known, what is surprising, however, is that Elias's interest in youth transitions and his only foray into large-scale government funded survey research were never fully explored until relatively recently. The Young Worker Project has received scant attention within the existing Elias literature and remains unknown outside Leicester or beyond those fully familiar with all aspects of Elias's life and work. Most introductions to Elias do not mention this research (see Fletcher 1997; Van Krieken 1998; Hughes 1998[4]) nor is it discussed in autobiographical writings (Elias 1994). The exception to this is Mennell (1992) who provides a brief, but tantalising, reference.

> In the early 1960s Elias also successfully applied for a major research grant ... to investigate school leavers' adjustment to working life. The results of this 'Young

---

4   With Dunning and Hughes (2013) being a more recent exception.

Worker Project' eventually appeared in publications by colleagues at Leicester,
not by Elias himself. (Mennell 1992: 21–22)

One possible reason why this project has received little attention is that it may have
been perceived by later scholars as a 'Departmental' project and not part of Elias's
body of work. Indeed, Elias referred to the project as a 'Departmental' project in
meeting minutes and the management of the project in its early phases involved
a number of members of the Sociology Department at Leicester including Ilya
Neustadt, Sheila Williams (later Allen), Percy Cohen, Richard Brown and Anthony
Giddens. However, there are problems with this view as the correspondence with
the Department of Scientific and Industrial Research identifies Elias as the grant
holder, Elias associates himself closely with the *Adjustment of Young Workers*
project in some of his Ghana correspondence and Ashton (1974) identifies Elias
as having led the research. Indeed, from the surviving background documents it
is evident that Elias was fully involved in the development of the proposal, wrote
a number of memoranda on the aims of the project, commented upon research
design and was central to the appointment of research staff. Elias also insisted
that his view and his approach to the research be adhered to, otherwise he would
resign from the research project (Elias 1963). Elias chaired numerous project
meetings before he left for Ghana and during his vacations. Whilst in Ghana,
Elias corresponded regularly with Neustadt and the other members of the team
about the research. In Neustadt's correspondence with Elias, Neustadt sought and
always deferred to Elias's views in relation to the research, despite Neustadt being
the head of department at the time (see Neustadt 1964a). In the final stages of
the research, it was to Elias that the original research team wrote to resign from
the project. Finally, Elias, after Ghana, returned to Leicester as a senior research
fellow and to supervise the Young Worker Project (see Neustadt 1964a).

Perhaps the main reasons, that discouraged a fuller discussion of this project,
are the problematic and difficult circumstances surrounding the end of the data
collection in 1964. As Brown (1987) suggests:

> Someone who had thought so long and to such good effect about sociological
> problems as he had could find it difficult to understand why others did not see
> things as he did, or to take on board ideas and points of view different from his
> own. There was in my experience one major disagreement about the conduct
> of a research project which proved quite damaging to all concerned and to the
> progress of the research. (Brown, 1987: 538)

Some of the problems surrounding this project have been considered elsewhere but
never published.[5] However, beyond Elias's remoteness in Ghana, communication
problems and other complications, there were three main areas of disagreement

---

5   See Allen, S., Brown, R., and Keil, T. *Working with Norbert Elias: Recollecting
Experiences.

between Elias and the research team. First there was an on-going argument over the researchers' right to publish. Despite the Research Officers' eagerness to publish the results from the research, the research team felt that Elias had vetoed the publication of an article they had written and Elias instructed that there should be no publications or interim reports based on the data. The following exchanges took place towards the end of the fieldwork:

> We are very disappointed that you, and Ilya, intend to concentrate on preparing a final report rather that to publish, in addition, interim articles on specific aspects which would not be fully dealt with in the one report ... unless it is the policy that we are free to submit such articles for publication after constructive criticism, the situation is unacceptable. (Keil and Riddell 1964: 1)

> ... you seem to think that I am a jealous man who wants to prevent you from publishing anything independently of me ... If you care to take up some specific part issue of the Young Worker Project and publish an article on it under your own name I have not the slightest objection ... If you are concerned for your future career, realistically speaking, I think nothing could be better for you than a really impressive final report on the Young Worker Project in which, you need not doubt, all due credit will be given for what you have done. (Elias 1964a: 1–2)

A second area for disagreement, and perhaps the main area of complication, was an on-going argument between Elias and the research officers about the theoretical framework and the composition of the sample. From the outset of the research, Elias was keen to capture their initial work experiences as he felt that the young people's experiences prior to work would not prepare them for employment. However, according to Elias, the researcher officers had interpreted the early discussions to mean that this research was to be a study of 'work' per se. They identified their problem as:

> ... given such a number of young people from known schools, home backgrounds, and work situations, what is their experience when they become workers? ... [We] do not think we should be content with knowing that they have difficulties and to what extent ... but wish to distinguish certain factors which make for certain types of experience in the work situation (Keil et al. 1963a: 2).

Elias argued the study should not be about work but instead the 'work situation' as many of the problems faced by young people rarely sprang from work *in isolation* of other situations. As for the research problem of the research officers, Elias suggested that their approach was simply trying to look for causal relationships between the different aspects of the sample. For Elias, such an approach was too conventional and ignored the relationships and processes surrounding the work situation that constituted the young workers' experience. Elias suggested:

It has been by now fairly widely accepted that this type of billiard ball causality: Billiard ball B (behaviour and attitudes) in its course determined by the movement of Billiard ball A (Features of the background ... features of the work situation, labour market), does not provide a very suitable model of thinking in relation to what one actually observes. I would suggest that the Research Officers think of the experiences of the young workers ... [and] that they cease to think in wishy-washy terms like 'Background' or 'Features of the Background' and learn to think in situations as wholes, in configurations ... (Elias 1963: 7)

For Elias (1963), the differences in the understanding of his ideas and concepts meant that the researchers were undertaking a different project to that originally proposed by him. The on-going misunderstandings over research direction and Elias's constant suggestion that the researchers lacked even a basic understanding of what the research was about, led the researchers to perceive that Elias had no real confidence in them or their ability. Furthermore, a review of the Neustadt–Elias correspondence also reveals some unease on behalf of Neustadt relating to the apparent lack of 'direction' received by the research team and the apparent contraction between their roles as researchers versus the amount and type of work in which they were engaged. Neustadt was clearly concerned as to how the working practices on the project were to be perceived. He writes:

It is a rather embarrassing situation which somewhat disturbs me as regards future developments and relations with D.S.I.R.: after all, their money is supposed to have been given for purposes of research by more senior people, and the research assistants are supposed to be research assistants. At the moment, however, the matter looks as though it is the research assistants who are, in effect, doing the research in every way and that the money has gone towards providing them with a research project. (Neustadt 30 January 1964)

Finally, the researchers and Elias also disagreed about broader methodological debates representing a collision of two different traditions.

... every meeting with you has ended in your saying that we cannot understand your ideas, that we are too concerned with numbers and statistics, too pedestrian, too inhibited by our training. I have thought a great deal about the source of such lack of mutual understanding and it seems to me to lie in a fundamental disagreement about the scope and limits of large-scale research which has resulted in such turmoil and acrimony over the Young Worker Project (Keil 1964: 1).

The officers came from the British tradition of empirical sociology with its emphasis on survey research and were recruited having previously worked on other large-scale quantitative research projects elsewhere. Elias came from a sociological tradition that was profoundly at odds with the abstract empiricism that was characteristic of social scientific research in Britain and America at that time. Elias was interviewed by Jennifer Platt for her book *Realities of Social Research* (1976) and he suggested that through the Young Worker Project he hoped to be able to demonstrate that statistical enquiry could also be undertaken within a dynamic framework and that it is only when the data is generated and analysed that the shortcomings of the survey can be seen. Based on these shortcomings one then can undertake a revised and improved investigation. In the interview Elias suggested the researchers did not believe his assertion that it was possible to develop a precise and straightforward questionnaire that could also access the 'experiential side' exploring the young workers' experiences. Elias's desire to use the survey data to identify further studies was translated by the research officers as the need to undertake additional 'case studies'. However, the research officers received the case studies approach very critically as they argued the value of the data resided within the fact that the survey was based on a large, properly constructed sample and a questionnaire designed to obtain factual information.

> Why else is there a need to interview 1,000+ young people if one is only concerned, in fact, with the experiences of 20 or 30 young people ... For me a large-scale survey is not a simple multiplication of a small one, but an opportunity to test certain hypotheses which cannot be tackled otherwise. (Keil 1964: 1)

For Elias the value of the study did not ultimately reside in the ability to produce statistically significant quantitative results but in the ability to explore the transition to work as the young people experienced and accounted for it themselves. These disagreements led to the failure of the project and to the acrimonious break up of the research team. They also possibly led to the research becoming lost within the history of sociology at Leicester.

Aftermath and Outcomes

Following the break-up of the research committee and the resignation of the researcher officers and fieldworkers, the project completely stalled. In his letter to Elias of 8 June 1964, Neustadt provides a 'frank' assessment of the situation with regards to the future of the research. He informs Elias that senior members of the research team have withdrawn from the project for a variety of reasons, including medical grounds, a lack of interest and 'dissatisfaction with the manner in which the research officers have been handled and the structure of "decision making"' with Neustadt, in the same letter complaining, 'The upshot is that the so-called "research committee" has disappeared altogether, formally and otherwise, and the whole matter is in my lap' (Neustadt 8 June 1964). For Neustadt, knowing that Elias's time in Ghana would end in the summer of 1964, the solution was more than clear. It was a solution that could (potentially) lead to a more than amicable outcome for both the Department and for Elias in relation to his future employment and place of residence. Neustadt writes of his desire to have Elias return to Leicester as a senior research fellow in order to get the research back on track.

> I have discussed the matter … and it is quite clear that more than ever your appointment to a Senior Research Fellowship is highly desirable. I have discussed the matter also with the Registrar, who was very favourably disposed to such an arrangement. I have at the same time requested an extension of the grant from 31st March to 30th September … Clearly there will be need for considerable assistance on the technical matters of coding, statistical analysis, computers, case studies and writing up. You might have a glance at the enclosed progress report which we have just had to send to D. S. I. R. If we make appointments of junior research assistants we shall have to make it absolutely clear what their tasks, responsibilities and privileges will be and what the lines of authority are. I can, of course, make no decisions in these matters until I have heard what your own views are as to the most appropriate arrangements with regard to this kind of assistance. (Neustadt 8 June 1964)

Neustadt was clearly relying on the outcome as he continues 'Needless to say, I shall be happy when I feel that the whole matter is solidly in your hands and under your control' (Neustadt 8 June 1964). As we have seen, by the time this letter was written, the data had already been collected, by the research officers and the interviewers, and a great deal of desk research had been completed. Elias could conceivably return to Leicester and with assistance in relation to what Neustadt refers to as 'technical matters', continue to manage the research to a satisfactory outcome. Such a proposal would have come has no surprise to Elias as, in his Ghana correspondence, he refers as early as 1962 to a 'Research Fellowship and a fairly big task, financed by the D.S.I.R, waiting for me in England if I return there at the end of this session' (Elias 1962d). Indeed, the correspondence records that Elias was keen to return to Leicester and regain leadership of the project. He writes:

> I have now booked passage for a boat leaving here on 5th August and arriving in Liverpool on the 17th. I shall probably stay then about a week in London and then come to Leicester and start working intensively on the Young Worker Project if that is still going. If not, I shall devote more time to my sociology series and to preparing my next book which I hope will be ready before Christmas. (Elias 4 June 1964)

And again in July 1964:

> What are the chances that D.S.I.R. will agree to continue the grant? Do let me know what the position is as soon as you can. (Elias 2 July 1964)

On 20 July 1964, Neustadt confirmed that D.S.I.R. had extended the project until 30 September 1965, awarded an additional £1,500[6] and had agreed Elias's appointment as research fellow. Neustadt continues:

> D.S.I.R. made it quite clear that unless the project is salvaged in some way and a report and a publication emerge from it, this Department will never again be in a position to apply to D.S.I.R. for funds. I suspect that it will not be in a position to apply to other organisations either. Secondly, they were not in any case willing to contemplate the continuance of the project in its last phase with more personnel than yourself fully in charge of the day-to-day operations, and one Research Assistant. (Neustadt 20 July 1964)

From this point onwards, it becomes less clear what happened next, the details relating to the completion of the project become very sketchy and the archive materials are incomplete. Amongst the archived materials there is a document, written by an unknown author but dated 8 September 1964, which documents some of the 'problems' with coding and classification. This is followed by a document written by Elias and dated 21 October 1964, entitled 'A Note on the Problem of "Typing" the Questionnaire', which could possibly be a response to the document of the 8 September, but it also contains some commentary on cases where there were 'high dream expectations which severely clash with reality'. In 1965, the correspondence contains a letter from Elias to Albert Cherns of the Science Research Council (the successor organisation to the D.S.I.R), in which he writes:

> Dear Cherns, I am on the point of leaving, but while going through my things I found a copy of a letter which I wrote to Ilya on 24th February, 1963. I feel I must send you a copy because I am very sorry indeed that the Young Worker project has not yet got as far as I hoped it would before leaving. I feel I owe it to you to say that I made every effort to get it into shape for a fuller report. As I said, the computer let me down, and there was little I could do. Now the materials is lying here – a great many tables which will probably never see the light of day … I have told some people about the preliminary results I have and they found it very interesting. I can assure you that I needed to do a great deal of thinking before I found ways and means to get results from the diffuse material with which the research officers had left me. I am sorry to have to leave it like that … I was sorry to hear that my going way means that the project is dead, but it seems there is nothing I can do. (Elias 9 November 1965)

---

6 Neustadt also wrote 'This sum, together with the large balance remaining in hand on 31st August 1964, provides adequate funds to carry on the project …' (Neustadt 20 July 1964).

From the letter it is clear that Elias had been working on the project since returning from Ghana in 1964 and had made some progress with the analysis but was leaving to take up a visiting position at the University of Münster. As Elias outlines, some of the material had been sent to the Department of Scientific and Industrial Research's computing facilities at Harwell.[7] Cherns replied that he remained optimistic that something would come of the research. In addition, the archived materials contained an undated letter, although it is clearly pre-1970, addressed to David Ashton, in which Elias acknowledges that David was doing some work with the *Adjustment of Young Workers* data and invites him to produce 60–70,000 words on the project. The substantive correspondence concludes in April 1966 with a request, from Elias to Leicester's vice chancellor, for additional support for the research. It is not until 1971 that further reference is made to the project, following the publication of a short editorial piece questioning the final outcomes of the project in the Times Education Supplement, under the heading 'Lost Property'.

> Mystery surrounds the whereabouts of a giant fact-finding report on careers for school-leavers which took four years and £15,000 to complete. It has become lost somewhere between Leicester University's sociology department and the light of day. The grant was originally made to Professor Norbert Elias and Mrs. Sheila Allen[8] in 1961 when they were both at Leicester University. Their brief was to investigate 'The Adjustment of Young Workers to the Work Situation and Adult Roles' ... Professor Elias, who is still at Leicester, claims that the report was sent to the Department for Scientific and Industrial Research ... Mrs Stella Thomas, press officer for the S.S.R.C, says that despite an extensive search she can find no trace of the report, of any evidence that it was ever sent to the former department. (Times Education Supplement 21 January 1971).

It still remains unclear what work was undertaken in the final years (1964–1966) on the *Adjustment of Young Workers* project, although it is evident that Elias and colleagues had tried, perhaps in vain, to resurrect and complete the research. It is also clear that Elias felt a significant amount of regret for what had happened during this research and, in a letter to Jennifer Platt (relating to an interview he did for her book *The Realities of Social Research*), Elias suggested 'the fact that a questionnaire designed and interviews conducted under the influence of divergent

---

7   Harwell, near Oxfordshire, is cited in the correspondence as being the location for the computing facilities. Most likely this was the Atlas Computer Laboratory and home of Atlas Computers at that time. The director of the laboratory was Jack Howlett. David Ashton recalls Elias discussing the computer analysis referring to the computer as his 'baby'.

8   Sheila Allen wrote a letter to the editor of the *Times Education Supplement* on the 1 February 1971 to challenge various factual errors in the editorial piece including the fact that she had left the project after only two years and that, as a junior member of the department, was not primarily responsible for the conduct of the research.

views cannot be salvaged by a later effort, was for me a lesson which I shall not forget' (Elias 1972a: 1–2).

Conclusions: Impact?

Yet despite this regret and subsequent publication of Ashton and Field's highly influential *Young Workers: From School to Work* book in the mid-1970s, the aftermath of this failed research was, perhaps, to have a lasting impact on Elias's reputation in British sociology. Despite Elias's centrality to sociology at Leicester, his ideas have not impacted upon British sociology until relatively recently (Kilminster 1987; Mennell 1992; Van Krieken 1998). This, it has been suggested, may have been due to the lack of English translations, the dominance of Parsons in 1950s and 1960s sociology, Elias's use of psychoanalysis, the increased specialisation amongst sociologists or even just a general lack of awareness (Kilminster 1987; Mennell 1992). Whilst these may be true, the failure of the *Adjustment of Young Workers* project may provide an additional explanation. It is not inconceivable that the way Elias developed, managed and implemented this project may have had a negative effective on his reception in British sociology. Many, if not all of the researchers originally involved in the *Adjustment of Young Workers* project went on to occupy senior roles within British sociology as professors, heads of departments or held senior positions within the British Sociological Association (see Platt 2003). Regardless of the rights and wrongs of the arguments that took place between Elias and the research team, the researchers felt aggrieved and some still reflect on their experiences with bitterness, regret and some anger. Such experiences and feelings must have impacted on their presentation of Elias to their colleagues within British sociology. As Neustadt (1964b) suggests in a letter to Elias,

> The research officers ... also created difficult and unpleasant situations here by agitating in a most unpleasant and vengeful manner with all sorts of people in the University here and in various other places in the country. (Neustadt 1964b: 1)

The difficulties that surrounded this project and its sensitivities, which remain for some of the original research team, have meant this project remained 'lost' for many years.

Chapter 2

Researching the *Adjustment of Young Workers to Work Situations and Adult Roles*: Conceptual Framework and 1960s Fieldwork

Introduction

Moving on from the problems surrounding the *Adjustment of Young Workers* project and its ultimate demise, it is important to acknowledge that the archived material does contain some examples of Elias's ideas relating to the transition to adulthood. Indeed, he articulated quite clearly aspects of the 'Shock Hypothesis' he was developing across the various memoranda and materials surrounding the research. He also discussed this at various research committee meetings with the aim of outlining the theoretical framework that should be used. Materials from the various archives also detail the actual fieldwork that was completed, both by those collecting data, as well as detailing issues around the pilot study, sampling frame and so forth. In this chapter we aim to explore the extent of the research that was completed after first outlining some of Elias's writings on the shock hypothesis. Although the separation between these two aspects of the research process – 'theory' and 'method' is somewhat artificial – and to do so runs counter to the empirical/theoretical approach to sociological practice that Elias himself advocates, we have presented the theoretical framework separately so as to reflect the division of labour that appears to have existed between Elias and the remainder of the research team.

As Figure 2.1, the Department of Scientific and Industrial Research project description, records,[1] the aim of the research is set out as being:

---

1   The project outline also names the lead investigators and those who were the initial 'staff' for the research project. Of those not already referred to in Chapter 1, as can be seen, the project staff also included Dr Percy Cohen and Mr Anthony Giddens. Percy S. Cohen was a lecturer at the University of Leicester between 1960 and 1965. In 1965 he was appointed to a lectureship at the LSE, where he remained until his retirement in 1992 (see Glasser 1999). Mr Anthony Giddens, later Lord Giddens of Southgate, worked at Leicester between 1961 and 1969 and is arguably the most famous British sociologist of his generation. The archived materials relating to the *Adjustment of Young Workers* project do not fully record the extent of the involvement of either Cohen or Giddens beyond their attendance at early project meetings in 1962 and 1963. Their involvement also seems to have declined with the recruitment of the research officers and once the data collection phase had commenced. Private correspondence between Anthony Giddens and the authors, in June 2001, confirms

... concerned with the problems which young male and female workers encounter during their adjustment to their work situation and their entry into the world of adults. When they go to work, or begin to train for work, young workers have to make a wider adjustment to a situation and to roles which are new to them, whose implications are often imperfectly understood by them and by the adults concerned, and for which they are in many cases not too well prepared.

This broad position was then translated into five specific areas of enquiry – *adjustment to relationships with older workers and supervisors*; *adjustment to job problems*; *adjustment to role as workers*; *adjustment to role as 'money-earner' in home relations*; and *adjustment to role as 'money-earner' in leisure time*.

At the heart of the problem for Elias was the idea that the adjustment to work and adult roles was not a straightforward transition from education to work or moving from school to a job, but was, instead, a more complex process of adjustment to the world of adults. This was a world, as outlined in the aims for the research, unfamiliar to young people. As a consequence of having to make these broader adjustments, Elias conceived of the transition from school to work as constituting a 'shock' experience and that young people may experience 'difficulties' in adjusting to their new role as adults and workers. As such, for Elias, the research could not simply focus on the young person's move from school to work but had to encapsulate the entirety of their experiences. A further point of departure was a view that much of the early research on youth of the time (such as Carter 1962), was essentially 'adult centred'. As Elias argued, this research would differ from other studies as 'adult investigators are apt to investigate either their own problems with regard to young people ... not problems which confront, and which are experienced by the young generation itself' (Elias 1962a: 1).

The adjustment 'as shock' motif is clearly evident throughout the archived meeting minutes, correspondence and memoranda associated with the project. Despite being developed over the course of two years, across a number of different media, whether they are recorded in minutes, correspondence or memoranda, the archive documents do indicate a consistency in Elias's thoughts on the 'problems of adjustment'. From these writings it is possible to ascertain that Elias identified

---

this. However, amongst the archive papers there is a seven-page document, dated 24 April 1962, entitled *Adjustment of Young Workers to Work Situations and Adult Roles: Some Preliminary Suggestions* written by Anthony Giddens. The document outlines, very early in the process, his suggestions for the general framework, immediate scope of the study and research methodology. It is unclear the extent to which the ideas presented in that document were adopted by the *Adjustment of Young Workers* project research committee, however there is some overlap in both themes and focus with the project proposal. Although named here, this does not imply that any of those named had any involvement in the difficult later stages of the project. Indeed, as the archive material suggests, almost all had moved on to other projects and concerns well before the fieldwork ended in 1964 (see Ilya Neustadt 8 June 1964, cited previously).

LEICESTER UNIVERSITY

The adjustment of young workers to work situations and adult roles

Investigators:	Dr. N. Elias
	Dr. J. Neustadt
	Mrs. S. Williams
Staff:	Dr. P.S. Cohen
	Mr. R.K. Brown
	Mr. A. Giddens
Period of research:	1.4.62 - 31.3.65

The project is concerned with the problems which young male and female workers encounter during their adjustment to their work situation and their entry into the world of adults. When they go to work, or begin to train for work, young workers have to make a wider adjustment to a situation and to roles which are new to them, whose implications are often imperfectly under- stood by them and by the adults concerned, and for which they are in many cases not too well prepared. The project will differ from other studies in investigating this wider adjustment which young workers have to make in their relationships with older workers and supervisors in the factory or workshop; to job problems and to their role as workers; and to their roles as money earners in home relations and in their leisure time. The factors to be examined will include differences between age groups, between sexes, in size of organisa- tion, in nature and status of job, and between young workers from working class and middle class home backgrounds. We intend to pay special atten- tion to the overall characteristics of industrial societies responsible for the specific problems of adjustment for people in this age group.

Figure 2.1   DSIR project description

eight specific problems relating to the transition to adulthood that contributed to the experience of transition as a shock. These are i) the prolonged separation of young people from adults; ii) the indirect knowledge of the adult world; iii) the lack of communication between adults and children; iv) the social life of children in the midst of an adult world with limited communication between the two; v) the role of fantasy elements in the social and personal life of the young vis-à-vis the reality of adult life; vi) the social role of young people is ill-defined and ambiguous; vii) striving for independence through earning money constitutes a new social dependence (on work rather than parents); viii) the prolonging of social childhood beyond biological maturity. There is a slight variation on these presented in Elias's 'Second Memorandum' (circa 1962), as nine problems that adolescents face when making the transition to work and adulthood. These problems are:[2] i) the problems arising from the need for earning and handling *individually* one's own <u>money</u>; ii) the problems arising from the need for dealing *individually* with one's *sexual* needs; iii) the problems arising from finding individually response and satisfaction in relation to the need for affection and friendship, in short, for a *personal circle of friends*; iv) the problems arising from the need for coping with close *impersonal* contacts particularly when in the work situation; v) the problems arising from the need to cope with adult competition and to learn *how and when to compete, how and when to co-operate*; vi) the problems arising from the need to learn how to *take* individually <u>decisions</u> for one's own life; vii) the problems arising from the need for a steady *control* of one's own *instinctive and emotional* impulses; viii) the problems arising from the need for learning *foresight*; and finally ix) the problem arising from the *quest for meaningfulness*. Combined, the two overlapping lists of the adjustment problems experienced by youth during the adjustment to work and adulthood are reflective of the need for young people to learn the 'behavioural standards' of adulthood at that particular time. Young people move from a position within their families where they are dependent upon family members, particularly their parents, to resolve issues and guide behaviour, to a situation where the young people have to deal with issues and situations themselves. In the second list, Elias emphasises this by underlining the key issues and the fact that the individuals themselves had to work through the problem of adjustment. However, this has to be understood in relation to Elias's broader sociological approach.

One of the central principles of Elias's processual sociology pertinent to this discussion is his approach '… to human beings as interdependent, forming figurations or networks with each other which connect the psychological with the social, or habitus with social relations' (Van Krieken, 1998: 49; Mennell and Goudsblom, 1998: 15). In *On the Process of Civilisation* ([1939] 2013), Elias examines the processes by which changes have taken place in the standards of behavioural expectations (Hughes 1998: 140) and the shift in peoples' behaviour towards higher degrees of self-restraint that accompanied the increasingly elaborate nature of etiquette codes in the Middle Ages. To explain this, Elias drew on Freud's notion of the super-ego and argues that through the civilising process, the psychic structure of people is transformed.

> The pronounced division in the 'ego' or consciousness characteristic of people in our phases of civilization, which finds expression in such terms as 'superego' and 'unconscious', corresponds to the specific split in the behaviour which civilized society demands of its members. It matches the degree of regulation

---

2   The underlining for emphasis presented here is as it appears in the 'Second Memorandum'.

and restraint imposed on the expression of drives and impulses ... This is what is meant when we refer here to the continuous correspondence between the social structure and the structure of the personality, of the individual self. (Elias 2000: 160)

However, for Elias, unlike Freud's (1930) approach, this process was not static and the super-ego changes constantly with the changing social code of behaviour.

... it is the web of social relations in which individuals live during their most impressionable phase, that is childhood and youth, which imprints itself upon their unfolding personality in the form of the relationship between their controlling agencies, super-ego and ego and their libidinal impulses. The resulting balance ... determines how an individual person steers him or herself in his or her social relations with others ... However, there is no end to the intertwining ... it never ceases entirely to be affected by his or her changing relations with other throughout his or her life. (Elias 2000: 377)

This process of constant change Elias conceptualised as the inter-relationship between *sociogenesis* and *psychogenesis*: sociogenesis being the processes of development and transformation in social relations, with psychogenesis being the processes of development and transformation in the psychology, personality or habitus that accompany such social changes (Van Krieken 1998). In this sense, habitus, or an individual's personality makeup, is not inherent or innate but 'habituated' and becomes a constituent part of the individual by learning through social experience and, according to Van Krieken (1998), develops as part of a continuous process beginning at birth and continuing through childhood and youth (Van Krieken 1998: 59). Given the interrelationship between sociogenesis *and* psychogenesis, Elias argued that the socialisation of children cannot take place behind closed doors and the learning of adult behaviours is only possible due to the presence of others. Indeed, Mennell and Goudsblom (1998) suggest that the individual civilising process is (more or less) a socialisation process, as children have to acquire the adult standards of behaviour and feelings prevalent in their society through learning. In 1980, Elias reflected fully on the individual civilising process, the socialisation of children and the changing relationship between children and their parents in his lecture *The Civilizing of Parents* (Elias 1980; Goudsblom and Mennell 1998). In this work, Elias suggested that despite a growing literature on childhood, the role of parents in helping children to enter a complex society, that demands a high degree of foresight and self-control, is not completely understood. However, for Elias, the fact that 'childhood' had been discovered suggested to him that children are different to adults and only become adults through an individual civilising process. The child, from early in life and through adolescence, is subject to an individual civilising process that shapes their behaviour and, in turn, emerge high degrees of self-restraint and foresight in line with the prevalent standards of behaviour at that time (Elias 1980). Van Krieken

(1998) argues that in Elias's work, childhood is the 'main "transmission belt" for the development of the habitus' (Van Krieken 1998: 156) of a given society.

> Today there is relatively little understanding of the fact that the problems of adolescents concern a combination of the biological processes of maturation on the one hand, that adaption to the current level of societal civilization on the other … Human social life in the form of urban-industrial nation-states encloses each individual person in a complex network of longer more differentiated chains of interdependence. In order to claim to be an adult … in order to fulfil and adults functions … it is necessary to have a very high degree of foresight, restraint of momentary impulses, for the sake of long-term goals and gratifications … it requires a high degree of self-regulating restraint of drives and affects (Elias 1980: 201–2).

Children have to learn the self-control of drives and affects through the course of relations with other people and 'according to the pattern and extent of socially given drive and affect regulation' (Elias 1980: 202). The more complex a society, the more complex this process of transition to adulthood or the learning of adult norms becomes. According to Elias, the more complex a society, the more differentiated the social functions are and the more interdependent people become. In such a society, to fulfil the social functions, more foresight is required in order to subordinate 'momentary inclinations to the overriding necessities of interdependence' (Elias 2000: 380; Mennell 1992: 96). For example, if one takes the social function of work, in a complex industrial society such as ours, the structure of drives and affects required for this adult behaviour is further from the behaviour of children than that required in a simpler societies. To illustrate this, Elias (1980) suggests that in what he describes as 'Eskimo' society there is direct developmental line between children's play behaviour (playing with bows and arrows or learning to treat skins) and adult behaviours of hunting, tent-making and survival (Elias 1980: 202). The child's or young person's behaviour corresponds to a high degree with adult reality, whereas in complex industrial societies it does not. As such, in a simpler society, Elias (1980) argues the individual civilising transformation is temporally shorter and less deep-rooted (Elias 1980: 202).

Although the archived documents contain details of the problems of adjustment, not all of the problems were explored in a consistent level of detail. While it would be useful to outline all of the 'indicators of shock', it is impossible to do so given the lack of detail in the materials – indeed one would assume that Elias would have developed a fuller account towards the end of the research process if the research had ultimately been successful. As it is, we have given particular attention here to three aspects – the separation of children and adults, with the attendant lack of 'direct knowledge of the adult world', the role of fantasy versus the reality in the adjustment to adult life and, finally, the adjustment to earning or 'handling' money of their own, as opposed to relying on parental resources.

Adjusting to Work Situations: The Separation of Children from Adults

In the *Adjustment of Young Workers* research, Elias wanted to examine how young people experienced the transition from school to work, not only how people learned to do a job, but also how the young workers acquired the prevalent adult standards or norms of behaviour. In doing so he focused on their problems of adjustment to work. Elias (1961) suggested that for young people:

> ... their entry into work places young workers into a different position not only in relation to parents or to friends, but in relation to adults who are strangers – adult workers, supervisors, managers etc. on whom they depend ... The norms, the behaviour and attitudes of the adults with which they now come into contact often differ considerably from those with which they are familiar in their own family circle or from their contact with masters at school. (Elias 1961: 1)

For Elias, the norms and attitudes or new codes of behaviour exhibited by the adults in the workplace, involved problems of competition and co-operation, conforming and non-conforming in factory and workshop and coping with tensions in social relations (Elias 1961: 1). The transition process and the adjustment to working life via the learning of adult norms, for Elias, was not a simple process. The difficulty arose in that the norms, the behaviour and attitudes of adults in the workplace differed considerably to those adults the young people were familiar with. In these 'already known' relationships, the position of the young person is clearer as a subordinate to the adult figure. For example, a child is subordinate to their parents and a 'teenager' is in a subordinate role to their teacher. Through the processes of sociogenesis and psychogenesis, over time a power ratio has emerged in these relationships, which supports the young person's subordination. In turn, the young person displays appropriate behaviour. However, in our current society, when the young person begins to make the transition to work and adulthood, their role becomes less clear. This, he argues, is due to the limited amount of contact between young people and adults over and above family, friends and teachers. For example, at a meeting of the young worker project team it was argued that:

> The central problem arises from the fact that a complex society such as ours requires customarily a prolonged period of indirect preparation and training for adult life. By indirect I mean from the age of 5 to 14, 15 or 16 the growing up children of our society are trained for their adult tasks in special institutions which we call schools, where they learn, where they acquire the knowledge about the adult world past, present and future not by direct contact with it, but largely from books. Their actual knowledge of the adult world, their only contacts with adults, are relatively limited. (Young Worker Project 1962a: 2)

Elias suggested that this is radically different from the children growing up in 'simpler' European societies of previous periods in which children and young people had more direct contact with adults. In our current society, problems or difficulties can arise in the adjustment to adult and work roles as the young workers are now neither fully adult nor fully children and they experience contact with different adults and different norms of adult behaviour. As such, Elias suggested that this research begin with the hypothesis that:

> ... nothing, or very little, that the school leaver has been taught has prepared him or her for the experience of starting work; that the experience was a 'shock' experience. (Young Worker Project 1962b: 2)

Elias's notion of shock is reinforced with comments made at the fifth meeting of young worker project team. Here Elias quoted an example of the shock experienced by a young worker at being told not to work too hard. The minutes suggest that Elias argued that the problem could be approached without first needing to find out the adult norm of not working too hard, instead the emphasis should be on 'what the young workers are faced with, as they see it and describe it in talking about their first few weeks in the factory' (Young Worker Project 1962b: 2). Elias wanted to understand how the young people *experienced* the norm of not working too hard. For example, it could be argued that shock emerges in that the young adults have moved from a situation where adults, in the form of teachers at school, have instructed the young adults to work hard and have administered punishments to those who did not, to a situation where unfamiliar adults are instructing, advising and encouraging the young people to behave in a way that was previously discouraged. The existence of the young worker is threatened by the fact that their social world changes and they come into contact with behaviours and norms that are totally unfamiliar to them. These changes to the 'social reality' of the young worker, experienced as part of the transition from school to work, according to Elias, caused anxiety or shock. These assertions by Elias build on points made in *On the Process of Civilisation*.

> Any other behaviour, any breach of the prohibitions or restraints prevailing in their society means danger ... And the peculiarly emotional undertone so often associated with moral demands ... reflects the danger in which any breach of the prohibitions places the unstable balance of all those for whom the standard behaviour of society has become more or less 'second nature'. These attitudes are symptoms of the anxiety aroused in adults when the structure of their own drives, and with it their own social existence and the social order in which it is anchored is even remotely threatened. (Elias 2000: 141)

Elias argued that the transition from childhood to adulthood, from school to work is one of the great anxiety arousing transitions, as the young person's social existence and social order are threatened. In previous societies, according to Elias, ceremonies or 'rites of passage' grew up around the transitions between social roles to help ease the anxiety. Indeed, Elias suggests that all situations, which were liable to arouse fear or anxiety, such as the transition from one socio-biological state to another, were marked by public ceremonies as means of helping the individual contain their fears and anxieties. However, Elias suggests that the 'communal ceremonies of passage formerly attached to the transition from childhood to adulthood have completely lapsed' (Elias 1962a: 2).

Adjusting to Work Situations: The Role of Fantasy

> Somehow the experience of many youngsters when they grow up in our society seem to me similar. They perceive more the wider choices of adulthood than its restraints and frustrations. (Elias 1962: 2)

A dimension of adult behaviour that children had to learn through their transition to adulthood was the difference between fantasy and reality. Like other aspects of knowledge and behaviour, the difference between fantasy and reality depends on prevalent standards at that time (i.e. it varies historically and between societies). For example, Mennell (1992) suggests that in industrial, complex societies, there is a very clear division between fantasy and reality and people have to behave accordingly as, if they act out their dreams in a way that conflicts with prevalent standards, their sanity will be questioned (Mennell 1992: 162). In other societies, the role of fantasy may differ. For example, for the indigenous peoples of North America, dreams and fantasy constitute a large part of their spiritual belief system. However, Elias (1993) argues that for children, the difference between fantasy and reality is blurred (Elias 1993: 56). In *What is Sociology?*, Elias wrote:

> Dreams often find short-term fulfilment: but in the long run, they virtually always seem to end up drained of substance and destroyed. The reason is that aims and hopes are so heavily saturated with fantasy that the actual course of events in society deals blow after blow, and the shock of reality reveals them as unreal ... (Elias 1978: 28)

Such themes were reflected in the adjustment of *Adjustment of Young Workers* research and, indeed, Elias wrote a considerable amount about the individual civilising process and the difference between fantasy and reality in his consideration of school to work transitions. He writes:

> I want to say that 'culture shock' is in my view a very inappropriate term for what we are getting at. It runs smoothly from the lips, that is quite true, it sounds nice. But we are not trying to find out about a shock which 'culture' gives to people. It is the work, the occupation, the whole undreamed of reality of the adult world which is responsible for the stresses of adolescents in that situation ... I have always preferred the term 'shock-experience', to the term 'shock'. The most precise expression of which I can think at the moment is probably 'reality shock'. That is, in fact, what it is likely to be. (Elias 1962: 1)

As part of acquiring the prevalent adult standards or norms of behaviour in the work place, the young workers had to also *learn* the prevalent standards in the differences between fantasy and reality at that time. For Elias, the gap between childhood and adolescent dreams and their adult reality is great and, given the absence of relationships between children and other adults (and the adult world), Elias suggests that children have developed fantasies about their future adult role. Children have to develop fantasies about their future adult role as they have not experienced it, nor do they have much contact (before they enter work) with adults who have. Elias (1962) goes on:

> Before they enter their job, adolescents have a highly selective and still rather unrealistic perception of the adult world and of their life in it. The encounter with reality enforces a reorganisation of their perception. This is a painful process for at least two different reasons. First, because every strongly enforced reorganisation of perceptions is painful. Second, to all intents and purposes the 'social reality' to which the youngsters have to get used, is unsatisfactory and the gap between the adult reality as it turns out to be is very great indeed. This is the objective situation … We are after the actual experiences to which it gives rise … 'shock-experience' or 'reality-shock' understood as something which may have a variety of forms, which may sometimes be sudden and biting and sometimes slowly coming over the years ending in a final shock of recognition that there will never be anything else but that, seems to me our best bet. (Elias 1962: 1)

For Elias, given the absence of relationships between children and other adults, the differences between the fantasies of future adult roles, the actual reality of adult life and the encounter with reality, which enforces a reorganisation of perceptions during the transition from school to work, all lead to this experience being one of shock. An example of this could be that the young person, before entering work, has a perception or fantasy that work will be a positive experience and will have no negative effect on them. In such a fantasy, the young person does not perceive the reality of adult working life as being one without long school holidays, short working days and extended 'break times'. The reality of work is different from the perceptions of the young person and, for Elias, the realisation that nothing will ever be the same in terms of school holidays or the general loss of the 'freedoms' that accompany childhood, lead the young person to experience a 'reality-shock'. Interestingly, Elias suggested that the reality shock was greater for girls as they have had a less 'realistic' upbringing as compared to boys.

Elias (1964) further clarified his thoughts on shock and suggested that it was possible to classify each 'interview' in terms of a particular 'reality type'. One of the reality types, Elias suggested, could be the 'types of relationship between expectation and reality'. Elias argued that there were three main possibilities that the young workers would experience. First, that expectations of the job would be more or less like school but the reality was that work was indeed very different. For example, the supervisors at work were not like teachers and, whereas at school it was possible to 'mess about' (or act in ways not approved of by adults) when not directly supervised, at work it was not possible to 'mess about' at all. Second, the expectation that work will be terrible and the reality was that work was not as bad as expected. For example, that work would be hard and the young person would be made to work like slaves, whereas the reality was different, with less control of the young person and great possibilities for controlling the pace of work. Finally, the expectation that the freedom from school would be 'marvellous' but the reality of work and adult life were less 'marvellous' than expected. Leaving school would be almost like an escape from the prison-like or controlled realities of education. However, on escaping, the young person finds that work is also controlled and provides little opportunity for the individual expression they so desire.

Adjusting to Work Situations: Handling Money and Striving for Independence

In Elias's writings, the earning of money is a fundamental adjustment for the young workers and represents a shift in dependency, from dependencies on parents and family, to a dependency on wage income. The acquisition and management of money requires the young worker to learn new behaviours and norms as the process of having one's own money, and having to work in exchange for this money, represented, for Elias, a further change in the social reality of the young worker. He suggested that the young people made the transition from a

> ... situation in which money, and food and clothing are given, and received as a right, without anything being given by the child in exchange, to a situation in which money is only given in exchange for work by the receiver. (Young Worker Project 1962c: 1)

The hypothesis here was that there would be adjustment problems in relation to money for various reasons. First, the child has never had to develop a full sense of reciprocity. That is money and resources are given relatively 'freely' by parents to children with limited expectation of the child giving anything in return. Upon entering work, the young worker earns money and then is expected to hand over wages to cover living expenses, in effect having to pay their own way. Second, the process is problematic, as earlier attempts at teaching/training reciprocal behaviours are not serious and cannot convey the actuality of the 'real' experience of earning money, for Elias, 'that the parents' teaching only becomes serious when the situation, of work not school child, means that they have to put it into practice' (Young Worker Project 1962d: 1). Third, there is an increased 'impersonal' dimension to the giving and taking of money, with the formalised, impersonal 'contact' controlled by rules replacing the informal resource allocation patterns of the family. Fourth, the need to manage income and plan for the future, require something beyond the immediate gratification of spending money, freely obtained, or immediate wish fulfilment. Instead, young workers needed to develop foresight in relation to money, not only for the long term but also for ensuring that their money lasts throughout the week and covers any obligations, such as 'bed and board' that they may have acquired since starting work. This is an adjustment from simply asking parents for money as and when the child experiences a 'need'. Finally, however, the adjustments made in relation to money may be

> ... in fact a relatively long drawn out process, beginning, for example, with a newspaper round, to earn pocket money, at the age of 12 of 14, and not being complete until the young worker married and left his [*sic*] parental home at the age of 21. This might ease the adjustment and dissipate the shock. (Young Worker Project 1962c: 1)

The research committee minutes record that the focus of the *Adjustment of Young Workers* research in respect of money was to 'concentrate on two areas of observation (i) the change from receiving without giving; (ii) the question of foresight in the use of money' (Young Worker Project 1962d: 1). However, the committee meeting minutes also record that the problems associated with the adjustment to earning and managing money may not be uniform across all young workers and may also vary by class membership.

Research Young Workers in the Field: Research Design and Implementation

Following the application made in 1961, the Department for Scientific and Industrial Research awarded the research team £15,081 for the *Adjustment of Young Workers* project, for three years beginning in April 1962. Initially the idea was for the data to be collected via interviews, informal discussions, case studies and participant observation; however, in the end, only interviews were used. The interview schedule was semi-structured with a mixture of open and closed questions. The schedule contained 82 questions organised in five sections: *Work, Family and Expenditure, Leisure, School and Work,* and *General* (see Appendix 1). The interviewers were asked to write all answers to questions verbatim, if possible, and always in as full detail as the time and circumstances allowed.

It appears that preparations for the fieldwork stage of the research began in 1962, with a pilot study being completed in Loughborough during the second part of February and the first half of March 1963. The pilot study comprised 28 interviews, including interviews with eight girls, and was written up for discussion by Teresa Keil, David Riddell and Colin Tipton in April 1963. Also, in the spring of 1963, the research team produced an extensive preliminary survey of the literature, comprising circa 200 books, articles and reports.

The sample of young adults was drawn from the Youth Employment Office index of all Leicester school leavers from the summer and Christmas of 1960 and the summer and Christmas of 1962. A full description of the sample, as written by David Riddell and Teresa Keil in July 1963 is included in the appendices (see Appendix 2).

The interviews themselves were undertaken in the respondent's homes and were tape-recorded. The fact that the interviews were tape-recorded would have been quite unusual for the time and, without doubt, would have been quite intrusive given the size of the reel-to-reel tapes that were used.[3] The use of audio-tape during this period represented a very significant technological advance in social research. The main advantage of the new technology was that for the first time it gave those working in the field the ability to systematically and faithfully record the words of the respondents. Such an approach allows the researcher to replay and reflect on the interview without relying solely on field notes. It also means the authenticity of the data can be maintained. Most contemporary methodological textbooks would recommend the recording of interview data for that very reason. However, not many texts actually reflect on the problems that technology may impose on the researcher. Yet, in practice, the process of recording an interview may not be so straightforward. The experiences of using the tape recorders and of conducting the interviews are often commented on in the interviewer notes. Indeed, a deal of insight into the research process can be gleaned from interviewer notes, as these accounts document the 'lived realities' of social research which contrast with the logical, smooth, rational and 'perfect' research process described in many textbooks (see Fielding 2000: 16). For example, the original interview team have recounted how, in the *Adjustment of Young Workers* project, large reel-to-reel tape recorders were used to commit the responses to tape and initially, they were used to seemingly good effect. 'We find each interview leaves quite a vivid impression, different from the next one, and it is hard to see general patterns at this stage. We are getting very good results with tape recorders' (Riddell, Keil and Green 1963: 2).

However, whilst the researchers were initially able to obtain good results with the tape recorders, the field notes reveal that the process of recording the interviews was not always straightforward and was often beset by technical problems.

> Tape recorder was used, but a flaw in tape recorder caused a distortion, but managed to write up most of the material although the last 1/3rd of the schedule's responses were based on memory as the tape went so slow and then very fast that it was impossible to decipher the interview. Any in-accuracy very slight as I wrote it up shortly after the interview.

> Tape recorder failed to record this interview which was written up next day from memory.

> A tape recorder was used for this interview but unfortunately it was not recording. As a result the schedule has been written completely from memory. Because of

---

3   Unfortunately none of the tapes survived. From the archived documents it appears that a Phillips recorder was purchased for the research at a cost of about 25 guineas.

this, it was very fortunate that the respondent had only had one job and that she had been to no classes, clubs or associations.

From the interviewer notes, it is clear that at times, the researchers experienced technological challenges. What we also see is a glimpse of the problems caused by human error (i.e. when the tape recorder is mistakenly not switched on or the problems of having to write up the interview notes from memory). What also becomes all too apparent is the sense of frustration with the technology.

Bloody tape recorder didn't record again – but could remember almost every word – wrote it up same evening.

Interestingly, the tape recorders also generated some unexpected interaction between the researchers and the young people being interviewed. Indeed, from some of the interviews it is clear that the respondents had as much, if not more, technological ability as the researchers.

The tape stopped after 5 questions – respondent kindly fixed it.

[He] had less to say than I thought he would have. He used his own little tape recorder for a bit, it wasn't very good.

At the end of the fieldwork in 1964, 882 interviews, plus a pilot survey of 28 interviews had been completed, of which we re-discovered 851 schedules in the attic office. Table 2.1 outlines the composition of the final sample.

Table 2.1   Sample descriptions and composition

Group	Original Target Sample	Archive Sample
Pilot Study	*28*	*0*
*Practice**	*–*	*16*
Actual Study:		
'A' – boys who had left school in summer or Christmas 1962, with less than one year of further education.	330	243
'B' – boys who had left school in summer or Christmas 1962, with more than one year of further education.	160	130
'C' – boys who had left school in summer or Christmas 1960, with less than one year of further education.	300	202

Group	Original Target Sample	Archive Sample
'D' – girls who had left school in summer or Christmas 1962, with less than one year of further education.	200	155
'E' – girls who had left school in summer or Christmas 1960, with less than one year of further education.	160	105
	1150 *(28)†*	851 *(16)†*

Notes: * The practice schedules appeared to by 'dry-run' interviews with actual respondents. Some vary in the degree to which they were completed.
† Totals including practice/pilot surveys.

Conclusions

To date, Elias's 'shock hypothesis' found little support within the literature of youth transitions or from the data. For example, in analysing data from the pilot study, Brown et al. (1963) suggested that the younger members of the sample had hardly had time to get over the excitement at not having to adhere to the rigid discipline of school and earning money, to experience the 'shock' to which Elias refers:

> Our examination of the previous work shows it to be an almost universal finding from actual investigations that, at the time of entry to work for young people, the excitement of leaving school and earning a wage over shadows other feelings, to a large extent. These preliminary attitudes reduce the impact of experiences of work and life as workers, for a time. (Brown et al. 1963: 1)

Brown et al. (1963) argued that the sample needed to be modified and the sample's length of time in work should be increased. They suggested that the sample should include a higher proportion of those who had been in work for two and three years and reduce the numbers who had been in work between six and twelve months. At a meeting of the research committee on 15 May 1963, these suggestions were agreed in Elias's absence. However, during the early part of the discussions, Neustadt had reflected that:

> … [at] our last research meeting when Teresa and Riddell were emphatic about the need to investigate young people at work 2–3 years, in the light of the literature, as well as those 6–12 months at work … Richard suggests a compromise whereby the bulk will be 6–12 months, and a portion of the sample 2–3 years … I was not very keen myself to fall in with these proposals, but there, I remembered after a while your strictures about my committee antics, and gave way to what the committee 'seemed' to want, subject to your being consulted first (Neustadt 1962: 1–2).

Likewise, Ashton and Field (1976) also argued that most young people did not experience severe problems of adjustment during the transition from school to work. They suggest that the view that young people experience shock due to the fact they are isolated from work in educational establishments and suddenly released into work is erroneous and at best common sense. They argue that previous experiences at home, school and amongst their peer groups actually prepare them well to fit in or adjust to the demands of starting work (Ashton and Field 1976: 12). There are also other criticisms of the shock hypothesis that can be used to question the legitimacy of this approach. For example, the actual origins of Elias's concern with the problems of adjustment and the adjustment as shock remain unclear and the lack of knowledge of work highlighted by Elias as being significant, may actually more accurately reflect the experience of middle class youth as opposed to working class youth. Likewise, the data also indicates that many of the young workers had actually worked before they had left school and had some understanding of what work entailed. However, despite these criticisms, a reanalysis of the data emerging from the Young Worker Project does provide some empirical evidence for Elias's shock hypothesis as the following quotations reveal:

> I think this respondent could qualify as one of Dr. Elias' 'Youth islanders', for she seems to live in a two-thirds dream world … Perhaps her maturity has been put off partly as a result of being an only child of rather old parents.

> An interesting character who seemed to typify Norbert Elias's 'Culture Shock'.

It is also the case that authors are beginning to explore some of the themes that Elias alluded to in his writings on the shock hypothesis. For example, Lawy and Bloomer (2003) reflect on the superficial understanding that the young people in their study had of their own futures and the fact that the future occupational opportunities anticipated by the young people were not forthcoming. The difference between perceived future opportunities (fantasy) and their actual experiences (reality) have consequences for the young people's identify formation and transformation. Likewise, Elias's concern for understanding the problems that young people experience in their adjustments in leaving school, becoming workers, entering unfamiliar situations for which they are unprepared, earning money, changing family relations and working with others beyond the close circle of school friends, has some overlap with the risk, uncertainty, insecurity and individualisation debates which are so characteristic of the current literature on youth transitions. We will explore these themes in subsequent chapters.

Chapter 3
Researcher Representations of the Young Workers

Introduction

The value of archiving qualitative data and making it available to other researchers wishing to undertaking secondary analysis has now been well recognised (see Hammersley 1997; Corti 1998; Laub and Sampson 2003; Fielding 2004; Heaton 2004; Savage 2005). However, in contrast to those reusing quantitative datasets where access to additional contextual data is vital (Dale et al. 1988), it remains relatively uncommon for qualitative researchers to carry out secondary analyses of associated project documentation such as correspondence, funding applications, meeting minutes, field notes and interviewer notes. With a few notable exceptions (Savage 2005; Evans and Thane 2006; Goodwin and O'Connor 2009; Gillies and Edwards 2012), qualitative researchers have rarely made use of such documents as data sources even though field notes and interviewer notes can provide illuminating insights in to the methods and processes of past research projects.

In this chapter we argue that if secondary analysis is to be effective then where researchers have access to project documentation such as interviewer notes, these should be subjected to the same secondary analysis process as the main dataset. We suggest this for three main reasons: first, interviewer notes provide essential contextual information required for the secondary analysis of the data; second, the interviewer notes provide a rare insight into the experiences of those collecting data in the field; and third, a secondary analysis of the interviewer notes may reveal factors that could have affected the data collection process. Without attempting to understand the thoughts, feelings, ideas and experiences of the interviewer, it would be difficult (if not impossible) for the secondary analyst to fully understand the data. For example, those in the field may have 'over emphasised' the factors in which they were interested in and, without access to the interview notes, this may go unnoticed. A similar view is offered by Fielding (2000: 21):

> Primary data analysis is always subject to the problem that researchers will have entered the field and collected their data with particular interests in mind ... This is probably more often an implicit or unwitting process, but this actually makes the problem worse, since the primary researcher may sincerely believe that such processes have not been at work and so may be blind to their effects ... Secondary analysis may have a legitimate claim to greater plausibility since it is

less likely that the analytic interests which are employed will have played a part in the interactional field from which the data were derived.

The chapter is organised in three main sections. Following the introduction, we consider the methodological and ethical issues that a secondary analysis of interviewer notes suggests. We then present data from the interviewer notes to explore the interviewers' experiences of data collection for the *Adjustment of Young Workers to Work Situations and Adult Roles* project, and to examine how the researchers' preoccupations with social class, income and wealth, the home environment, the physical appearance of the respondent, and respondent's family and friends, may have affected the research process. We then conclude the chapter by reflecting on the importance of secondary analysis for educational and sociological research.

Using Interviewer Notes as Qualitative Secondary Data

The secondary analyst has an anonymized, ready-made dataset that requires none of the moral considerations that are a constant worry for the qualitative researcher carrying out interviews in the field. (Dale et al. 1998: 56)

As we have suggested above, in order for secondary analysis to be effective, the researcher needs to have a clear understanding of the process through which the data was collected. Dale et al. (1988), in their discussion of secondary analysis, support this view and argue that the analysis of qualitative data involves not only an analysis of the data per se, but also an understanding of the process through which the data was collected and the interactions that took place during this process. Central to understanding the process, are the accounts written in interviewer notes and produced by researchers whilst in the field. However, with the exception of Wolfinger (2002), there are very few discussions as to how researchers' experiences are documented in interviewer notes and considerations that offer a secondary analysis of interviewer notes are fewer still. There could be a number of reasons for this, including the methodological and ethical issues surrounding secondary analysis per se or, as others suggest, the fact that many qualitative data sets and accompanying interview notes have simply been lost or destroyed, leaving little opportunity for such secondary analysis to take place (Corti et al. 1995; Hammersley 1997). Despite the trend towards the archiving of qualitative materials, the loss of data may have been accelerated in recent years with the greater emphasis placed on ethical usage and the stricter enforcement of data protection legalisation. Indeed, in many countries, legislation and ethical guidelines demand the destruction of data at a given point in time after the completion of the research. The loss and destruction of qualitative data and interviewer notes aside, however, we do feel that it is important to consider the methodological and ethical concerns that such an approach suggests. There are three broad concerns relating to confidentiality and anonymity, the nature of qualitative research and the problem of 'auditing'.

First, in qualitative research, the researcher responsible for data collection is usually also responsible for writing interviewer notes and analysing the data (Dale et al. 1988). During the research process the original researcher would have provided guarantees as to how the data would be used and given assurances relating to anonymity and to representation of the respondent. Indeed Corti et al. (1995) found that a main concern with secondary analysis relates to the promises made to respondents regarding confidentiality. Additionally, it is possible that the respondents only revealed certain information because of the relationship they had developed with the original researchers. No such relationship exists with later researchers and those who are undertaking the secondary analysis of the data may be unaware of any of the assurances that were given. Such issues are compounded when the secondary analysis process also involves an analysis of accompanying interviewer notes. Problems arise in that the interviewer notes not only contain confidential information about the respondents, but also reveal much about the interviewers. As such, the secondary analyst has to be concerned about maintaining anonymity and confidentiality for both the researcher and the researched and be mindful that the data contained within the interviewer notes was perhaps never intended for secondary analysis. However, Corti et al. (1995) do suggest that a number of steps can be taken to preserve the confidentiality of the research material. Such measures include having a closure period for the material, specifying restricted access to the material so that usage can be vetted, and that the data is anonymised and all personal identifiers are removed. It is also essential that permissions to use the interviewer notes are sought from the original research team.

A second concern for the secondary analyst is that in qualitative approaches the researcher often *becomes* the research instrument (Dale et al. 1998). Here the researcher cannot be separated from the data or interviewer notes and, as such, one must question the ability of a secondary researcher to re-analyse the data. In the case of the secondary analysis of interviewer notes, the notes may only provide an incomplete picture of the data collection process or, as Dale et al. (1988: 15) suggest, 'in these circumstances it seems unlikely that the re-analysis of either interview transcripts or field-notes by an outsider could give more than a partial understanding of the research issues'. Yet despite these concerns, the secondary analysis of qualitative data and interviewer notes has much to offer the educational and social researcher, including the discovery and examination of additional examination of themes, issues, concepts or ideas. Heaton (1998), cited in Fielding (2000), suggests three analytic approaches: 'additional in-depth analysis; additional analysis of a sub-set of the original data; or to apply a new perspective or a new conceptual focus' (Fielding 2000: 16). Likewise, it is not unusual for more than one person to be involved in data collection and analysis. As such, the relationship between respondent and researcher may not be an insurmountable problem for the secondary analyst. As Heaton (1998) argues, whilst one of the limitations with secondary analysis of qualitative data may be the inter-subjective relationship between the interviewer and the interviewee, it is often the case that more than one researcher was involved in the generation of the data.

A final concern is raised by Hammersley (1997), who suggests that the secondary analysis process may lead to an 'auditing' of social research, raising ethical problems for the researcher as well as the researched. Hammersley suggests that 'the audit model could be taken to imply that the efficiency and competence of researchers can be assessed on the basis of archived material' (Hammersley 1997: 136). Corti et al. (1995) also report that researchers are concerned about secondary analysis due to the possible methodological criticisms that could be made of the original research. Again, when the secondary analysis process also involves an analysis of interviewer notes, these issues are further compounded. In the majority of cases, researchers produce interviewer notes for themselves and not for consumption by others and, therefore, making such notes available to secondary analysts must heighten concerns about judgements being made regarding the efficiency and competence of the original researchers. However, Corti et al. (1995: 3) also suggest that 'whilst this concern is understandable, it is probable that secondary users will be more interested in using data for their own specific research rather than replicating the original analysis'. More simply, the intention of most secondary analysis is not to highlight the flaws in the original analysis or to pinpoint any problems with research design or implementation in the field. Instead, the concern is more with using the data to explore new ideas.

It is, nevertheless, important to be mindful that there is a risk that the secondary analyst may be critical of the original research. Geiger et al. (2010) highlight Evans and Thane's (2006) work as a case in point. Evans and Thane revisited publically available archived data originally collected by Dennis Marsden (1969) in his 1960s study of single mothers, *Mothers Alone*. The archived dataset includes his notes on the interviews in the form of observations and reflections on both the interviewee and the context of the research encounter. These notes have much in common with the interviewer notes that we go on to describe in this chapter and are, in many ways, indicative of research practice at the time. By today's standards, many of the comments are judgemental, disparaging and 'unacceptable' (Evans and Thane 2006: 80). However, the context of the original research is crucial here and as Savage (2005: 21) has argued, much social research of the 1950s and 1960s took place during a period when sociological research reflected the:

> ... tradition of Victorian social work, concerned with evaluating the moral capacity and household circumstances of particular families [and] the researchers were quite happy to pass judgements about the respondents.

We, like Geiger et al. (2010: 20), were surprised at the approach taken by Evans and Thane who appear to judge 'past practices ... in terms of their conformity to present practices'. Such a starting point seems to us to ignore the very issue that is so valuable about having access to project documentation – that it provides contemporaneous context. Marsden was carrying out his research in a particular context and time where research practice was very different to now so it comes as no surprise that his work 'depart(s) from current good practice in social research'

(Geiger et al. 2010: 20). Indeed, as Gillies and Edwards (2012: 327) posit, current research practices which are viewed as 'gold standard' now may well come to be viewed in a very different light by future generations of researchers.

The preceding discussion raises a number of issues that need to be considered in the light of this particular project. Dealing with Hammersley's (1997) concern first, it was not our intention to produce an audit of 'the efficiency and competence of researchers', nor was it our intention to imply in any way that the original research design was incorrect or invalid. A replication of the study or a re-testing of the findings (inasmuch as most of the data was never originally analysed), was also beyond our concerns. Our concern was more about understanding the data collection process and examining the original research context and any factors that may have affected it. Indeed, without undertaking a secondary analysis of background material, such as the interviewer notes, it would be impossible to fully understand the context of the research or the data collection process and its attendant problems. In terms of confidentiality, the historical location of this data affords us the closure period that Corti et al. (1995) suggest. In 2004, when the data analysis commenced, the majority of this data was over 40 years old. In usage terms, we were well beyond the current practice at the UK Public Record Office (2001), which opens files for public inspection after 30 years (unless there are specific reasons not to do so). Furthermore, in order to obtain permission to use the data (and to offer reassurances about the purpose of this research), members of the original research team were contacted. Finally, in order to understand the research process more fully, we have discussed the secondary analysis with the original research team. The original research team were also present when some of the data from the interviewer notes were presented at a conference. Being able to discuss the research with the original research team was advantageous, as they were able to provide background material, offer insights into the research process and comment upon our interpretations.

We now move on to look at the themes emerging from the interviewer notes, focusing initially on how the interview process was documented. Particular attention is given to the researchers' experiences of using 'technology' in the field, access issues and the problems of collecting interview data. Following this, the discussion explores how the respondents were represented in the interviewer notes. We pay particular attention to representations of physical appearance and clothing, personality and intelligence, and employment status, reflecting on the impacts that these may have had on the data collection process.

Representations of the Respondents, Class, Gender, Homes and Households

The Young Worker project was primarily a project about the transition from school to work and the adjustments made by young people on entering work and becoming adults. It was therefore surprising to find that each interview included detailed reflections on the interview encounter itself focused not only on the experience of transition but also on seemingly peripheral information about the domestic life of the respondent (home, family, relationships, money). This led us to question why this section of the interview schedule was framed as such and why the interviewers gave such detailed comments on aspects of the young person's life that were beyond the scope of the interview. There are two inter-related reasons which explain why this data was recorded. The first reason relates to the time period in which this project was carried out and the approach to social research at that time. Much social research in the post-war period retained characteristics of an earlier period where it was common for researchers to focus on and highlight the social problems encountered in the field. This is evident in similar studies of the time, particularly community studies such as Young and Wilmott's (1957) *Family and Kinship in East London,* Marsden's (1969) *Mothers Alone* and Goldthorpe et al.'s (1969) *The Affluent Worker.* In all of these studies similar contextual data about interviewees was collected and the form of this data was consistent across these projects. Gillies and Edwards (2012) and Evans and Thane (2006) draw upon interviewer notes from *Mothers Alone* and Savage (2005) uses examples from archived studies such as the *Affluent Worker,* which reveal that other researchers working at the same time were using similar methods.

The second factor relates to the role of Norbert Elias as the principal investigator. Elias was interested in the 'figurations' or inter-relationships and interdependencies between aspects of the young people's lives and the impact of these on the transition to adulthood. These interdependencies were centred on the relationships between home, family, school, employment, income and leisure. This interest goes some way to explaining the directive given to interviewers at the end of the research encounter, to provide a 'general impression from the interview, noting any problems connected with work, family and leisure'. The interviewers were urged by Elias to comment on their impressions of the interview, in particular the attitude of respondents, the atmosphere of the interview and any problems connected with work, family, or leisure. The interviewers also used the interviewer notes to record their own reflections on the research process as *they* experienced it (Goodwin and O'Connor 2009).

The interviewers commented at length on aspects of the interviewee's domestic circumstances: the type and condition of housing, household ownership of material goods, the appearance and behaviour of their parents, siblings and others present at the interview, class status, appearance and perceived level of intelligence and so on. As the quotes below will reveal, these reflections were often derogatory and judgemental and surprisingly candid, particularly when contrasted with present day research practice where such reflections, if made, would certainly not be written down.

In the Field: The Realities of Social Research in the 1960s

One of the benefits of having access to such detailed field notes is that these notes reveal so much about the reality of social research in the 1960s, the 'hidden ethnography' (Blackman 2007), which would otherwise have been concealed or 'written out' of the accounts of the study. Practical concerns dogged many of the encounters, as the relatively advanced (for the time) technology was frequently problematic for the interviewer. It was not only the technology that caused the interviews to run less than smoothly. In some cases, the respondents themselves could present challenges and at times the researchers reported a certain amount of hostility or indifference from interviewees.

We learn a great deal about the atmosphere of each research encounter and the behaviour of the interviewee and others present during the interview from the interviewer notes. The field researchers were asked to indicate whether the interviewee was hostile, indifferent or friendly and to reflect on whether the atmosphere surrounding the interview was poor, moderate or good. Of the 854 interviews, 15 interviewees were recorded as 'hostile' and 139 were indifferent. In terms of atmosphere, 50 interview situations were described as poor, with 219 being recorded as moderate. Part of the hostility may have in fact been due to the reality of undertaking this kind of research in the field with respondents who were just not interested. The interviews were undertaken in the respondent's home after s/he had returned home from work. It is conceivable that the respondents had no interest in answering questions, or speaking to the researchers, after what had been (for them) a full working day.

> Appointment had been made by Mother (after Father had made a mistake in the shift respondent was working). Respondent was alone when I called and seemed to have made up his mind to say no. Talked round the subject, told him about the project and the content of the schedule and he said he would answer if I did it quickly as he wanted to continue mending his bike ... and in any case was waiting for someone to call round. He refused to let me use the tape recorder and stood over me in a very hostile way as I asked the questions and noted the answers.

However, in other situations the hostility shown by the respondents to the research increased when other family members or friends were present during the interview.

> Respondent was indifferent to take interview at first and positively hostile towards the end when his father was present. He left the room immediately. Father started to ask me questions about the research and returned only to see me out. The interview was the shortest I have ever done – 25 minutes tape – but even that seemed too long to hold the boys interest.

> Father was rather critical of the project, and it was only after lengthy persuasion that he finally agreed to the interview being conducted.

> Parents entered at about Q65 and were, especially the father, vividly hostile. Tried hard to intervene and spoil interview atmosphere which had been good up to then. Boy became more cautious with his answers.

More problematic than mere hostility, it is clear that the presence of family members and friends during the interview ensured that some respondents either did not answer the questions fully or that they adapted their answers to become more 'acceptable' to those present.

> Mother was quiet at first, positively hostile when I began to ask questions about the family and I am convinced she indicated to Respondent (she was standing behind me) to refuse to answer. I explained again and again but she was not reassured and we missed out the money/home questions.

> I first talked to respondent's father who was very difficult. He scrutinised the schedule. It took me nearly 45 minutes to convince him that I had no ulterior motive … The respondent was told by his father not to answer anything he didn't want to. Respondent obviously didn't want to be interviewed at all. He refused to answer 2 questions for no obvious reasons I could see apart from bloody mindedness.

> The mother didn't help at the start of the interview by saying 'I shouldn't find **** easy to talk to, he was a funny lad', this in front of him. His younger sisters also kept poking fun at him during the course of the interview, because of some of the words he used e.g. bloke, owt and nowt, and his younger brother was the cause of quite a bit of embarrassment to his mother (not to me).

> A very subdued and inarticulate respondent. This might have been due to pressure of parents, particularly Father …

As in most research, those undertaking the interviews and knocking on doors in order to gain a response were confronted by a range of problems relating to access. It appears that for some of the respondents' parents, there was an anxiety that the researchers were actually sales people intent on selling everything from tape recorders to encyclopaedias.

> Father was very sceptical about the interview and he demanded that I show him my 'permit'. After assuring him that I was not from the police and was not trying to sell him a tape recorder he was keen for me to conduct the interview.

> Mother was interested (perhaps I should say suspicious). She stopped me on way out of house to ask for more details of purpose of interview. She told me after our conversation she thought I might be trying to sell something and warned Respondent against being persuaded to buy something.

> I had considerable difficulty in convincing Respondent's mother that I was not selling encyclopaedias. Respondent had not come home so I called again later. Another quite lengthy explanation followed before I was taken into the front room.

Mother described an experience with two self professed educationalists which had resulted in them buying £30 worth of encyclopaedias – this accounting for the initial suspicion and hostility I encountered in a pre interview call.

Mother brought in coffee, and apologised for nearly having shut the door in my face at first because she'd seen my car around the neighbourhood for several nights and had presumed I was selling books or something.

The researchers had obviously experienced this response so often that they themselves began to 'jokingly' reflect on the issues of selling:

... friendly and welcoming family though father a bit stern and I felt it would have gone badly for me if I'd turned out to be selling encyclopaedias!

Representations of Respondents: Class, Wealth, Home, and Appearance

The importance of social class to this study cannot be ignored. The class status of respondents in the project, as judged by the interviewer, was given great importance and this becomes very clear in the notes made by the interviewers. Class status was identified in a number of ways, including school leaving age, parental occupation, young person's occupation and home address, each of which are explored below.

One of the main indicators that was utilised by the interviewers, related to the age at which the respondent had left school. This information was available to the research team prior to the interview, as the sample was stratified according to gender and age at leaving school. The vast majority of the sample (groups A, C, D and E) left school at the earliest opportunity, usually at the age of 15, without qualifications and only those in Group B, all boys, had stayed on at school beyond the legal school leaving age (see Table 2.1 for more information on the sample).

The stratification of the sample meant then that the interviewers were likely to arrive at the interview with a preconceived idea of the class status of the respondent based on what was known in advance, namely whether the respondent had stayed on at school or not, which school s/he had attended and their home address. Certain assumptions may, therefore, have been drawn in advance of the interview before data on parental occupations and respondent occupation was collected, based upon the sample into which the individual had been categorised.

Once the interview was complete, the interviewers made detailed notes on each respondent with a particular emphasis on family background, home environment and parental (usually the father's) occupation and income. The comments made about the young workers (male and female) who had left school at the earliest opportunity and, broadly speaking, came from more socially deprived backgrounds, tended to be of a more negative nature, often irrespective of each individual's personal achievements. The residential area in which the respondent lived was a signifier of social class that was used extensively by the interviewers.

As the sample was drawn from all school leavers across the city, the interviewers found themselves visiting homes ranging from those in the inner-city which had been ear-marked for demolition in slum clearance programmes and where living standards were extremely deprived, to newly built council estates and more prosperous suburban neighbourhoods.

The following quotes illustrate the type of points noted and illustrate the way that the interviewers were able to add detail to their initial impressions and assumptions relating to the local neighbourhood:

> It is what one would call a lower middle class area – certainly respondent would be classified as such by his occupation, dress, speech and by his peer-group ties.

> Looked like a private semi in an unmade up road, but in the middle of a council estate, with working class sort of family good friendly interview with attractive girl.

> A rough and ready household, as we might expect with such a big family.

> The front room was leading off to another room which had been piled high with rubbish and it was very dirty. The living room was dark and the wallpaper was peeling. The TV dominated and was on throughout my visit.

It was not only the living conditions of respondents and their families that attracted comment from the interviewers. The physical appearance of respondents and other family members was frequently described in detail, with an emphasis on unusual physical characteristics, as illustrated by the following quotes.

> Respondent is a tall, thin lad, looks physically rather awkward and a bit self conscious.

> Respondent is the smallest person I have met in the sample – apart from rather tired eyes he looked about 12 years old.

The following set of interviewer notes is amongst the most descriptive and most negative of the sample:

> One cannot avoid commenting on the physical peculiarities of the boy and his mother. She was an extremely small mouse like woman who seemed to have all sparks of life damped out of her – she let me into the house hardly questioning my purpose and Respondent started answering my questions with the same lack of enquiry. He too was undersized, pitifully, pale and unglamorous looking dressed in a holey sweater and mucky jeans.

His complete lifelessness seemed to be a combination of environment [a miserable back street terraced house furnished with the barest of essentials and so dark] and congenital low intelligence … We conducted the interview in what appeared to be the junk room. Yet it was difficult to understand why the family was still so poverty stricken now that all three children were working and the eldest son had been for 9 years … This is his father's line, but it is difficult to say whether Respondent was going to do something about this as a career or whether it is just a daydream.

The physical characteristics of both the respondent and his mother are graphically recounted and the lack of interest in the survey is attributed to the poor home environment and congenital low intelligence. As neither the respondent nor his family changed the interviewer's opinion during the interview, the resultant notes are negative and critical. However, in other cases, physical descriptions were often positive, identifying desirable physical features. Perhaps not surprisingly, the comments again tended to be social class based, with positive physical attributes identified primarily amongst boys in sample B and girls who were perceived by the interviewer to be 'attractive'.

Respondent was friendly but a little reserved, I think probably inhibited a bit by the tape. He was V good looking.

A very confident good-looking individual whose intelligence was used for making a rationale of life – yet he wasn't bigoted.

Respondent was a quiet, rather attractive girl but was very nervous during the interview – physically trembling at times. She was, however, determined to play the hostess – preparatory to her marriage this year – and invited me to stay for tea.

A well dressed good looking blonde who was reluctant at first to answer my questions but who thoroughly enjoyed it at the end. She was very talkative and confident.

Assessments of the respondents' level of intelligence were provided in the more extreme cases, for example, if the interviewee appeared to be either somewhat lacking in intelligence or particularly 'bright'. The extracts below illustrate the type of notes made in the case of respondents who were thought to be of low intelligence.

Respondent is mentally backward and was not able to answer any questions which required thought – I asked the simple questions but did not pursue any which I thought were unsuitable.

A pathetic little boy. At a guess I'd say 'D' stream or worse of a secondary modern. Yet his Father repeated several times that he was very shy and it may have been more nervousness than sheer stupidity that produced these poor questionnaire results.

The perceived high intelligence of other respondents was commented upon in a positive way, as highlighted by these quotes:

He was an extremely intelligent boy, he used for example, such words as jubilant and extrovert quite naturally. On leaving the house he said 'I suppose you are going to use the old psycho on all this'.

An alert young man, full of ideas and confidence in himself, learns quickly from experience.

The respondents were also subject to judgement of their personality traits, again focusing on extremes, for example shyness, or at the opposite end of the spectrum, 'cheekiness'.

His mother told him to be sure to be serious in giving answers so he probably tends to be cheeky.

Respondent was extremely shy, would not answer the door, or look at me or speak to me at first.

Very shy at first and so answers were very limited but became more interested and confident gradually. She hasn't very much confidence in herself, maybe because she has an elder sister (20) who is cleverer than her, according to the parents.

Certain personality traits, for example, cheerfulness, charm, and extraversion were seen as positive characteristics.

Respondent is a cheerful likeable friendly lad, v co-operative and open, looks if anything a bit younger than his years and not very interested in his appearance, though clean and not exactly untidy.

Respondent was most charming the whole time, and if he continues to use this charm for his own ends, he should do very well as a sales rep. His answers to Q76 give the impression that he is perhaps rather immoral. I would not say that this is not the case however. I think he answered the question in this way because he felt that it was the way a 'gay young man' should answer such questions. He rather fancied himself as a 'Tom Jones'.

The detailed, highly subjective and frequently disparaging and critical descriptions of many of the respondents, seems vastly at odds with current standards of research practice. However, it is important to recognise that these research notes were not unusual at the time and similar, indeed almost identical comments, can be found in the majority of sociological studies of the period, for example, Jackson and Marsden (1966), Goldthorpe et al. (1969) and Marsden (1969). The value of such detailed accounts is that these tell us so much about the concerns of the period and the process of social research at the time allowing us to reflect on what has changed, how it has changed and what we can learn from earlier sociological concerns when viewed through a contemporary lens.

Aspirations, Occupations and Orientations to Work

It was not only the appearance and living conditions of the respondents that were used to make what are, essentially, class-based assumptions by the interviewers. Another area of interest was based around the individual's occupation and orientation to work. The role of the respondents' parents was important here, with parental intervention in to career decisions being viewed as positive, middle-class behaviour:

> Respondent's father seems to have been very systematic and helpful when R decided to leave school. Respondent also showed signs of a clear middle class appraisal of jobs and prospects and the need to have help in decision-making.

> A comfortable, semi-detached house – which would be classified as working class, however, in terms of furnishings, general impression of the home … She reflects the type of unambitious, passive young worker common amongst factory girls and the antithesis of the conscious chooser of occupation – with work of peripheral significance in one's life.

> Respondent was a friendly, attractive young man in a good class of house – certainly lower middle. There was a friend of the family there who seemed well-educated and had a daughter doing social psychology at the University. The mother was articulate and well spoken also. This is not therefore a working class family in the sociological meaning of the term.

In these cases, positive comments were made regarding those interviewees seen as middle class, whilst the working-class respondents were often described negatively. Where the interviewer's class-based expectations were not borne out during the interview, this seemed to feature prominently in the interview notes.

> Respondent was friendly and intelligent – though not verbally accomplished. The home was untidy warm and comfortable – Father was very much a background figure – it was Mother with arms akimbo who broke into the interview and

demanded to know about what was going on. Having being reassured she became friendly and made a cup of tea. Respondent has aspirations towards a white-collar job – being specifically attracted by the cleanliness of the draughtsman's work. No other members of his family have such a job – neither do his friends but he seems to have been influenced by his school in the sense of having stayed on and worked hard for the extra year. This argues some identification with teachers. The parents gave no impression at all of wanting to be thought middle class [the sons were wandering about with bare torsos during the interview – Mother did not bother about the mess on the table where we were sitting – Father sat munching a huge pile of toast in front of the TV speaking only to his dog]. It is not a socially mobile family unit as far as one can see. Perhaps the aspiration is merely towards a clean, interesting, well-paid job with no social status considerations.

This respondent clearly fitted the interviewer's expectations of a middle-class background. However, the working-class home environment and the parents' apparent lack of middle-class aspiration appear to surprise the interviewer. Perhaps as a result of this, the interviewer sympathised with the respondent who, by contrast, had aspirations. For example, his ambition to become a draughtsman was admired and he was deemed to be intelligent. This was reinforced by the fact that he left school with qualifications. The interviewer saw no evidence of family support or encouragement. Instead, the role of the school environment is highlighted, suggesting that his experience there led him to identify with the teachers rather than his family.

In general, it is evident that the observations and comments made about the respondents who had stayed on at school and tended to come from middle-class backgrounds were positive. In cases where middle-class respondents had not progressed as well as might be expected, there is little criticism and in each case the respondent is portrayed positively. However, assertions were sometimes made about 'respectability' and in many cases, the working-class label was qualified with a comment about the 'respectability' of the family. Wight (1993) locates respectability for working-class males in hard work, being disciplined at work, having good timekeeping in employment, having a trade, 'right living', being decent and having self-respect, being well groomed, managing ones resources wisely, being restrained in drinking and gambling and going to church. These criteria can compare very favourably to those rough or disorderly males, 'wasters' or those in Wight's (1993) study who are labelled as 'a bad lot', rough, lazy, 'immune to work', promiscuous, anti-social, poor, and unemployed and not actively seeking work. This seems to be what the researchers were suggesting about the following respondent:

Respondent is one of those little rogues called a 'handful' by teachers, parents and anyone in authority. He didn't seem to be either school or career minded but more concerned with getting out with the boys, and spending his money.

The parents didn't seem to have much influence or control over him and the general impression, from both them and his brothers, was that he was a bit of a black sheep.

Respondent had an adolescent disrespect for his parents – 'oh they don't do any work' – and seemed to regard it as right and proper that he should rebel, whether against teachers, parents or employers … Irish, he was a scruffy little character who 'gave plenty of cheek' to more than just the butcher he had worked for.

His mother confided that he was going through 'that difficult age' and although their flat was one of the most tatty I have been in – lino floor and no carpet, food left out on table, washing and cooking facilities on the landing – the parents were extremely mild, polite and quite well dressed. That peculiar Irish mixture of caring less for surroundings than personal relationships.

This is one of the few respondents whose family had migrated to Leicester, coming from Ireland four years earlier. The description of the respondent and his home environment has explicit undertones of anti-Irish sentiment which was common in the UK during this period. The family home is described as being poorly kept due to the family being Irish and not caring about their surroundings. The respondent left school without any qualifications and had no wish to stay on longer. Although the parents are not blamed for the respondent's lack of interest in school and career, their negative role is perhaps implied by their lack of 'influence or control' over his behaviour. In this description, the social class of the respondent is not explicitly referred to. However, the comments regarding the family background imply this. There were no surprises for the interviewer and the notes are accordingly negative.

Amongst our sample, the employment status and individual attitudes towards work appear to have been highly significant in influencing the interviewer's perception of the young worker. As in Wight's study (1993), such attitudes seemed to have a greater bearing than all other factors, including class status. For example, judgements on personality were often linked to the respondents' thoughts and feelings about their employment status and, as the following quotes illustrate, those who expressed disappointment about their employment situation tended to be criticised for having a poor attitude, irrespective of social class.

Respondent seems to have a bit of a chip on his shoulder, because he hasn't got the kind of job he wanted, road construction. I thought for a grammar school boy he didn't show much initiative over leisure.

I got the impression that he goes around with a chip on his shoulder, that society owes him a good job with short working hours and plenty of money.

Likes to think of himself as a frustrated artist, writer and film star all rolled into one. Perhaps his background was responsible for his inability to realise his

ambitions but he had an unhealthy desire to pin all his failings on to other people
– his parents, his girlfriend, his boss.

Conclusions

We have argued that for the secondary analysis of qualitative data to be effective
in educational and social research, researchers need to also analyse interviewer
notes where these are available. It was suggested that a secondary analysis of
interviewer notes was crucial in providing insight into the research process and
the experiences of those working in the field. However, we acknowledge that
any secondary analysis of the interview notes needs to be set in the context of a
discussion of the ethical and methodological implications of qualitative secondary
analysis, including issues relating to confidentiality, anonymity, the nature of
qualitative research and the possible problem of auditing.

Despite these ethical and methodological concerns, it was felt that the
secondary analysis of interviewer notes was essential if the researchers were to
fully understand the data collection process. In the current research, a number of
important themes and issues relating to the data collection process emerged that
would ordinarily have remained hidden if we had not analysed the interviewer
notes. Each of these themes could have had a potential impact upon the actual
interview data and may have had some affect on any subsequent analysis. First,
it is clear that many of the interviews and the responses that were collected, were
'viewed' through a 'middle-class lens'. What emerges from the secondary analysis
of the interviewer notes is that that the researchers often described working-class
respondents more negatively as compared to the middle-class young workers
they interviewed. Comments on physical appearance, family, income and home
environment all clearly fell along rigid class lines. Characteristics such as
educational achievement, staying on at school, living in a 'nice' home, having
supportive parents, having middle-class career aspirations and displaying middle-
class behaviours were always viewed positively, and appeared to be what the
researchers were looking for. If, for some reason, a middle-class youngster had
not achieved, rational justifications were found and recorded in the interviewer
notes. Yet, these characteristics were seemingly not at all present in many of
the interviews with the working-class youngsters in the sample. Likewise, the
'fault' for any failures or having limited aspirations was clearly recorded as the
respondent's own.

One possible explanation for this has to be the class background of the
researchers. It appears that all of the researchers and interviewers were educated
to at least degree level or were currently registered for degrees. The researchers'
own lifestyles, educational and career achievements or aspirations must have
contrasted sharply with those respondents who were living in relative poverty and
who had limited aspiration beyond their immediate circumstances. The researchers
recognised in the middle-class young workers, educational and career patterns

similar to their own and, arguably, as a consequence, recorded more positive perceptions and observations in the interviewer notes. Such a middle-class lens must have mediated the data collection process and the subsequent write up.

Alongside the lens of class, there was also some evidence that gender and gender-based prejudices influenced the interview process. From the outset of the research, the inclusion of girls in the sample was contentious, with an assumption by the male researchers that the girls' experiences were less important than the boys. However, despite their inclusion, it is clear that during the fieldwork gender-based assumptions were made about the female respondents. For example, the interview notes reveal some evidence that male researchers made assumptions that the girls would give up paid employment for marriage and motherhood at the first opportunity. Likewise, assumptions were also made about the need for male respondents to secure higher paid jobs in order that they could 'provide' for their future families – an issue we discuss in more depth in a later chapter.

The researchers' reflections on each interview provided us with insights into the research process that we would not have had from the questionnaire data alone. Indeed, the lack of interviewer notes available to us in the reanalysis of later datasets, from the 1980s, has been a source of frustration. The researchers described and reflected on a process that involves using imperfect technology and the resulting frustrations of constant technological breakdown. They documented very clearly the hostility that they faced trying to access and eventually going into the young people's homes to interview. They described a research process that was imperfect, but where they tried to collect authentic data even in the midst of interruptions, mild intimidation, indifference and personal scrutiny.

Overall, the interviewer notes have provided a glimpse into the process of data collection, the attitudes and experiences of the researchers, and have highlighted a number of clear limitations with the youth transitions data that we have. Without first analysing the interview notes, we would have been unaware of the middle-class lens of some of the researchers and would not have known that some of the interviews were written up from memory. Highlighting these issues, however, is not to question the professionalism or competence of the original researchers, but more simply to locate our secondary analysis in its original context so that our analyses and discussions are as meaningful and as useful as possible. For the secondary analysis of sociological data to be as effective, we recommend that other researchers also submit any accompanying interviewer notes to the secondary analysis process.

Chapter 4
Complex Transitions in 1960s Labour Markets

Introduction

The way youth transitions are conceptualised has changed over the last 30 years or so (Layder et al. 1991; Roberts 1995; Evans and Furlong 1997; Lawy 2002). Evans and Furlong (1997) reflect on this change by documenting the metaphors emerging from the different theoretical approaches of the last 30 years. They argue 'each metaphor represents ways of analysing and understanding the young person's interactions with his or her social milieu and typical sequences of events between adolescence and adulthood' (Evans and Furlong 1997: 17). For example, they suggest that youth transitions were categorised first, as niches in the 1960s and then pathways in the 1970s, as trajectories in the 1980s, before moving on to the more reflexive and post structuralist metaphor of navigation in the 1990s. In turn, these metaphors have given rise to newer metaphors such as structured individualisation (Nagel and Wallace 1997) and rationalised individualisation (Furlong et al. 2002).

However, underpinning these different metaphors is a view that the individual experience of the transition *has* indeed changed and that the transitional experience of contemporary young people is markedly different to the experiences of previous generations of youth. The implication is that school to work transitions have moved from being a mass, straightforward, linear and 'single step' process (albeit mediated by family background, class and gender), to a complex, fragmented and individualised process dependent on the navigational and negotiating abilities of young people (Furlong and Cartmel 1997; Cartmel et al. 2002). Whereas once young people could leave school, often without qualifications, now young people face uncertainty and have to navigate their way through a variety of experiences and transition options, always reflecting on the risks involved. Young people entering a local labour market no longer share common transition experiences with others, as transitions have become more individualised.

> Analysis of the contemporary situation of young adults highlights an increasing fragmentation of opportunities and experience; the processes of youth are highly differentiated, reflecting and constructing social divisions in society in complex ways … As possible pathways out of school have diversified, young people have to find their own ways forward and their own values in education, consumption, politics, work and family life. (Evans and Furlong 1997: 33)

The evidence put forward to support the view that young people's transitional experiences have changed usually appears in the form of drastic labour market transformations (Ashton et al. 1991; Roberts 1995; 1997b), the rise in youth unemployment (Furlong 1993; Roberts 1997a), the emergence of youth training schemes, the increased availability of post-compulsory education (Furlong 1993; Roberts 1997b), changes in social security legislation (Pilcher 1995; Furlong and Cartmel 1997), and the increased complexity (and risk) of choice (Nagel and Wallace 1997; Lawy 2002). However, with new studies collecting reflexive accounts of past transitional experiences and via the secondary analysis of historical young worker data, it has become possible to re-examine the individual transitional experience and question the extent to which past youth transitions were individualised and complex. For example, Vickerstaff (2001: 3) has explored the assumed linearity and uncomplicated nature of transitions for post-war apprentices. In this research she has demonstrated that past transitions were anything but straightforward, unproblematic or single-step. For some of the respondents in her study, the experience of apprenticeship was unpleasant, violent, fragmented and as much the result of 'chance' as choice. She suggests, compared to contemporary transitions, that:

> The range of choices may have been different, leading to a greater homogenisation of possible pathways and individuals may have had less expectation of being able to design their own trail but the individual still had to negotiate and manage their own trajectory, whether it was of their own choosing or not. Indeed, the absence of apparent choice might be hypothesized to have brought its own risks and dilemmas. (Vickerstaff 2001: 3)

Using data from the little known project from the 1960s, in this chapter we used data from the Adjustment of Young Workers project to examine the complexity of past transitions and to question their assumed linearity. The argument offered is that previous research on youth transitions has understated the level of complexity that characterised youth transitions in the early 1960s and 1970s. From the secondary analysis of the 1960s data, the individual level complexity that underpinned school to work transitions is documented. For many in this study, the transition process was not as smooth, uncomplicated or as linear as has been previously argued. Throughout this chapter, the concept of a 'golden age' is used as a shorthand term to describe the post-war period (between the 1950s and the late 1960s), which has been characterised by many authors as a time of mass employment and straightforward school to work transitions (Vickerstaff 2003). Certainly in Leicester, the focus of this chapter, the 1960s, was a period of excellent employment prospects for young unqualified workers with the wealth of low skilled jobs available and a low rate of unemployment (Pye 1972: 375). However, this orthodox view of the past ignores the fact that many local labour markets were characterised by large fluctuations in their buoyancy and prosperity. Even in the Leicester labour market of the 1960s, our data reveals that there was a fear of unemployment regardless of those accounts which suggest that during this 'golden age', jobs for school leavers were plentiful (Kiernan 1992; Roberts 1984; 1995; Unwin and Wellington 2001). Indeed, as Pollard (1983) has argued, unemployment elsewhere was substantial during this period, suggesting that the young workers' fears were justified.

In this chapter we explore the following questions:

i.   to what extent were transitions in the 1960s 'non-linear', involving breaks, changes of direction, extended or repeated periods of unemployment, frequent moves between jobs, returns to education and training after labour market participation and any unusual sequences of events (Furlong et al. 2002)?;
ii. to what extent were transitions in the 1960s homogenised or differentiated at the individual level?;
iii. to what extent were transitions in the 1960s single-step or prolonged?

From School to Work: Linear and Smooth or Non-linear and Complex?

Furlong et al. (2002) reflect on transition experiences that can be defined as either linear or non-linear. They suggest that linearity involves fairly smooth, straightforward transitions from school to work in which there are no major breaks, divergences or reversals (Furlong et al. 2002: 7). However, they note that this has changed over time and once uncommon experiences, such as unemployment, have become normalised. They suggest, for example, that few young people have managed to avoid unemployment altogether and a young person now 'who has a short period of unemployment between leaving education and gaining a job can still be seen as having made a linear transition' (Furlong et al. 2002: 7). Conversely, they argue that non-linear or complex transitions 'involve breaks, changes of direction and unusual sequences of events' (Furlong et al. 2002: 8) and can include extended or repeated periods of unemployment, frequent moves between jobs, returns to education and training after periods in the labour market (Furlong et al. 2002: 8).

Using this typology, Furlong et al. (2002) have successfully questioned the assumed non-linearity and complexity of all *contemporary* transitions and argue that some young people still follow smooth and linear routes. They suggest that the routes young people take still depend, to some extent, on educational attainment, gender and class, arguing that 'those who experience complex transition tend to be disadvantaged educationally and socially and are over represented in areas of deprivation' (Furlong et al. 2002: 13).

Given Furlong et al.'s (2002) critique of the assumed non-linearity of current transitions, it is possible to question the assumed linearity of past transitions using the same typology. This typology implies that the transitions of the 1960s were linear and straightforward involving no major breaks, divergences or reversals.

It would also be fair to suggest that a linear transition of the past would not have involved any periods of unemployment or employment breaks, changes of direction, frequent moves between jobs or returns to education as, at this time, these were relatively uncommon experiences.

Frequent Job Moves

Data relating to the number of jobs held immediately after leaving school and prior to the interview is presented in Table 4.1. Usually the respondents were interviewed within one to two years of leaving school and as such, the number of jobs broadly represents the numbers of jobs held in their first two years of working life. Data on the number of jobs held is presented by gender, age and education.

At the time of the interview, the majority of the young workers were still in their first jobs, although a sizeable group had worked in at least two jobs. Interestingly, the numbers of young people who had held four or more jobs is not insignificant. Whilst the data provides no evidence of young people returning to education, this data does suggest that some of the young workers did engage in frequent job moves, with many of those interviewed changing jobs anywhere between every month and every four to six months. Indeed, taking the sample as a whole, there were a small number of individuals who had held between seven and 11 jobs between leaving school and the time of the interview.

There is an important gender difference here, with girls experiencing a greater number of job changes than boys in the same period. Over 43 per cent of the girls interviewed were on their second or third job and 10 per cent were on their fourth job or more, whilst the majority of young males were still in their first job, 37 per cent had held more than one job and nearly 6 per cent had held four or more jobs. Given the fact that the majority of these young workers were actually in their first year of employment, for this small group it implies a job move at least every three months.

Table 4.1   Number of jobs by gender, age and education

Number of Jobs			
Gender	1	2	3	4+
Male	63.0	22.1	9.2	5.7
Female	46.1	27.3	16.5	10.1
Age				
14*	33.3	–	66.7	–
15	57.5	30.0	5.0	7.5
16	61.8	22.4	9.9	6.0

Number of Jobs				
17	62.1	29.1	5.8	2.9
18	49.8	24.1	16.6	9.6
19	68.9	17.8	8.9	4.4
20*	100.0	–	–	–
21*	–	100.0	–	–
Education				
More than one year of Further Education	77.7	18.5	2.3	1.5
Less than one year of Further Education	53.8	25.0	13.2	8.1
Total Percentage	57.3	24.0	11.5	7.1
N Missing = 1	488	204	98	60

Note: * The numbers in each of these categories was very small (2–3 in each).

From Table 4.1, it appears that most young people had remained in their first job. However, of those aged 18, 16 per cent had held three jobs and nearly 10 per cent had held four jobs or more. Educational experience also had an impact. The data appears to suggest that those young workers with less than one year of education (in this sample, the majority) were more likely to be onto their second or third job, whilst those with a higher level of education were more likely to have remained with their first employer.

Frequent Moves and Changes of Direction

The changes in direction that such frequent job moves entailed are also evident in the data presented in Table 4.2. Although not fully representative of the sample, this data provides some insight into the early career histories of the school leavers interviewed and individual level complexities. This data is typical of many of those young workers who had not remained in their first job. The data in this table is presented in order of job, reading from right to left.

The data clearly indicates that some of the young people interviewed did experience significant changes in direction during the early part of their career. For example, respondent A464, aged 16 and interviewed in April 1964, had had a total of seven jobs since leaving school 16 months earlier. On average, this respondent changed jobs every two months. He started work as a shop assistant before spending one month as a machinist in a large boot and shoe factory. He then went to work in a crisp factory, returning to boot and shoe work for three months before subsequent moves through positions in a plastics factory, a sweet factory and an engineering works, before becoming unemployed.

Respondent E87 is similar. Aged 18 at the time of interview, this respondent had held nine different positions in just over two years in the labour market. On average, she stayed in each job for just under three months. She began her working life as a shop assistant before moving into a position as a cutter in a hosiery factory.

Table 4.2   Job movements

ID	Job Types		
A464	Shop Assistant Boot and Shoe* Engineering Works	Shoe Machinist Plastic Works Unemployed	Inspector of Potatoes/ Crisps Manufacturing
A544	Boot and Shoe Leather Worker	Bakery Assistant	Hosiery*
A601	Apprentice Joiner Shop Assistant	Trainee Hairdresser Trainee Caravan Fitter	Farm Worker
A762	Shop Manager Trawler Fisherman	Apprentice Butcher Hosiery	Boot and Shoe
A806	Apprentice Carpenter Grocery Worker	Apprentice Butcher Labourer	Grocery Worker Boot and Shoe
B207	Warehouse Man TV Repairs	Chemist's Assistant	Milkman
C331	Pattern Maker Boot and Shoe	Army Packer	Tyre Fitter Labourer
C510	Van Boy Shop Assistant	Painter Army	Shop Fitter
C538	Car Sales Warehouse Man	Warehouse Man Shop Assistant	Butcher's Boy Assistant Shop Manager
D579	Hosiery	Shop Assistant	Nurse
E87	Shop Assistant Machinist Groom	Cutter Chamber Maid Hotel Assistant	Domestic Assistant Maid Shoe Machinist
Practice	Boot and Shoe Car Wash Foreman Driver's Mate Labourer	Painter Gardener Hosiery	Driver's Mate Ice-cream Seller Driver's Mate

Note: * Boot and Shoe and Hosiery has been summarised here as it could involve a number of different functions including cutting, overlocking stitching, etc. All other jobs are recorded according respondent's definition.

She left the hosiery factory because she wanted to become a nurse and then spent six months working as a domestic assistant in a nursing home. She went onto become a machinist in a boot and shoe factory. Subsequently, she moved into positions as chambermaid, maid, groom and a hotel assistant, before returning to work as a shoe machinist.

Breaks and Unemployment

A further factor identified as being central to a linear smooth transition from school to work is the absence of periods of unemployment or breaks in employment from work histories. The assumption in much of the literature is that young people in the 1960s moved seamlessly from school to work without a break. From the data it appears that many of the young people did not experience any significant breaks in employment and avoided unemployment. However, this may mean that for some, unemployment and the fear of unemployment added to the individual level complexity of their own transition from school to work. Indeed, although while perhaps not the norm, individuals in this study did experience breaks in employment and periods of unemployment.

> The respondent gave the impression of being very insecure. He had 7 sisters and 4 brothers, but his mother was a widower. For the last few years of his school career, he had lived at a council home because he often played truant from school while he was living with his mother. Since he had been out to work, he had had 7 jobs but he was now out of work ... At the end of the interview, respondent mentioned that he may get a job with a fair that was due to leave Leicester in the next few days.

> **** had a good school career, and with five passes at GCE started out with the intention of making a good career for himself. He was very pleased to get the position with a firm of chartered accountants and felt he was on the road to becoming a professionally qualified man. It came as a great shock when he was dismissed for having a Saturday job on a market stall. He was unemployed for five weeks and had to take a job simply to earn some money.

It also appears from the data that the fear of unemployment was a real issue for some of the young people. As the quotes below illustrate, a group of the respondents professed their anxieties about being unemployed when leaving school or becoming unemployed in the future. For some, the concern was so great that they took the first job that they could.

> ... respondent has had fears of unemployment and general economic insecurity. It came out several times in the interview. As his father realised ... respondent has also been afraid of becoming a drifter, if not a 'delinquent' ...

Worried when it came to leaving school in case he didn't get a job: took the first he could get because it was better than being unemployed.

I used to worry that I would get the sack because I wasn't underlined. [Did any boys get the sack?] Oh yes.

In this study, the respondents were asked whether they had secured a job whilst they were still at school or whether they secured the job after leaving school. Over 170 respondents reported that they did not secure a job until after leaving school. The length of time after leaving school until they found work could vary anywhere between two and five weeks or between two and six months. This suggests that quite a sizable group did not leave school and walk straight into a job. As the interviewer notes record:

… after leaving school – he couldn't get a job to start with so he had an uncle in carpentry who took him around with him and gave him pocket money.

Or as a respondent suggested:

Long time after I left. Two months [didn't you have job during that time?].

In terms of movements between their first and second job, of those who were in their second job, 117 suggested that they have only heard about the current position after leaving their previous position. It is also clear that some of the young people in the survey experienced periods of unemployment.

Straightforward Transitions?

A key characteristic of non-linear transitions is the risk and uncertainty experienced by the young person. Again, the assumption here is that young people making school to work transitions in the 1960s did not experience the process as being characterised by risk and uncertainty. Instead it was relatively straightforward. However the data for this study suggests that some of the young people did indeed perceive the risks and uncertainties of life beyond the school playground and, as with Vickerstaff (2001) and Carter (1962), quite a large proportion of the young workers did not feel that they had been prepared for entering employment for the first time. The respondents were asked 'when you were at school, what were you told about work?'

That it was terrible, had to work long hours. Pretty general idea that it was a horrible thing to do, that nobody would ever want to leave school when been to work.

We had a few talks but very little really until you come to the real thing. Went on a few trips but they never really told you much.

> YEO told us it wasn't as easy as it seemed to be. When at school tend to see just payday side – don't look into hours and how hard you have to work.

> That I would wish that I were back at school.

For many, their preparation for working life was ad hoc and was largely dependent upon the whims of teachers, schools and youth employment officers. For others, the mere prospect of entering employment brought with it feelings of risk and uncertainty.

> I had no idea what it would be like. It's like going to a new town – you just don't know what it's going to be like.

> I thought I'd have to work quite hard – If I didn't work fast enough I'd have to leave the job.

> I was a bit frightened going into big factory and not knowing anybody, and people being older than you, – not quite sure what to expect.

During the first few months of work, the risk and uncertainty remained for many. For example, a large number of those who had left school to become apprentices experienced real anxiety and a heightened sense of risk in simply getting their apprenticeship papers actually signed. The risk for these young workers was that without the signed apprenticeship paper they could lose their job, have difficulties in gaining access to college or, as one respondent reported, they would be 'mucked about, the new lads are used as cheap labour'.

> … you have to push them to sign your apprenticeship … [what did you do?]. You tell them and they put your name down and they forget it you have to keep urging them on and keep telling them till they get fed up and they let you go. [Is yours sorted out?] Yes I keep going up and telling them, but me dad has gotta go up and see him and sign them. [How soon?] It has to be done not much before and not much after 16 because your apprenticeship finishes when you're 21 1/2 years.

> The only difficulty was getting my apprenticeship papers. It wasn't difficult getting into tech but I had to go to my boss and ask about apprenticeship on a years approval to start with and if you are satisfactory you start apprenticeship … [What did you do?] Asked my boss … he said that at the moment the problem is getting into tech. There was a meeting of apprentices with the boss and he said he could only let a few go and it was a question of who … the first thing I knew was a member of staff coming to me with the papers and telling me to get them signed. As far as I know there has only been trouble about being an apprentice.

I was worried about my apprenticeship papers not being signed. After I had been there about 9 months I went to see the boss about it. He said he would make it all right and he backdated the papers for me.

Homogenised or Differentiated Transition?

A crude measure of individualization is the proportion of age peers in a person's social network with whom he or she shares a common biography having grown up in the same district, attended the same schools, and entered similar types of employment at the same ages. Virtually everything that every individual does and experiences is still shared with many other people, but nowadays in a variety of individualized sequences and combinations. (Roberts 1995: 113)

As suggested above, alongside the debates relating to the relative complexity of school to work transitions is an assertion that transitions in the past were more homogenised and less individualised. Roberts (1995) provides a useful discussion of this, pointing to the shared characteristics of a homogenous transition – same biography, similar education, growing up in the same area and entering similar types of employment.

The relative homogeneity of transitions can also be explored using the *Adjustment of Young Workers* data. During the interviews, the young workers were asked two questions that could be used as broad indicators of the homogeneity thesis. First, the young workers were asked 'did anyone else you know have the same sort of jobs as you?' Such a question touches upon notions of individuals sharing a common biography, growing up in the same area, attending the same schools and entering the same types of employment, as the question is specifically directed at the respondent's relatives, friends and neighbours. Likewise, the same 'type' of employment that Roberts refers to is also captured in this question as the question deals with types of jobs rather than dealing with specific employers. The second question deals with the latter issue by asking the respondents 'was there anyone you knew working in the same firm?' The data relating to these two questions is presented in Table 4.3.

Table 4.3   Working with friends, family and neighbours

	Yes	No
Did anyone else you know have the same sort of job as you (any relatives, friends, neighbours)?	410	423
Was there anyone you knew working in the same firm?	372	449
N 851		

From Table 4.3, it is clear that approximately 50 per cent of young workers in 1960s Leicester may not have made the homogenised transitions suggested by authors such as Roberts. For example, 49 per cent of the respondents suggested that they did not work in the same sort of job as their friends or relatives. Although such a question may underrepresent the ability of respondents to fully differentiate between types of jobs in terms of their 'similarities', such as working conditions and rewards, and should be treated with some caution, the findings do suggest that past transitions may not have been as homogenous as previously thought. Likewise, the fact that 52 per cent of the respondents indicated that they did not know anybody working in the same firm raises questions about the extent to which biographies were shared by those growing up in the same area.

Single-step or Prolonged Transitions?

Vickerstaff (2001) argues that earlier studies assume that transitions in the 1950s and 1960s were 'single step'. It is suggested that the buoyancy of the labour market in the early 1960s enabled young people to make a direct and single-step transition from school to work. Once the young people had entered work, they tended to leave home, achieve some state of financial independence, marry and have children in a relatively short period of time, making what Coles (1995) has called three interrelated transitions; from school to work, from family of origin to family of destination and from childhood home to independent living. This pattern was particularly true for the working class (Jones 1995; Furlong and Cartmel 1997), with working class youth more likely to become economically independent earlier than middle class youth (Pilcher 1995).

However, 40 years later it has become widely accepted that youth transitions are now extended and more diversified, with young people remaining dependent on their families for a longer period of time (Roberts 1995; 1997b; Furlong and Cartmel 1997; Pilcher 1995; Lawy 2002). The protracted transition from school to work has left young people remaining dependent on the family and state for longer (Pilcher 1995; Furlong and Cartmel 1997; Lawy 2002), as the possibility of early financial independence has become more remote. Furlong and Cartmel (1997) also suggest that domestic and housing transitions have become more complex. Explanations for such extended transitions range from labour market restructuring, the rise of youth unemployment, changes in social welfare legislation and the increased numbers of young people staying on in education, either because of limited employment opportunities or because of family pressure.

There is little evidence to suggest that the young workers in Leicester were prolonging their transitional experience by staying on in education, as the vast majority left school at the first opportunity. Indeed, instead of family pressure to stay in education, there was a great deal of pressure from family and friends to leave education as soon as possible. Yet the single-step hypothesis, relating to past transitions, is questionable when one considers the data relating to dependence on the family, financial independence and housing transitions.

One characteristic of independence or self-responsibility, we suggest, would be the ability of the young people to make decisions about their own futures and resolve any difficulties that arose in work or life. However, many of the young people interviewed in the young worker project still relied heavily on family members in obtaining work or in resolving difficulties of conflicts at work.

> ... The forewoman has to sign the ticket if you make your own price out – she signed the ticket and I sent them down then swore blind she hadn't signed them. My Dad went up because they'd accused me of putting the tickets in which I didn't.

> Father went to see Mr ****** and the Station Master and it was settled by them.

> We started at Tech for one year and then he stopped us going the following year. My father got the TU in and the secretary went to see the boss. [Father] got it so that we shall carry on at Tech next September.

> [Have you had any difficulties in this job?] Not really – if I have, I talked to mother or people at work, e.g. problems with tax.

In these examples, the young workers did not attempt to resolve their difficulties themselves or display independent behaviour. Instead, they relied heavily on the interventions of family members. There are other examples in the data where parents intervene in obtaining employment, getting apprenticeship papers signed, negotiating pay and even helping the employers to discipline the young workers. When asked how they got to know about their first job, such responses were typical:

> My dad got the job for me. My dad's in the job and I've been interested in it since I was at school.

> Dad got me the job. At least he got me the interview, which I had to go to. Dad works for the gas board.

> My mum used to work there and they said I could have a job if I wanted it.

The influence of personal networks was extremely important amongst this sample and many of the young workers did indicate that their parents, siblings and members of their wider family network had helped them to find their first jobs. Friends were also important sources of information about workplace vacancies. This pattern of obtaining employment through personal contacts has been noted in other studies and can, perhaps, be attributed more to strong community ties (Grieco 1987) than to dependence on family. However, we would argue that this pattern, combined with the tendency of the young workers to talk over problems at work with their parents, was an indicator that the important transitional step of 'disengaging' with their families of origin (Hubbard 2000) had not been made.

The single-step hypothesis is also questionable in terms of economic independence. When asked what happened to their wages, the data reveals that far from being domestically and financially independent, fewer than half the respondents kept the money themselves. Rather than paying a certain amount of board and lodging as if they had moved to alternative accommodation, many had to pass their wage packet to their mother or to share it equally with her or, for a small number, give it to their father. Their parents would then allocate a small proportion of the pay packet to the child as 'pocket money'. For many, their own money was not spent on the pursuit of an independent life style, but on 'sweets', 'going out' and buying clothes, records and cigarettes.

> I have £1 she has the rest – she buys my food and clothes out of that. It's better than if I kept her and gave her board, she'd want my packet and everything else besides. So at [the?] moment better to give it to her.

> I get £7 and bring home £6–11 according to tax and I give it to her and she gives me £2–15 spending money.

> Give it all to her [mother] and she gives me spending money – about a £1 and if I want something.

> For a start until my 17th birthday gave Mother all my wages and she gave me spending money. Started paying board at 17. Now has £2 a week.

These quotes suggest that the young workers had not financially 'disengaged with their family of origin' (Hubbard 2000: 9–7) and illustrate the way in which the young workers, to some extent, remained financially dependent upon their parents. Equally, in some families, the parents were financially dependent on the young worker and relied upon their wages as essential family income, supporting parents, siblings and other relatives.

> Respondent has morning paper round and keeps this for pocket money.

> Mother explains that she keeps the money and gives him what he needs as he is not responsible with money.

Jones (1995) has argued that historically, young workers made the transition to domestic independence soon after beginning full time paid work, however, domestic or housing transitions were not a feature of the young workers' lives. These young workers had neither financially disengaged with their families of origin, nor disengaged domestically, either by leaving home to live independently or by becoming part of a family of destination. Certainly none of the respondents had made a housing transition; all of the interviews were undertaken in the family home where the respondents continued to live, despite the fact that many were aged 18 or over and three had already married.

Conclusions

In this chapter we have attempted to demonstrate the complexity of past school to work transitions via a secondary analysis of data from the 1960s. Despite assertions that past school to work transitions were single-step, simple and homogenous, data from the *Adjustment of Young Workers to Work Situations and Adult Roles* project provides clear evidence of frequent job moves (often to very different job roles and different industries), with many young people having four or more jobs within the first year or so of employment. The findings also question the assumed seamless transition from school to work, as it appears that transitional experiences during this time period were not straightforward. The data reveals that many of the young workers already felt disillusioned with work and were anxious about their future prospects or concerned about their lack of training. Some of the young people had experienced periods of unemployment either before entering work or between jobs. The young people interviewed also clearly felt increased levels of insecurity (and risk) brought on by being out of work or when threatened by unemployment. Likewise, the view that young people in the past made homogenised transitions to work, sharing the same experiences with friends, neighbours and relatives is also problematic. For example, over half of the sample interviewed here clearly had individualised experiences entering different firms at different times during the first years of their working life. The data also suggests that many of the young people in this survey had not made the step of disengaging with the family of origin and consequently they remained very dependent on their parents and family for housing, money and decision-making long after they had made the transition from school to work.

However, there are also three broader conclusions that can be drawn from our analyses. First, whilst most authors agree that youth transitions have moved away from a process that is linear and smooth or uncomplicated, to a process that is both non-linear and complex or problematic, many authors have merely confirmed an established view about the past. Indeed, as Furlong et al. (2002) and Vickerstaff (2001) suggest, the consensus view on the changing nature of transitions, from linear and smooth to non-linear and complex, has largely remained unchallenged. Given the individual level complexity uncovered in the transitional experiences outlined above, one has to question why this is. Why have ideas relating to the 'golden age' of employment and notions of smooth transitions remained unquestioned? Moreover, why did sociologists at the time choose not to highlight the complexities contained within the data? These can perhaps be explained by the changing nature of the theoretical and methodological approaches to transitions over the last few years, as outlined above. This conceptual shift from exploring the impact of social structure to the more contemporary individualised approaches actually means that in conceptual terms we are not comparing like for like when we compare current and transitional experiences of 40 years ago. To put it simply, those currently involved in trying to understand transitions have become concerned with different phenomenon and have different academic pre-occupations. Past scholars were *not looking* for the individualised, subjective, complex transitional experience, and the over-concentration on macro process as being central determinants of the transitional process meant that the individual experiences were largely ignored or hidden in a broader analysis. For example, in Ashton and Field (1976), the over-riding concern was to explore how an individual's social and educational experience led to a continuity of experiences at work. Likewise, the dominant structural view of the 1980s viewed labour market destinations as being determined by social forces outside the control of individuals. Evans and Furlong (1997: 18) suggest that, with the collapse of the youth labour market, transition experiences were explained 'more in terms of structural forces such as social class, race, gender, educational attainment and labour market conditions rather than by reference to individual characteristics or aspirations'.

A related conclusion, therefore, must be that a secondary analysis of old sociological data and the re-reading of classic studies are both worthwhile and insightful. Being able to interrogate historical data with contemporary ideas and concepts has obvious value and can change (or contribute to) previous understandings of the social world (Roberts 1997b). However, with the exception of Vickerstaff (2001) and the current study, the value of applying and exploring contemporary notions and ideas against the transition experiences of youth for previous generations, and questioning the assumed linearity has not been considered.

Finally, and again a related conclusion, is that the interrogation of historical sociological data, facilitates reflection on the adequacy of contemporary theories and debates. For example, this data does question aspects of the youth, risk and individualisation debates so dominant since the publication of Beck's *Risk Society* (1992). When Beck locates the problems of risk and individualisation in late modernity, there is an assumption that the experiences of young people during this time are essentially different to the experiences of those who have gone before and the notion of late modernity implies a unique time period separate from other epochs – what Furlong and Cartmel (1997) refer to as the 'epistemological fallacy of late modernity'. Again, the data presented above challenges this assumption. Past transitional experiences were not uniformly simple, linear or as single-step as previously suggested and many transitions were characterised by individual level complexities similar to those of contemporary youth. This is not to suggest that all past transitions were 'individualised', but more simply that the past could be a complex, risky and problematic place for young people making the transition from school to work. Given Elias's (1987) assertion that 'one cannot ignore the fact that present society has grown out of earlier societies' (Elias 1987: 226), the past cannot be ignored and it needs to be re-interrogated.

Chapter 5
Gendered Transitions

Introduction

The transition from school to work has been a major focus of research on young people in Britain since the early 1960s (Wilson 1957; Carter 1962; 1963; 1969; Douglas 1964; Watts 1967; Willis 1977). This chapter aims to build on these debates by focusing on the gendered nature of school to work transitions, examining how young women and men experienced the transition process in the early 1960s. The gendered nature of transitions is an important area of enquiry, not least because the transitions of girls have been neglected in the literature whereas the experience of boys is well documented.

In this chapter we examine the boys' and the girls' reflections on their education and their thoughts about work before they left school. The data reveals how the young people experienced the transition process in terms of reflections on school, thinking about work, finding and adjusting to work and thinking about the future. In exploring this data we place emphasis on their actual lived experiences of work and the transition process. We examine the influence of career determinants both at school and home. We continue by looking at the long-term plans held by the respondents and consider the extent to which the prospect of marriage and motherhood impacted upon early career choices for the girls. This leads us to conclude, in the final section, that although this cohort of school leavers did not face the later problems of unemployment, their transitions from school to work were often far from simple.

Gendered Transitions from School to Work

Existing research from the post-war period and up to the 1980s tended to either disregard gender differentials or to focus almost exclusively on the experience of young males in the transition, leaving the female experience largely unexplored by sociologists in Britain. As Ashton and Field (1976: 35) acknowledged in the mid-1970s '... at present there is a marked absence of research into and knowledge about the perspectives and experiences of young women ...' The extent to which the transitions of girls were ignored in post-war period empirical research is well illustrated in the documentation relating to the composition and selection of the sample of young people who participated in this research. Whilst we feel that the data is valuable and provides a fascinating snapshot of school to work transitions in the 1960s, it is not without limitations and some of these relate to gender. There are, for example, concerns relating to the composition of the sample. As Table 2.1 revealed (see Chapter 2), the number of girls in the target sample was significantly lower (under half) than the number of boys in the sample. In addition, the sample of girls did not include any girls who had had a further year of education. The girls included in the survey were generally perceived as being 'non-academic', having attended secondary modern or technical schools until reaching the minimum school leaving age of 15 and entering the labour market. Therefore, whereas we have data on high-achieving boys (or, by default, more middle-class boys), we do not have comparable data for the girls. Although not covered explicitly in the schedule, gender was an issue for debate and discussion amongst the research team itself. Initially the idea was to include only boys in the sample; however, this became hotly debated amongst the research team and is documented in the minutes of their meetings:

> Are we going to confine the study to boys only? No. Too much has already been written about male attitudes and too much generalisation about girls. We should investigate girls also. There are certain differences between the adjustments of boys and girls – different attitudes because girls have the expectation of getting married and not going out to work. (Young Worker Project 1962a: 1)

It was not until the mid-1970s that teenage girls began to receive attention in the academic literature. The work of McRobbie and Garber (1975) was something of a breakthrough at the time, as they recognised and criticised the existing literature on youth subcultures and teenage lives as being concerned only with boys. This, they argued, ignored the importance of gender as a 'structural inequality that materially affects the life chances and experiences of individuals' (Nayak and Kehilly 2008: 53). Although McRobbie and Garber (1975) were concerned with youth subcultures, their work signified a change in how youth was explored by sociologists. At the same time, authors such as Sharpe (1976; 1994), and later Griffin and Wallace (1986), focused attention on the transition experience of girls. With the publication of Griffin's study *Typical Girls?*, which she describes as '… a sort of female version of Paul Willis's research …' (1985: 2), the research gap around the employment of girls began to be addressed. However, in common with other research on female transitions, which had aimed to redress the existing gender imbalance (Wallace 1986; Sharpe 1976; 1994), Griffin's research was carried out at a time when fundamental changes in the youth labour market were taking place. The context of the research was one in which rising youth unemployment had become a key issue and, as such, the girls had a set of very different concerns to those leaving school in the early 1960s (Roberts 1995: 89).

Although we can see that there is good reason for going back to the 1960s data to explore girls' transition experiences first hand, what is to be gained from re-examining the data on the boys' experiences? Indeed, for some, discussions of how young men experience the transition from school to work may not appear to be a new aspect of social enquiry and, as suggested above, it has been argued that many of the earlier studies on the transition from school to work focused almost exclusively on the experiences of young males (Roberts 1984; O'Connor and Goodwin 2004). Yet closer inspection of the literature on youth transitions reveals that the actual experiences of boys often remain hidden within broader class or education narratives. For example, in studies such as Carter (1962) and Ashton and Field (1976), the authors tended to over concentrate on structural issues at the expense of exploring the individually complex and gendered transitional experiences of the young men involved (Goodwin and O'Connor 2005a). As such, it has not usually been the transitional experiences of young males per se that were of interest, but the experiences of young males as members of certain class or educational groups. An additional problem occurs in that where gender has been specifically raised as an issue (for example Roberts 1984: 26), it has been used as 'shorthand' to describe the experiences of girls rather than to also problematise boys' gendered transitional experiences. In many respects this reflects the practice in social science research at the time, of interpreting 'gender studies' to mean the study of women (Brod 1987; Goodwin 1999).

Conceptual Framework: Linking Men and Work

The process through which boys learn their gender identities has been the subject of a great deal of research and is an area supported by an ever increasing body of literature where it has been argued that paid employment is linked with the very nature of men's identity (Harris 1995; Connell 1995; Edley and Wetherell 1996; Collinson and Hearn 1996; Nilan 2000; Goodwin 2001; Haywood and Mac an Ghaill 1996; 2003). There is also now an emerging literature on how young men are socialised into work (Dennehy and Mortimer 1993; Goodwin 1999; 2002; Lloyd 1999) and how men experience the transition from school to work as a gendered process (McDowell 2001; Paechter 2003). These authors draw upon a range of theoretical perspectives to explore and conceptualise the gendered nature of boy's transitions, including hegemonic masculinity (Haywood and Mac an Ghaill 1996; Goodwin 2002), communities of practice (Paechter 2003), occupational socialisation (Lloyd 1999) and multiple masculinities (Collinson and Hearn 1996). The conceptual framework informing the present discussion draws upon a number of these authors, as well as others such as Elias (1998) and Wight (1993).

According to Goodwin (2002), Connell's approach to masculinity is valuable in that it highlights the relational nature of its construction via interaction with other masculinities and femininities. Central to Connell's analysis is the concept 'hegemonic masculinity', which refers to a 'configuration of gender practice which embodies the currently accepted answer to the problem of patriarchy … which guarantees the dominant position of men' (Connell 1995: 77). However, hegemonic masculinity is not fixed but is defined socially and historically at any given time, as Connell (1995) suggests, 'at any given time one form of masculinity rather than others is culturally exalted' (Connell 1995: 77). Elias (1998) develops a similar approach to Connell emphasising that the 'interdependent relationships between people and groups as power relations' (Smith 2000: 191) and that gender relations emerge via changes in power configurations throughout history. Goodwin (2002) suggests that the configuration of hegemonic masculinity that is currently culturally exalted, continues to emphasise the externality of men to the home and the clear association between being male and paid employment, arguing 'in most Western societies it appears that notions of what it means to be male and work external to the home are inextricably linked' (Goodwin 2002: 154). Alternatively, as Wight (1993) suggests, the words 'work and men are continually merged in everyday speech' (Wight 1993: 101). Lloyd (1999) confirms the association between masculinity and paid work in his study of young men and the labour market. He suggests that when the young males in his study were asked what were the most important attributes and roles that defined a man, they identified 'having a job, defending their family and being a good father' (Lloyd 1999: 26).

The hegemony of masculinity organised around paid work and capitalism, has implications for the transitions from school to work that boys make and there are three interlinked gendered aspects of transition that are of interest in this chapter. First, the transition from school to work highlights and reinforces gendered vocational preferences. As Harris (1995) argues, men's behaviours are shaped by environmental and social cues from their families, friends, the media, schools, teachers and work colleagues. All of these cues shape to reinforce a man's gender identity within a specific culture at a specific point in time. Families and, in particular, fathers have been highlighted in numerous studies as being significant in boys' transitional experiences (for example Carter 1962; Maizels 1970; Ashton and Field 1976; Harris 1995). Following in 'father's footsteps' has been seen as a significant issue in reinforcing hegemonic masculinity through the transition to work. Indeed, fathers and other male relations have often been cited as being significant in helping young males enter the labour market (Lloyd 1999). Likewise, schools reinforce different cultural values, dominant masculinity types and, via the curriculum, link types of knowledge and skills with masculinities and femininities (Bowles and Gintis 1976; Willis 1977; Dart and Clarke 1988; Harris 1995; Lloyd 1999; Connell 2000). In early studies, authors such as Carter (1962) and Maizels (1970) highlight the role of school in the gendering of vocational preferences and, indeed, the differing ways the schools prepared boys and girls for work. Later studies also clearly link boys' experiences of school with occupational outcomes (Willis 1977; Roberts 1984; Banks et al. 1992).

A second and related theme is that the transition from school to work is often experienced as a confirmation of breadwinner ideology. As suggested above, the linkage between men and work is often expressed by males in notions of breadwinning or 'providing' for the family and the male breadwinner versus the female homemaker model remains culturally dominant in most Western economies. Although the breadwinner/homemaker dualism has been questioned (Pollert 1981; Griffin 1985; Haywood and Mac an Ghaill 2003), youth transitions research has highlighted notions of breadwinning as being important to young males entering work for the first time (early examples include Carter 1962; Maizels 1970).

Finally, the transition from school to work reinforces an employment ethic amongst boys that emphasises hard work and careers over and above familial aspirations. Linked to the emergence of notions of being the breadwinner, the 'employment ethic' is summarised by Wight (1993) as being a man's ability 'to earn money for himself and his family' (Wight 1993: 106). In exploring this theme, Wight (1993) differentiates between the 'respectable' and the 'wasters'. He locates the employment ethic for respectable males in hard work, being disciplined at work, having good timekeeping in employment, having a trade, 'right living', being decent and having self-respect.

Linking Women and Work

By contrast, girls' transitions to employment were historically viewed in a very different way. Wallace (1986) and others have argued that traditional models of social reproduction have placed women firmly within the family, implying that although most women seek employment on leaving school, this is only viewed as a stop gap until marriage and motherhood take over. Griffin (1985: 50) for example, found that amongst her respondents, there was an acceptance that marriage and children were an inevitable part of their lives ahead and that this would also signal the end of their time in the labour market until their children were older. As Roberts (1984: 26) comments, during this period '... neither the girls nor the wider society regarded routine ... jobs as anything other than sensible stop gaps between school leaving and motherhood. Women had already been emancipated, or so it was believed ...'

These girls were, then, faced with a complicated transition to work and adulthood, fraught with contradictions. On the one hand they were expected to enter employment on leaving school and on the other they had been socialised to believe that their paid work was somehow not as important as men's. Both at home and at school, social structures tended to operate in such a way that girls have held low occupational aspirations and generally have a lower commitment to school and to their future employment, because they accepted that their long term prospects placed them in the home as wives and mothers (Wallace 1986: 95). However, a small number of other studies of this period had begun to focus on the role of women in the labour market, with a particular emphasis on working-class women who, it is well-recognised, have a long history of employment outside the home. Work by authors such as Jephcott et al. (1962), Klein (1965) and Myrdal and Klein (1956; 1968) sought to address the issues faced by working women in the 1950s and 1960s. Myrdal and Klein's (1956) study 'Women's Two Roles' explored the challenges faced by women in the 1950s and 1960s who were combining paid employment with the demands of domestic life. Similarly, Klein's (1965) study, *Britain's Married Women Workers* was concerned with understanding the labour market participation of women with a focus on wives who had, for the most part, raised their children before returning to the workplace. Jephcott et al.'s study, *Married Women Working* (1962) focused on the labour market experiences of women in one specific community and one main workplace – the Peek Frean biscuit factory in Bermondsey, London. These studies reveal that the concept of women at work was not unusual at the time, Myrdal and Klein, writing in 1968, go so far as to comment that 'the practice of going out to work, at least part-time, has become so widespread among women in their thirties and forties, irrespective of social class, that those who fail to do so now have almost to give an explanation for staying at home' (xi). Yet, it was still assumed that young women would enter the labour market only briefly on leaving school and, therefore, their plans, aspirations and career hopes were somehow less important than those of the boys.

Gender and Employment in Leicester: The Historical Context

Leicester's economy in the 1960s was dominated by engineering, textiles, clothing and footwear manufacture. Engineering was Leicester's leading industry, employing 67,960 employees in 1967, followed by textiles and clothing and footwear manufacture, employing 55,970 and 16,500 respectively (Goodwin and O'Connor 2003). However, it would be incorrect to view these industries separately, as the manufacturing concerns of these three industries were closely connected. For example, the British United Shoe Machine Company was concerned with producing machinery and tool parts for the city's footwear manufacturers.

These industries were buoyant in Leicester in the 1960s and, as Brooks and Singh (1978) report, Leicester's economy was characterised by high employment, prosperity and opportunity. The availability of relatively well-paid manufacturing jobs meant that unemployment remained at around one per cent. Despite the domination of Leicester's economy by three main industries, it is interesting to note that many of the city's firms in the 1960s actually employed fewer than one hundred employees. For example, Keil et al. (1963) report that over 30 per cent of the total number of those employed, worked in firms with less than one hundred people and these small organisations attracted 44 per cent of the total number of school leavers during the period 1960 to 1962. Keil et al. suggest that:

> ... the fact that so many young entrants to industry get their initial experience in firms of under 100 employees affects both their attitudes to work, and the quality of their industrial training ... (Keil et al. 1963b: 411)

In the 1960s, Leicester had a mixture of secondary modern schools, technical schools and grammar schools catering for around 80,000 school children. From the mid-1960s to the early 1970s, it is reported that the percentage of pupils attending secondary modern and grammar schools remained fairly constant at 73 per cent and 27 per cent respectively (Brooks and Singh 1978). According to Ashton and

Field (1976), those young people unable to obtain a place at a grammar school were unlikely to leave school with any qualifications and would leave as soon as possible at age 15. In 1960, there were 1,750 school leavers who left school aged 15 and with no qualifications and by 1962, this figure had increased to 2,053.

Leaving School

One of the key sections included in the original interview focused on education. The responses to this set of questions are central to this analysis as they serve to illustrate the way in which aspects of the future career trajectories were often put in place at this early stage, prior to any formal guidance from careers advisors or the gaining of any formal qualifications. The responses show that many had already decided that school was not of any long-term benefit and they had taken the initiative to prepare for their futures, not through education, but by seeking employment well in advance.

Respondents were asked a series of questions about their experience of school and to reflect on their feelings about school with the hindsight of at least one year in paid employment. This section of the interview began by asking the young people to consider how they had felt about school *before* they had left. The majority recalled that they had been keen to leave:

> I didn't like school very much. It just was a bore, dragged on, just didn't suit me at all.

> Couldn't bear school – hated it. Disliked everything – I was fed up every minute I was there. I was really glad to leave.

> I wanted to leave. I didn't like school and wanted to go to work.

Not all had such negative reflections on their experience of education; some had enjoyed it and had been less keen to leave:

> It were lovely at school. Let's face it, I were really good and top of the school and somebody, but now I'm at work.

> If I'd have stayed I'd have got a better education. I liked school tremendously, I didn't want to leave.

For others there was ambivalence at the thought of leaving school, almost an unquestioning acceptance of the next stage of the life cycle:

> I didn't sob me socks off, or put the flags out, just took it that I was leaving, said goodbye and left like.

Didn't want to do it at first – quite liked school and thought about all the lovely holidays you've got. But just have to think … got to leave at sometime might just as well get used to the idea.

Many felt that school had become a 'waste of time' in their final year and that they were largely being taught subjects which were irrelevant to their lives ahead. Most had already secured future employment, for which qualifications were rarely required, and were therefore confident that further education was not a worthwhile investment of their time:

I wouldn't have wanted to stay on for GCE. It would have been a wasted year really.

Because I'd learnt what I wanted for this job – I couldn't have learned anymore for the job itself – I'd only have learned more Geog. & History and you don't need it really.

I was sorry to leave my friends, but I didn't like school – felt as though I was learning a lot of things that I didn't need to know.

I don't know, I didn't like school. They used to learn us things I don't think helped us, like PT and games, social studies, RI, I don't see how that's helped us.

The young people were also asked whether in retrospect they wished they had stayed at school for longer. The majority indicated that they did not regret the decision to leave school primarily because the financial incentive of becoming employed workers was hard to resist. Certainly notions of becoming breadwinners were highly significant (Carter 1962; Maziels 1970) for many boys in the study:

Wanted to leave so could get out and earn own money.

Looking forward to it very much, I always wanted to go to work and to earn my own money.

I wanted to leave school. I grew fed up – the attraction of earning my own money also helped.

For the girls, too, the idea of earning their own money and becoming more independent was significant:

No I just wanted to leave to earn my own money; to buy own clothes.

Fabulous, I thought it was a great idea. (Why?) Because I thought I would get more clothes, more of everything.

However, not all were so positive about entering the world of work and some explained that they had been anxious or even frightened of leaving school going to work for the first time:

> I was anxious, confused, worried. I think we're all like that on leaving school.

> I was frightened. It was a big change. At school you have nothing to bother about, but at work you may get the sack.

> I wasn't glad to be leaving. I liked school but I wanted to get a job. But I was a bit worried about what things would be like – what the people would be like and if I would get on alright.

For some of the young workers there was a sense of regret about leaving school and this was true even of those who had been too keen to leave school at the time. Like the boys in Willis's (1977) research there seemed to be a realisation of the value of education only when it was too late to reconsider the decision to leave. As Willis (1977: 107) suggests '... ironically as the shop floor becomes a prison, education is seen retrospectively and hopelessly as the only escape'. The respondents in our sample were asked the question 'Do you wish you had stayed on longer at school?' and their responses, below, illustrate Willis's argument:

> I wanted to leave when I was at school. But when I was at work I wanted to go back to school. I wish I had taken my GCE.

> Half of me does, half of me doesn't. I'd like to have a career as an air hostess, I'd learn languages and I'd like to be on [an] international GPO switchboard.

> I wanted to get away and earn the money. I suppose everyone does. Once I'd left and been at work a couple of years I started thinking – we didn't really take advantage of it.

> When I go into business on my own I'll need to know more about English, how to speak proper grammar, more about maths, it would be useful now.

> I didn't want to leave, I would have liked to go to school still as part time, I think it ought to be compulsory to go to school for perhaps two days a week and to work for the rest of the time for a while, it's too big a step straight from school to work.

Some of these quotes demonstrate that alongside the recognition of the value of education there was also a realisation that qualifications would have served as a 'short-cut' to achieving the desired career. The revelation that education was important came late to many of the sample but motivated some to attend evening classes to improve their qualifications and in turn improve career prospects.

However, it is important to realise that within this group of school leavers very few would have had the chance of staying on at school, even if they had wanted to, as this 18-year-old office worker describes, 'I couldn't stay any longer; you had to leave at 15. If I'd had the chance I should have stayed – think I'd have benefited in the long run'. Most of the schools attended by respondents did not offer the option of studying for GCE O-levels. As Ashton and Field (1976: 290) explain, those schoolchildren who attended secondary modern schools as opposed to grammar schools, were 'unlikely to obtain any certificates and were destined for manual work'. Invariably it was the working-class children to whom this applied.

Job Aspirations

As we have already seen, these school leavers were eagerly anticipating the perceived freedom working life would bring and before they began the search for employment, they often had relatively ambitious career plans. Many had thought a great deal about their futures and had a clear idea of the type of job they did and did not want to accept. The data allows us to move beyond what are often stereotypical views of the past, for example, the view that girls would not attach a great deal of importance to the labour market, as it was expected that marriage and motherhood were the destination for most and examine the aspirations expressed by these young people.

At the time this research was carried out, the Leicester labour market was buoyant and employment was widely available. The local labour market was dominated by engineering, textiles, clothing and footwear manufacture, underpinned by a large number of craft-based occupations and apprenticeships. This meant that employment prospects for male and female school leavers in the city were good and there was relatively little anxiety over unemployment. However, there was not a particularly wide range of occupational choice as most of the available entry level jobs were located in these industries. Table 5.1 contains data on the boys' and girls' career aspirations and actual labour market destinations and it is here that we see a mismatch of reality and expectations begin to emerge, particularly for the girls, as it becomes evident that the types of jobs which were widely available were precisely those that the girls did not want to enter.

Having left school and started work some 12 months previously, the young people were asked in the interview to reflect back upon their original career aspirations. Table 5.1 lists the range of jobs cited in response to the question: 'Was there any job you wanted to go into when you were at school?' and the first job destination of each respondent.

Table 5.1   Career aspirations and first job destinations of boys and girls

Job description	Boys		Job description	Girls	
	Aspiring	Actual		Aspiring	Actual
Engineering	62	92	Hairdressing	56	11
Mechanic	46	31	Office work (e.g. telephonist, receptionist)	36	70
Electrician	34	28	Working with children	24	4
Joiner/carpenter	29	12	Doctor/nurse	19	1
Draughtsman	24	12	Factory (overlocker, hosiery worker)	19	109
Navy (Merchant and Royal)	20	1	Shop work	18	47
Factory worker	18	69	Working with animals / on a farm	14	0
Painter and decorator	18	16	Artist (commercial)	10	0
Police	15	1	Teacher	9	0
Farming	15	2	Dressmaker	8	3
Office work (e.g. clerk)	14	62	Air hostess	7	0
Artist (commercial)	13	1	Window dresser	6	2
Printer	12	14	Police force	3	0
RAF	11	0	Model	2	0
Accountant	7	6	Journalist	1	0
Plumber	7	7	Ballet dancer	1	0
Railway worker	7	6	Cook	1	0
Radio and TV technician	7	4	Tailoring	0	2
Shop worker	7	42	Dental nurse	0	1
Army	6	0	Bookbinder	0	1
Footballer	6	0	Baker	0	2
Architect	6	0	Metallurgist	0	1
Builder/labourer	5	8	Warehouse work	0	1
Bricklayer	5	5	Upholsterer	0	1
Journalist	5	0	Photography processing	0	1
Butcher	4	6	No opinion	36	N/A
Doctor/dentist	4	0			
GPO	4	3			
Lorry driver / driver's mate / van boy	4	9			
Fire officer	4	0			
Chef	3	1			
Hairdresser	3	1			
Insurance sales	3	0			
Teacher	3	0			
Advertising	2	0			
Gas fitter	2	4			
Gardening	2	1			
Jockey	2	0			
Work with animals	2	0			
Solicitor, air steward, fishing, miner, actor, chemist, researcher, warehouse, projectionist, probation officer, waiter, laboratory assistant, scientist, window cleaner	1	10			
No opinion	155	N/A			

Note: Some respondents mentioned more than one job and all preferences were counted, hence the total here is greater than the number of respondents.

For the girls, the list is immediately striking both in its lack of diversity and its reflection of traditional non-aspirational, 'feminine' occupational trends (Rauta and Hunt 1972; Ashton and Maguire 1980; Furlong 1986; Bates 1993). Such positions within the labour market have been traditionally viewed as low skilled and low paid; job characteristics which have historically symbolised 'women's work'. In accepting jobs such as these, women have been seen to hold low initial career aspirations, becoming 'trapped' at the bottom of the labour market hierarchy (Furlong 1986). However, the top four jobs aspired to (see Table 5.1), are of great interest because, we would argue, these reveal a far greater degree of ambition than would first appear. Certainly the occupations aspired to by our cohort were generally low skilled and low status, but they do suggest that many of the girls were actually quite ambitious, particularly given their relatively closed spheres of influence.

It is important to recognise that at this time the range of jobs on offer in Leicester was severely limited and the majority of women known to these girls as family and friends worked within the key industries based in the city. The range of jobs held by the respondents' mothers, for example, was far narrower than the list of jobs aspired to by the girls, with the majority working in factories and shops or as housewives. Furlong (1986) has shown that mothers, female friends and relatives play a key influential role in girls' job choices. For the girls in his research, mothers, female friends and relatives were the 'single most important influence on occupational aspiration' (Furlong 1986: 66). Significantly, amongst our sample, many of the girls actively wanted to avoid taking the type of jobs held by their mothers and female friends. What becomes clear is that, initially, these school leavers, in aspiring to very different careers than those of their mothers, were attempting to resist the mechanisms of social and cultural reproduction. Factory work, so widely available in Leicester, was particularly spurned, with only 19 girls citing this as a career choice and others making comments such as:

> I've been in the factory where mother works, I didn't like it, it was noisy and dusty.

> Just didn't fancy factory work, saw mother's factory, old factory, messy.

Further to this, when asked 'Was there any job you didn't want to go into when you were at school?' many cited factory work, which was seen as boring, dirty and hard. As the quotes illustrate, respondents worried about the high levels of noise and expressed fears that they would feel 'trapped', rather as they had felt at school. There was also a view that factory work was 'low class' and the people who worked in factories were 'rough'.

> You're too hot in a factory, you're closed in, it's too noisy. When we went round the shoe factory it was very hot and noisy.

[I didn't want to work in a] factory. I just don't like being closed up, obeying the whistle …

A factory. The work people are rough and the work is monotonous.

A factory. The noise. I didn't think the people were my type. I suppose I am a snob. Most of the people in a factory are illiterate.

This attitude towards factory work was not confined to Leicester or to this particular time period. Griffin (1985: 100) found that amongst her school leavers in Birmingham, some 20 years later, a job in a factory was perceived to be 'boring, insecure and unpleasant … "not a nice job for a girl"'. Similarly, amongst Wallace's (1986) respondents in Kent, factory work had a poor image, despite the potential for earning high wages in this environment. For the few Leicester girls who expressed an interest in pursuing a factory-based occupation, the potentially high earnings were the key motivation:

I just wanted to be an overlocker, I thought it was a good job.

Corah's [hosiery factory]. Heard money was good.

Shoes, everybody told me the shoes were better paid than the hosiery – that was main reason I went.

Hosiery, I had heard there was good money to be earned and it was a useful trade.

Overlocking. You hear more about overlocking than any other thing in the hosiery and everybody reckons overlocking earns good money.

Conversely, referring back to Table 5.1, we can see that hairdressing was by far the most popular career aspiration with more than 50 girls citing this profession as being desirable. As the quotes below suggest, hairdressing was seen as a glamorous, creative job. Other popular ambitions for the next generation were working with children, either as nursery nurses or teachers, or working in offices; all jobs which very few of the girls' mothers were employed in:

Hairdressing. I liked doing people's hair. There wasn't any vacancies, everybody wants to go into hairdressing.

Hairdressing. I think every girl likes to think 'Oh' a hairdresser, making gorgeous styles of hair – creative imagination.

> I wanted to be a hairdresser in my 2nd year. Then I always wanted to work with children, I don't know.

> Nursery nurse, I like working with children and it was a job where you could work with children.

Although hairdressing was the most popular aspiration, office work was also frequently mentioned with 36 of the girls keen to seek employment in offices. Given that in later studies office work was seen as the career of choice for many (Sharpe 1976) it is perhaps surprising that it was not ranked even higher amongst the Leicester group. There are a number of possible explanations for this.

One explanation may have been that as Ashton et al. (1988) note, Leicester, as a base for manufacturing, had a lower proportion of white collar jobs available than other cities. The research was carried out at a time when factory work was the predominant employment sector in Leicester and this group may not have considered office work as a possibility. This is not entirely satisfactory as an explanation, because hairdressing was clearly ranked as the number one choice regardless of the fact that every respondent seemed to be aware that there were few jobs available in this sector.

An alternative explanation is that office work had historically required a relatively high standard of education and there was certainly a perception in this sample that office work was hard to obtain. As the quotes below reveal, given in response to the question 'Was there any job you didn't want to go into when you were at school?', some girls did not think that they were 'clever' enough to work in an office. However, others clearly had considered the option and concluded that life in an office would be very tedious:

> An office. I haven't got the brains.

> Office work. Wouldn't be able to do it. Wouldn't be brainy enough. I'd had enough of school. It reminded me too much of school you know.

> Didn't think I was clever enough from a secondary modern school.

> Office work. I didn't fancy sitting at an office desk all day.

> Didn't want office work. I think it would be a boring job.

Those who cited office work as desirable did so because of the perceived nature of the work environment or more commonly because it seemed to be the only alternative to a factory or shop work:

> I thought it was light, clean, not too long hours.

My aunt was in it and she liked it. It's a nice job for a girl.

I felt I couldn't mix with people in a factory. I couldn't be stuck in a factory all the while. I just thought I'd like office work.

I thought if I worked in a factory (rather than an office) I would get a dead end job.

Overall then, what emerges very clearly from the data included in Table 5.1 is the mismatch between the jobs aspired to and the eventual employment taken. We have argued that this group of school leavers, though generally seeking typical 'female occupations', were, at the same time, expressing great ambition given their circumstances and backgrounds. Clearly to aspire to work as a hairdresser or a nursery nurse, or even in an office was, at this time, in this Midlands city, quite ambitious and, in the event, often unlikely to be achieved by many.

Although seemingly realistic and modest aspirations were held, few of the girls were able to realise their ambitions. This was, in part, because the social and economic structures in place proved too strong to resist and the jobs the girls dreamt of were just not available in the local labour market. As Bates (1993: 21) suggests:

> ... at the crucial juncture of school leaving, the structures to which they had so far been exposed had not brought their aspirations in to line with labour market opportunities ... Whilst oriented in the general direction of gender-stereotyped, working class jobs, they were still seeking jobs a 'cut' above what was possible.

In addition, the girls' own circumstances, particularly their generally low levels of educational achievement, had already conspired to militate against their ambitions.

Amongst the boys, the mismatch was less marked and many of their aspirations reflected the reality of local labour market conditions, with large numbers of boys aspiring to enter a range of craft-based occupations, such as engineering, mechanical and electrical trades or joinery and carpentry (Carter 1962; Brooks and Singh 1978). The appeal of such craft-based industries seem to reside within the opportunity to be creative and make things that were useful:

Mechanic. I liked pulling things to bits and sticking them back together again.

I have always been interested in cars, I used to like wood – carving and clay modelling, I like doing things with my hands.

I was interested in making things out of metal.

Interestingly, many of the boys aspired to these occupations because of their own experiences of subjects at school, such as metal work, woodworking and electronics (Carter 1962; Maziels 1970; Ryrie and Weir 1978). Their apparent creative successes in these subjects spurred them on to seek careers in which they could pursue these skills:

> Yes, I always fancied the engineering. Well I think because ... I enjoyed the metal work classes at school.

> We used to do wood work quite a bit at school and in our spare time we used to do it.

> ... used to get on all right at metal work and thought if I could get on alright at school [I] could get on alright in engineering firm.

> I done lot about electricity in Science at school and wanted [to] have [a] go.

These quotations provide some evidence that the transition from school to work reinforces gendered 'appropriate' preferences. Many of the boys in the study were pushed toward subjects such as woodwork, metalworking and engineering whilst at school and. in turn. these experiences shaped the boys' work and occupational choices. Similarly, regardless of their aspirations prior to entering the labour market, the girls were pushed towards traditionally feminine occupations such as hosiery manufacture and this shaped their eventual occupational choices.

However, whilst most boys successfully entered employment soon after leaving school, many did not achieve their original occupational aspirations. As Table 5.1 illustrates, the most significant job destination was the engineering industry. Some 96 boys ended up working in this industry, either as apprentices or in roles such as trainee fitter, store keeper, lathe operator and general labourers, although only 62 had expressed a preference for working in this environment. Although more boys ended up in this industry than those who aspired to enter it, there were many who had ambitions to work in engineering:

> I was good at metal work at school, my dad was in it and my brothers.

> Yes, I always fancied the engineering. Well I think because it were put into my head by my brother and because I enjoyed the metal work classes at school.

> Interested in engineering and my father is an engineer.

Again, from the quotations above, it is clear that engineering was seen as an occupation to aspire to, given the boys' experiences at school or because of their relationships with other significant males who were engineers themselves. Likewise, the importance of 'getting a trade' cannot be ignored for the boys in this sample. As Roberts (1984) argues, studies of school leavers in the post-war period all stress the significance of getting a trade and parents of boys, in particular, frequently advised their sons of the security associated with learning a trade (Ryrie and Weir 1978). Many of the boys took this advice and sought jobs in trades such as engineering because of the good prospects such careers were seen to offer:

> Good job, prospects, stable and got trade if do decide to leave.

> I never had the brains to do anything else. I didn't want to be a navvy or anything like that – I wanted a trade in my hands.

> I tried a few places and then I went to Freers and they do coppersmith so I tried there cos I liked the idea of coppersmiths, it's a good trade like.

This is in direct contrast to the girls, for whom apprenticeships were highly unusual and 'getting a trade' was seen as unnecessary. The girls were more likely to be encouraged to pursue well-paid work, such as overlocking, which existed in hosiery factories at this time. For girls, the pursuit of short-term high financial rewards was seen as desirable because this would maximise the benefit of their potentially curtailed period of active labour market participation.

Amongst the boys, the next three actual first job destinations were, in numerical order: factory work, office work and shop work. Few boys aspired to work in any of these occupations, for example, only 18 boys wanted to work in a factory, whereas factories were the first job destination of 69 respondents. When asked if there were any jobs that they did not want to take, factory work was mentioned the most frequently and 125 boys identified that they did not want to work in a factory.

> I didn't fancy working in a big factory. I don't think I'd be able to stand that. It's too big you're like a number. Just made my mind up I weren't going into a factory that's all. Just didn't fancy it that's all. Seemed a bit of a hard life as you got older. [F] My influence drove you on. Having a father been on the factory floor it influences you against it, in a way, I doctrined him against the bench work. What I've seen of the factory life [it's] always beneficial to be on the salaried side of things.

> The factory we went round, shoe machinery. Dirty, damp, noisy machinery – little kids doing men's work getting low wages – men pulling a lever and getting £20 a week it was like a workhouse.

> Not into a factory. Because factory jobs to me were always dead end jobs.

Similarly, although for 62 boys office work was their first employment, only 14 boys had aspired to office work. Generally, such work was seen as boring and being too similar to school life:

An office job. I just think it's boring and I think it's far more satisfying to do something with your own hands and then see the results of it.

I didn't want to work in an office. I thought – I'd been cooped up in a school since I was five, an office wasn't much difference I couldn't sit at a desk all day, I wouldn't be happy.

Shop work was also unpopular. Only seven boys aspired to work in a shop although six times as many (42) ended up entering shop related work. Before entering the labour market, many boys felt that shop work was 'dead end work', 'boring work' and as far removed from a 'trade' as one could get. Again, as with Wight (1993), the issue of having a trade as part of being a respectable working man seems very important, as the following quotes illustrate:

Shop. There's no trade behind it.

Well it isn't a trade being in a shop.

No trade in a shop anybody could do it, just gotta be good at maths and talking to people.

You really have no trade, you can't change to a factory or anything. You can only move to another shop.

These first job outcomes; factory work, shop work and office work, are striking in the close resemblance to the girls' first job destinations. Amongst girls, factory, office and shop work were seen as being the least desirable occupations, yet it was mainly this type of work they ended up with (O'Connor and Goodwin 2004). Like the girls who were unable to achieve their ambitions of becoming hairdressers (O'Connor and Goodwin 2004), many of the boys could not easily obtain access to learning a trade of their choice.

However, there is little evidence to indicate that the boys had unrealistic aspirations. Although Table 5.1 does reveal a diverse range of career aspirations, with some of the boys aspiring to become pilots, footballers, journalists, doctors, teachers and jockeys, the numbers hoping to achieve unrealistic jobs were low. In general the boys were aspiring to obtain jobs which matched the immediate demands of the local labour market. They were aspiring to become mechanics, carpenters and electricians, but such jobs often proved difficult to obtain as relevant opportunities were lacking:

I wanted to be a mechanic. But in the end it (stock-keeper) was the only job I could get.

I said want to be a mechanic. I went round and looked but couldn't get one.

Actually I first wanted to be a carpenter and joiner but at the time there was no vacancies so the YEO [Youth Employment Office] says I ought to take a temporary job.

I was going as an apprentice electrician but didn't pass test – they offered this instead.

For these young people in Leicester, the occupational reality was rather bleak in some respects. As Roberts (1995) has argued, it is rare for occupational aspirations and the reality of job opportunities to correlate, and 'choices' about work are limited. Although some of these boys obtained apprenticeships (156), mainly in engineering, many others took jobs that they had originally spurned. As Furlong (1993: 60) suggests, such a pattern is not unusual amongst school leavers in general and 'more often than not, young people fail to enter the specific types of work that they had hoped for whilst at school'. Certainly for this group, once they began to look seriously for work, many found that they had less choice than they had first assumed and consequently had to lower their aspirations in order to enter the labour market. As Roberts (1995) has proposed, the notion of occupational choice was something of a myth and the opportunities available in the local labour market largely dictated the employment destinations of most school leavers.

The majority of the female cohort eventually took the precise jobs they had fought so hard to avoid, in factories, shops and to some extent, offices. These were the jobs that the girls had known were available and, importantly, jobs which were easily attainable because qualifications were generally not required. Almost half of the sample (109) began their working lives on a factory floor and even those who went into office work tended to be based within factories. Their working lives turned out to be very similar to that of their parents.

This group of Leicester girls were certainly not unusual in their lack of success in achieving their occupational ambitions. Job aspirations held by school pupils are often not the jobs they are ultimately employed in and the jobs that children aspire to are not the jobs that they really expect to do (Carter 1962; Roberts 1975; 1995; Kelly 1989; Furlong 1993; Francis 2002). As Furlong (1993: 60) has argued:

By the age of sixteen most young people have some idea of the sorts of work they want to enter once they leave school. However, at this stage their ideas about future jobs are often tentative and as they make the transition from school to work they will tend to modify their ideas as certain jobs prove difficult to enter and as new opportunities arise.

Bates (1993) found that amongst the YTS (Youth Training Scheme) girls she interviewed in the early 1980s, there was a general aspiration for unrealistic occupations, unrealistic partly because of the high unemployment at the time. These girls mentioned their desire to work as hairdressers, beauty therapists, to look after children or work in department stores. In reality they became care assistants looking after old people, a much less desirable job, rather like many of the Leicester girls who eventually took jobs in factories. Bates goes on to suggest that in previous decades, when unemployment had not been an issue and the school to work transition was seen to be a more linear, simple process, this 'mismatch' may have been unusual. However, our data indicates that this was not so and even in the 1960s the career ambitions of many girls were not necessarily achievable.

Similarly, Wallace (1986) has questioned the relevance of the notion of 'functional convergence' whereby school leavers in the post-war years, prior to high unemployment, did not find their entry into work a 'shock' because their previous experiences at school and at home had prepared them for this. In contrast, she argues that those who left school during periods of high unemployment '... had to accept jobs lower than their expectations due to a decline in opportunities in the local labour market ...' (Wallace 1986: 99). Our data, on the other hand, indicates that, in fact, even at times of high employment and with a buoyant local labour market, this mismatch was common. Taking hairdressing as an example, only 11 girls found work in this sector against the 56 who aspired to this role.

What is revealed by this data is that regardless of whether or not initial aspirations were achieved, the girls in this sample tended to be ambitious. There is evidence that for around half of this sample of girls there was a strong commitment to career and they were prepared to invest heavily in the future, indicating that not all of them believed that marriage and children would signal the end of their working lives:

> Daren't really think but I hope to own my own salon. I'm going to be apprenticed and have courses on different aspects of hairdressing.

> Don't know, hoping I'm going to be a typist in authority, I hope I might take my Father's firm over later on.

> I hope to be in America (had plans to work as nanny in USA).

> Hope to be married and get a shop – me own salon.

> I hope to get [a] secretarial position. Don't want to get married too early, and I'd like to travel before I settle down.

Securing Employment

The decision to leave school was made at a very early stage and as we have seen, most school leavers either were not able to or did not want to continue with education, investing their time instead in investigating the local labour market and securing employment in readiness for their exit from education. Although some had enjoyed school and were worried about leaving the security of the familiar environment, the lure of money, independence and adult life proved difficult to resist. Even in this time of high employment, however, the respondents believed securing a job before leaving school was a key consideration and not something to be left to chance. This suggests that the school leavers had few illusions about the world of work – they knew what awaited them and understood the need to be organised in finding work. There was some anxiety about the prospect of unemployment and even when jobs had been secured, there were concerns for some over the frequent lack of job security (Goodwin and O'Connor 2005a). This is, perhaps, surprising given that this period has been seen as a 'golden age' of employment, when jobs were plentiful and young people made a smooth transition to work (Kiernan 1992; Roberts 1984; 1995). However, as Goodwin and O'Connor (2005a) have argued elsewhere, some individuals in this study did experience frequent breaks in employment, periods of unemployment and difficulties in securing employment.

For the vast majority who were able to arrange work in advance of leaving school, kinship networks played an important role in helping these school leavers find their first jobs. For many of the boys their early introductions to work were via male relatives, particularly fathers, who informed them of suitable vacancies in their own workplaces. As Lloyd (1999: 28) suggests:

Traditionally young men have been introduced to the workplace by their fathers often finding them jobs in the industries in which they themselves worked ... the young men rarely sought/received direction from their mothers.

Ashton and Field (1976: 46) also stress the importance of informal and kinship networks in seeking employment, explaining that the role played by 'word of mouth from family, friends and relatives', cannot be ignored. Certainly this was a pattern which was important amongst this group and the boys' fathers played a key role in helping them find work and gain entry into workplaces – this appeared to be particularly true when the boys entered apprenticeships, craft and trade type jobs or factory work. This is in direct contrast to the girls in the study, none of whom found their first job through their father, relying instead on their mothers and female networks:

Me dad knows this man at work. His mate and his dad worked there and got me the job.

Dad works there – works on machines so got me a job.

Through my father. [Mother] – He couldn't have got in otherwise, it was difficult to get a job.

My dad took me down to the manager in 1960 to Mr Holmes, and it was arranged that I should start 2 weeks after leaving school.

Mothers and other female relatives were less helpful to the boys than male relatives (Carter 1962). Often mothers played a more passive, advisory role than the fathers, suggesting places to apply or using personal contacts to introduce their son to an employer.

> 2 weeks before leaving school I was going with mother for an interview at [a] shoe factory when [an] Imperial Van passed by – mother said how about trying there so I did – called at firm and got a job.

> I told my mother I was interested. One of the women she works with her husband said there was a job going so I went to see.

The pattern of a strong parental influence which emerges from this data fits with Ashton and Field's (1976: 97) assertion that for boys who had had a poor experience of school, only attaining a 'low position' educationally, the role of the parents in assisting the transition into work was of paramount importance. They suggest that working-class parents were likely to 'use their knowledge and connections in the local labour market to gain his (the son) entry in to an occupation'. This was not the case with their daughters as 'their future well-being … is often seen as largely dependent on making the "right" marriage'.

Although family contacts were clearly very important to many respondents, another main mechanism for finding work was through the Youth Employment Office (YEO). As Maizels (1970: 122) comments, those school leavers with 'weaker … parental influence' were most likely to be users of the YEO. As the quotes below suggest, the boys in this study were relatively positive about the help they received from the YEO, in contrast to the girls, who were often disparaging about their role.

> Asked me what I wanted to do. I told him and he arranged an interview.

> YEO suggested Co-op. after R had said he wanted shop work without Saturday afternoon work, YEO arranged interview.

> He asked me what I wanted to do and I said not in a factory and he gave me a list of jobs – a shop cropped up. (What kind of shop?) Well grocery cropped up so I go and have 2 interviews.

This suggests, perhaps, that the YEOs were more helpful to boys and perhaps saw girls as needing a job only to 'fill in' until they married and gave up work (Ashton and Field 1976; Roberts 1995). However, the data also suggests that the YEO were giving gender appropriate advice by steering girls towards Leicester's traditional feminine occupational sector and away from their modest career aspirations and steering boys towards craft-based trades rather than their initial occupation preferences:

YEO said cars should be a hobby and I was not well built enough for police, suggested GPO.

Yes – YEO more or less persuaded me to [work in a factory].

I wasn't actually certain what I wanted to be, and there's not many lads want to go into [the] building trade, and of course he thought well he's good at woodwork so I might as well see if I can get him to go into that trade, yes he definitely made up my mind.

Oh yes definitely it was him who made me do engineering.

Conclusions

We began this chapter by suggesting that school to work transitions needed to be considered as gendered experiences from the perspective of both female and male school leavers. It is well-established that post-war accounts of entry to employment tended to disregard girls' experiences to focus on boys' experiences. The focus on boys was primarily due to the nature of sociological research at the time and the tendency for empirical studies to disregard the experience of girls and women (Delamont 2003). However, the focus on boys was not grounded in a gender perspective per se but focused instead on the impact of class and education rather than gender and did not, therefore, account for the individual complexity of boys' transitions to work any more than those of the girls.

The data presented in this chapter, however, provides some insight into the school to work transitions of both genders entering work for the first time in the 1960s and it reveals a great deal about their early work experiences. First, the majority of the young people in this study wanted to leave school as soon as they possibly could, to earn money and provide for themselves and, for most, staying in education was not an option. They saw school as a 'waste of time' and it was not until they had left school that they realised the true value of educational qualifications. For many this realisation came too late.

Second, the local labour market was relatively buoyant in the early 1960s and the respondents in this study did give careful consideration to their future careers. They had a wide range of occupational aspirations and, for many, these aspirations were realistic given the conditions of the local labour market. However, the individual experiences reveal that, although realistic, many were not able to realise their ambitions. The data also reveals that job choices were highly gendered and, on the advice of school, family and the Youth Employment Office, the boys entered male dominated careers that were trade-based and the girls entered female dominated roles. The data also suggests that fathers and other significant males played a crucial role in the final job destinations of the boys, where mothers and female networks were key to securing employment for the girls.

Finally, all the boys in the study highlighted the significance of work for their own futures and only a few identified home, marriage and family as being something they were aspiring to in the future. Those who did feel that they would be married in 10 years' time linked this to future job prospects and their ability to provide. By contrast, although few of the girls assumed that marriage and motherhood would permanently exclude them from the labour market, the majority did expect to give up work at some point. At the same time, nearly all of them also anticipated the resumption of waged work once their children started school. Contrary to widely held beliefs about young women's work in the 1960s, it was common for the girls to have relatively sophisticated career aspirations which did not reflect their immediate frames of reference. Many chose jobs that offered the best training and, therefore, future career opportunities over and above employment which offered immediate financial gratification, suggesting that the girls had long term plans to develop their own careers.

Chapter 6
Youth Culture and Leisure in the 1960s

Introduction

The 1960s is widely perceived as the decade during which the phenomenon of the 'teenager' emerged and changed the lives of young people forever. As has been well-documented elsewhere, the 1960s represented a period of huge significance for the lives of young people, both then and subsequently. This era saw the birth of the 'affluent teenager' a product of:

> full employment, narrower differentials between teenagers' and adults' earnings, teenagers going 'on board' at home from the beginning of their working lives, and the affluent teenager becoming a market segment. (Roberts 1997a: 6)

Young people had, for the first time, a significant amount of disposable income thanks to a period of economic boom with an associated buoyant labour market. They were benefitting from the great changes that had taken place in the immediate post-war period resulting in higher wages and more freedom, leaving many better placed to express themselves through their leisure time activities, interests in fashion and music, and being 'teenagers'. Indeed, Dyhouse has described the 1960s as a 'teenage revolution' and a decade which, significantly, ended with a legislative change to the definition of an adult. The introduction of the Family Law Reform Act of 1969 saw the age at which 'children' were legally treated as 'adults' reduced from 21 to 18 (Dyhouse 2013: 6).

In this chapter we explore the emergence of the teenage lifestyle and the extent to which the changes associated with the 1960s impacted on school leavers in a provincial city. Had the youth subcultures so widely discussed in the media at the time 'arrived' in the provinces or were youth cultures, such as Teddy Boys, mods, rockers and Beatlemania, confined to the big cities? To what extent did young people in provincial towns and cities have access to the kind of leisure pursuits supposedly enjoyed by all young people in the 1960s? Similarly, were the 'moral panics' of youth subcultures, of juvenile delinquency, teenage pregnancy, excessive drinking, smoking and drug-taking, and the 'problem of youth' (Cohen 1972; Clarke et al. 1976: 72) evident in Leicester? We also explore the more 'mundane' aspects of becoming an adult, applicable to all young people at all times regardless of the social mores of the period; the change in relationships to the family of origin, to leisure pursuits, to education and to work.

The following discussion explores different aspects of youth culture and leisure amongst this group of 1960s school leavers. We begin with a brief review of the large body of sociological literature concerned with youth and youth cultures. We then go on to explore the leisure pursuits evident in this study and the changes that occurred in the everyday lives of teenagers once they had left school and started work, gaining some measure of independence. This leads us to examine the patterns of consumption amongst this group, their money management practices and the true extent of 'disposable income'. Leisure time activities and spending on fashion, music and going out are similarly documented. Finally, because changes in household relationships are also an important aspect of the transition to adulthood, we explore the aspects of parental authority and control in relation to teenagers' sense of freedom and independence.

The Study of Youth

The growing interest in the lives of young adults is evident from the abundance of studies of teenagers which emerged during this period. One of the earliest studies was Pearl Jephcott's (1942) study *Girls Growing Up*, in which she recognised that the changing lives of young women were worthy of closer study. This early study of youth was followed by two further studies: *Some Young People* (1954) and the later study of youth leisure in Scotland, *Time of One's Own* (1967). Jephcott's early work was followed by other landmark studies of the time, such as Abrams's (1959) research on teenage patterns of consumption, *The Teenage Consumer* and Laurie's (1965) *Teenage Revolution*. At the same time there were other empirical studies of youth being carried out across the UK, for example, Carter's (1962) *Home, School and Work* and Veness's (1962) *School Leavers*, which mapped the transitional experiences of young people.

Since the 1960s, studies of this period of young people's lives have been commonplace and have generated numerous works with an emphasis on either youth cultures or youth transitions (Nayak and Kehily 2008: 12). The cultural studies perspective has resulted in a range of studies around youth subcultures and teenage fashion, music and consumption (Hall and Jefferson 1976; Hebidge 1979; Frith 1984). The growth of youth cultures was a defining feature of this period and a feature closely associated with working class youth rather than the middle classes. As Roberts (1997a: 7) highlights, 'young people on working class trajectories were making the most rapid transitions to adulthood and earning the 'good money' that enabled them to participate in the new commercial scenes at the youngest ages'. Young people on more middle class career trajectories tended to earn less money, as they were more likely to pursue roles with longer periods of training that were poorly paid by comparison, yet offered greater long-term rewards (Ashton and Field 1976). The study of youth transitions to work, in contrast to the cultural studies perspective on youth, has tended to prioritise the understanding of structural constraints that shape young people's moves to independence through leaving education and starting work. Studies such as Ashton and Field (1976), Willis (1977), Brown (1987) and Roberts (1995) were at the forefront of youth research which illuminated the huge structural changes to the youth labour market beginning in the mid-1970s.

Much of the early work on youth subcultures, dating back to the 1970s, in common with early work on the transition to work dating from the 1960s, prioritised the experiences of young men at the expense of young women. In the texts cited above much of the focus was on boys; their experience of leaving school and starting work and their participation in youth cultures. The increasing profile of the affluent teenager in the 1960s and the associated youth cultures focused on Teddy Boys, mods and rockers, and tended to be male dominated. Although girls were also enjoying more affluent lifestyles and 'there were indeed signs of a new independence among young women in the 1960s ...' (Dyhouse 2013: 161) their leisure time was more likely to be spent at home, 'based around bedroom cultures' (Roberts 1997a: 7). McRobbie and Garber (1976: 213) describe the 1960s teenage girl bedroom culture as one of 'experimenting with make-up, listening to records, reading the mags, sizing up boyfriends, chatting, jiving'. There was, therefore, an assumption that girls were far less likely to participate in youth subcultures than boys and tended to spend their leisure time 'at home' (Jephcott 1967; McRobbie and Garber 1976). There was also a belief that transitions to work were less significant for young girls as they were more likely to perceive paid work as simply a stop-gap between school, marriage and childrearing. This perception led to the experience of girls being omitted from many studies of this period with, perhaps, Jephcott's (1942) early work as an exception to this. It was not until female sociologists recognised the exclusion of young women from many studies of youth that the gendered experiences of transition began to receive due attention (Sharpe 1976; McRobbie and Garber 1976; Griffin 1985).

In the following section, we begin to explore the lived experience of teenage life for both young women and young men in Leicester in the early 1960s. The main focus of the data we draw upon is concerned with the changes brought about to the young people's lives through their entry to work, for example, their newly acquired 'wealth', their spending patterns, social lives and independence.

Earning and Managing Money

One of the defining features of the lives of the post-war teenage generation was that the economic prosperity of the period had created a generational group with spending power. For the first time many young people were earning significant amounts of money in relatively well-paid jobs with few financial responsibilities or obligations. This era saw the birth of teenage consumers who began to be targeted by specific industries relating to their interests: fashion, music, cosmetics and so on. The late 1950s saw the publication of Abrams's (1959) influential study of teenage spending and a recognition that the social and economic implications of this newfound wealth were to be hugely significant. Indeed, in Laurie's (1965: 9) work he begins by attempting to define the term 'teenager' concluding that chronological age, biology and marriage are not the important markers of teenagehood. For him, economic behaviours defined teenagers as those who '... spend a lot of money on clothes, records, concerts, make-up, magazines: all things that give immediate pleasure and little lasting use. In contrast, adults spend more on food, rent, washing machines, furniture – the equipment of a stable and continuing existence'.

Given the level of interest in the spending power of young people and the rise of the teenage consumer it is not surprising that the young workers in Leicester were asked about their incomes and their outgoings. They were asked a series of questions relating to pay, allocation of resources, consumption and leisure time, which were designed to understand more about the practicalities associated with becoming wage earners. However, these questions were also focused, in part, on understanding more about how the young person's relationship with their families, particularly their parents, had altered since s/he had left school and gained more independence, as this was a key concern for Elias.

As we have seen in earlier chapters, some of the young people were earning significant amounts of money in Leicester. Jephcott (1967), researching youth in Glasgow during the same period, found that very few earned over seven pounds a week and most earned around three to four pounds. In Leicester, it was common for young workers to be earning around £10 per week, sometimes more, although the wages in different jobs varied enormously. Amongst the highest paid workers in this sample were the skilled factory workers, who had learnt a particular role in the boot and shoe, hosiery or textile industries. High rates of pay were common for both male and female young workers who had secured work in busy factories. The success of the particular factory was important, as most of the highly paid workers were employed on piecework rates. Therefore, full order books meant the potential for earning higher wages. So, for example, one respondent who was an experienced hosiery worker at the time of interview explained his high wages:

> Pairing ladies nylons! (what?) well, I don't know if you know anything about it but the stocking machines cannot always make them the same length when they're dyed. By the time they are finished they are different lengths and sizes and you can't sell two different stockings and so you have to pair them up. All depends on how many hours I do. It will change but now on average I earn £9–£10. It will go up of course when I'm on my own time, when you get paid by how much you do and not by time.

For those who had completed a formal apprenticeship or had been trained for a specific role within a factory, the potential rewards once training was complete were high:

> I was under apprenticeship – £3.11.6 when I started, got 5/-rise every 6 months. There? Started £3.10.0 but after fortnight on own time earned about £5. Machining – finishing off jumpers cardigans, about £11 per week.

Amongst the boys, the highest rates of pay were found amongst those who were employed as labourers or, by contrast, as qualified skilled machine operatives, for example, working a toe-lasting machine in a footwear factory or mending machines in the same factories. However, it tended to be the young women who earned the highest wages in the city. Many of the girls were employed in very lucrative roles – skilled roles in textiles, hosiery and footwear commanded high pay and most were able to earn around £12 per week up to as much as £16, which was considered a very high wage. This was significantly higher than the wages earned by hairdressers, for example – a job seen as far more desirable and fashionable but with very low levels of pay, usually around two to three pounds a week. Office work, unskilled factory work and shop work paid far less money. Trainee positions also paid much lower wages but these roles came with the promise of skilled jobs at the end of the apprenticeship phase of learning – with the exception, perhaps, of hairdressing jobs, which were hard to secure and low paid even when the young worker was fully trained.

The high wages paid to many of the young women in Leicester were unusual, as typically teenage girls have been seen to earn less money than their male counterparts and to have less disposable income (McRobbie and Garber 1976; Roberts 1983). For many in Leicester this was not the case. In McRobbie and Garber's (1976: 217) exploration of teenage and girls and subcultures they describe how young girls were often attracted to what were perceived as new and glamorous jobs relating broadly to the industries created by the increased spending power of teenagers. Jobs in the fashion and cosmetic industry, and jobs in offices, where it was possible to 'dress-up for work', were poorly paid but the associated 'glamour and status often compensated for poor wages'. In Leicester, as elsewhere, the glamour of hairdressing attracted many girls and the appeal of office work, as opposed to 'dirty' and hard work in factories, was considerable (Sharpe 1976; Griffin 1985). Nevertheless, skilled factory work was well paid and the draw of high wages and the ease of obtaining a job proved hard to resist. Teenage girls in Leicester took jobs producing the fashions that were consumed by other teenagers around the country though, ironically, through these roles they earned a great deal more money than their contemporaries employed in more glamorous roles.

Teenage Patterns of Consumption: What Did They Spend Their Money On?

Further questions about money were focused on how wages were managed by the young worker, with a particular emphasis on understanding how the money earned was spent, allocated to parents or saved. Respondents were asked to explain how their money was allocated on a weekly basis: whether the wage packet was given in its entirety to a parent in exchange for an allowance or pocket money, or whether the young worker paid a set amount for board and lodging. Part of the reasoning for these questions derived from a desire for the project team to gain a greater understanding of how the earning of money impacted on the young person's independence and changing relationships at home – an area we explore later in this chapter.

Whilst Frith (1984: 10) suggests that the rise of the teenager was in part due to greater disposable incomes created by young people having well-paid jobs 'and less obligation than previous generations to contribute their wages to the family income', our data paints a different picture. The data reveals that just over half of the respondents (51 per cent) maintained responsibility for their own pay packet, allocating a prescribed amount for board and lodging to their parents as the majority were living at home. Most of the remaining respondents (40 per cent) gave their entire wage packet to their mothers and were given 'pocket money' back for themselves:

> Mother: £5 – I have more if she earns it, she always gets the same rate of spending money unless she does a particularly good week and then I give her more, of course she doesn't buy her own clothes, that's why she doesn't pay her board.

> (Long pause and embarrassed cough from respondent.) [Mother – she gives it all to me and I give her spending money.] (How much?) About £3–10–0 pocket money.

> £2– 5– 0 (M: I don't want to take too much from her, there are so many things a young girl wants & she pays her own expenses, of course I didn't have as much as that when she was earning less.)

> Well I really only pay her for my bed each week it's £1–10–0. She doesn't have anything to do with myself because I buy my own clothes and everything.

Strikingly, the young people frequently talked about the difference their income had made to family finances. It was clear that for many families at this time, the impact of an additional wage on household income was significant. Indeed, a number of young people had explained their decision to leave school as having been driven by the financial needs of the family. Interviewers often commented on this, particularly in larger families where the young worker had a number of younger siblings or where the family had only one parent working. Contributing money to the household income also had an impact on relationships within the family, with young workers describing feeling more 'respected':

> You seem more important in the house when you bring money in. You see other people's situations better.

> We've improved the house now there's more money coming in.

> I think there's more respect for me now. The extra money in the house has made the place more comfortable.

Have been able to afford more things and give the kids a better time (son in household with single mother and five younger siblings).

Mother has more money to spend on house and children.

The research team also explored patterns of consumption amongst respondents. Teenage spending habits were a topical issue in the early 1960s. Abrams (1959) had identified teenagers as a new group with disposable income and free time, 'a new "teenage culture" ... defined in terms of leisure and leisure goods – coffee and milk bars, fashion clothes and hair styles, cosmetics, rock'n'roll records, films and magazines, scooters and motorbikes, dancing and dance halls' (Frith 1984: 9). In view of the level of interest in teenage consumption patterns during this period, it is of little surprise that these respondents were asked about their spending habits and their ownership of certain material goods. Respondents were presented with a list of consumables and were asked to identify which, if any, they owned and to specify whether they had bought the item themselves or not. The list ranged from high ticket price items such as a car, motorbike or scooter, to smaller goods such as cameras, radios and record players. Few of the respondents owned the most expensive items; only 6 per cent owned a car, 14 per cent a motorbike and 5 per cent a scooter. Ownership of cars and motorbikes was more likely amongst the boys. For example, in the case of the car owners, from a total of 48 only three were girls and one of these owned the car jointly with her boyfriend. Not surprisingly, less expensive items were more widely possessed. For example, 60 per cent owned a bicycle, 50 per cent a camera, 45 per cent a radio and 45 per cent a record player; although only 19 per cent owned a tape-recorder, which, we would suggest, is indicative of the high cost of such technologically advanced equipment in the early part of the decade.

Having established the extent of ownership of material goods, it is of interest to explore the day-to-day spending activity of this group of young people. Most young people, having already paid for their board and lodging, had a certain amount of disposable income and others, who gave their wages to their parents, were given 'pocket money' to spend as they wished. We were able to compile a list illustrating the consumption patterns of these young workers based on their responses to the question 'what sort of things do you spend your money on?' This list throws up few surprises and mirrors teenage expenditure patterns in other studies of the time (Abrams 1959; Laurie 1965), with a focus on going to the cinema, transport, clothes, make-up, music and saving. Thirty years later, these patterns had not changed drastically and young people were still spending money on clothes, music, going out, saving up, transport and cosmetics (Stewart 1992, in Furlong and Cartmel 1997).

A high percentage of the young workers (77 per cent) managed to save some money each week. This high figure was surprising when compared to responses to a later question as to whether their money lasted all week, to which only 58 per cent were able to give a positive response. Some 17 per cent indicated that they often had to borrow from others, usually their parents, towards the end of the week. When asked what they were saving for, answers tended to be vague and non-specific. However, saving for clothes, expensive one-off purchases such as cars and particularly holidays was commonplace and some mentioned that they were saving to get married and buy a house. Again, this mirrors closely the teenage saving habits identified by Furlong and Cartmel (1997) some 30 years later.

The most common answer amongst young people in this study was that they spent their money on 'going to the cinema'; some 40 per cent of respondents mentioned this. This was followed by: sporting activities (bowling, snooker, football, fishing), buying clothes, going dancing, buying cigarettes, buying sweets, tea, coffee and food, buying drinks (presumably alcoholic as opposed to tea/coffee and soft drinks), buying books, records and music, stockings, cosmetics and hair and, for a significant number of young people, saving:

> Clothes, haircut, dinner money, cigarettes, dancing, pictures, drinking.

> Pay some to father who lent me money towards motorbike, records, clothes, pictures, bowling, sweets.

> Tools for work, pictures, dancing, beer, clothes, lemonades and things at work, a few cigarettes.

> Have a drink, dancing and dancing lessons, clothes, pictures and football.

> I just bought a Beatle jacket and a pair of pointed shoes, clothes, pictures, cigarettes, sweets.

The list of consumables gives an indication of the status of these young people as being in transition from childhood to adulthood. It was common, for example, for answers to this question to include more adult spending behaviours such as buying alcohol and cigarettes, and work-related items alongside the purchase of more childlike products: sweets and lemonade. Other expenditure fell more neatly in to the teenage spending patterns of dancing, cinema and fashion.

Fashion and Youth Cultures

The significance of fashion, hair and make-up as a way for young people to differentiate themselves from their parents, was beginning to be recognised during the late 1950s and early 1960s. As Dyhouse (2013: 154) has commented, 'the style revolution of the early 1960s could scarcely be ignored by contemporaries: it had obvious links to the widening gap between generations'. Without doubt, fashion played a key role in the lives of many of these young workers and is key to understanding the youth cultures and teenage behaviours of the time. This was, in many ways, the starting point of teenage fashions becoming central to the process of transition to adulthood and, as Hodkinson (2009: 281) has suggested, now 'the notion of youthful style as a response to the particular transitional circumstances of adolescence is broadly accepted'.

One of the most visible fashion trends of the post-war period related to the birth of youth subcultures. Furlong and Cartmel (1997: 59–60) suggest that during the post-war period there was 'a close correspondence between fashions and class membership' and the 'predominant styles of the time, teddy boys, mods and rockers were seen as adaptations of working class cultures'. However, the majority of young people, and in particular young women, did not necessarily participate in subcultural youth groups yet were interested in fashion. As has been suggested elsewhere, a consequence of the excessive research focus on 'spectacular youth' has been that the behaviours of 'ordinary' youth have been neglected (see Hodkinson 2009). Certainly in this study we find examples of young women whose leisure time pursuits clearly fit with McRobbie and Garber's (1976) descriptions of 'bedroom cultures', whereby there was a tendency to stay at home, listen to music and experiment with fashion and make-up, rather than evidence of any participation in youth subcultures.

> Arrived in the middle of a pop tune session. Mother seemed to be doing household jobs while respondent and friend danced, listened, or moved in time to the music.

> At first interview was difficult as respondent was watching pop-record programme on ITV and setting her hair at the same time.

We also find very few comments about teenage boys engaging in what could be termed youth subcultures in terms of fashion or behaviours noted by themselves or the interviewers. The tendency for the interviewers to make detailed comments on the fashionable appearance of some of the young people would suggest that membership of youth subcultures or adhering to the more 'spectacular' fashion trends of the period, was somewhat unusual in the early 1960s:

> This interview got off to a bizarre start; respondent opened front door to me with large guitar in one hand and a cigarette in his mouth and although he stopped smoking he kept strumming his guitar.

> Respondent was really 'with it' when I first met him, wearing a Beatles collector's suit.

> A rather bizarre character looking worn and tired dressed in skin tight pale blue jeans, boots, a thick leather belt and a black T-shirt. With long blonde hair styled in a Tony Curtis fashion and may well have been dyed.

However, as we have seen already in this chapter, it was common for disposable income to be used to buy clothes and many of the respondents said that they were saving money to buy clothes. This was particularly true among the girls who were less likely than the boys to rely on their mothers to buy their clothes. As Dyhouse (2013: 162) describes, fashion in the 1960s became far more of a feature of young women's lives than was previously the case: 'Girls began to dress differently for their mothers, in Quant-inspired dolly-dresses, high boots and miniskirts'. Although miniskirts and Mary Quant style fashion were still some time away, it was evident that expenditure on clothes was becoming a significant feature of teenage patterns of consumption. We learn a great deal about the fashions of the period from the interviewer comments – where respondents were dressed in fashions of the time, the interviewer invariably commented on this:

> She seems to live in a two-thirds dream world. This consists of black leather coats, coffee bars, Art and Tech, etc. She obviously yearns to be one of the college set and was proud of her affiliations to it. An attractive girl – with the pale faced look and dressed conventionally 'off beat'.

> Respondent looked young and immature (in spite of/because of carefully waved hair and leather pull over).

> Respondent wore his hair in a subdued Beatles style.

> Respondent would definitely be disapproved of by the conventional. She looked a little wild (long absolutely straight black hair) and unkempt but also 'sexy' – short straight tight skirt, and tight sleeveless jumper.

> Although he hoped to be getting married soon, he did not treat the problem seriously since he was still going out every night and saving only £2 a week. His clothes were in the latest 'Beatles' style.

> Respondent seems to be treated as adult member of household and allowed plenty of freedom. She is a very small, slender girl, skillfully made-up with sophisticated, artificially blonde hairstyle.

While it is clear from these comments that teenage fashions such as Beatle suits and tight skirts were not confined to London, the fact that the interviewers described in some detail the more fashionable teenagers, suggests that such following of fashion was not yet commonplace in Leicester. The interviews took place in the early 1960s and in March and November of 1963 the Beatles appeared at De Montfort Hall in Leicester. These dates fell within the period that the interviews took place so it is to be expected that their visit would be mentioned during some of the interviews:

He likes the Beatles but wouldn't queue up all night for a ticket. However he intends to stand outside the De Montfort Hall to see the crowd 'tear it to pieces'.

The local newspaper, the *Leicester Mercury*, recently noted that the first appearance by the Beatles in the city did not attract much media attention and they did not even send a photographer to record the event in March 1963. This gives some indication that the unfolding popularity of the Beatles and the musical fashions of the period had not fully registered in Leicester at the time of the interviews.

> The Leicester Mercury's records show that, while some young girls queued all night for tickets for the show at De Montfort Hall, full-scale Beatlemania had not yet hit the East Midlands. The De Montfort Hall booking record for the show on March 31, 1963 does not even mention the Fab Four. This apparent indifference to the lads from Liverpool is supported by the fact that the Leicester Mercury picture desk did not deem it significant enough to send a photographer. When the Beatles returned to De Montfort Hall in December 1963, their popularity was on the increase … Mercury photographers had also learned their lesson and took pictures of virtually everything that moved. (*Leicester Mercury* 30 March 2013).

By November of the same year, interest levels had increased and Beatlemania in the city was evidenced by record queues for tickets and to enter the venue on the night being covered in detail by the local press, suggesting that the trends that started in the bigger cities took longer to reach provincial Leicester.

Independence and Going Out: Friends and Leisure Time Activities

Transitions from school to work in the 1960s have been viewed largely as a single-step process by which young people left school and started work at a time when jobs for young people were widely available. Alongside this transition to work, young people also began the transition to independence largely due to moving from being school children dependent on their parents to becoming wage earners in their own right and contributing to the family income. Most young people were expected to contribute to the household economy once they began to earn their own money. Some gave their entire wage packet to their parents and were given 'pocket money' in return. Others paid a pre-arranged amount of board and lodging and retained the rest of the money to spend as they wished. This economic transition has subsequently been viewed as part of a process of 'becoming adult': 'leaving education and collecting the first wage packet was symbolic for both young people and their parents and tended to be accompanied by the granting of greater freedoms and responsibilities' (Furlong and Cartmel 1997: 42). Nevertheless, as the quote intimates, it was not just freedom that increased; young people often found their new responsibilities increased at the same time. For some this meant new, additional responsibilities at home, for example, being expected to clean their own rooms, buy their own clothes and do their laundry, whilst others found that their household chores decreased once they started to contribute to the household income. Perhaps the most burdensome responsibility was the financial one. For some families, as we have seen, the wage of the school leaver in the home was crucial and, therefore, earning money took on a different importance as it came with the responsibility of becoming a contributor to the household rather than simply a consumer.

Without doubt what we see in the data from this study is that the young workers were afforded a greater degree of freedom from parental restrictions that were in place for many when they were still at school. Having left school and started work, their increased independence was evident. Some 88 per cent indicated that they were able to go out as often as they wished. This did not vary greatly between the boys and the girls, with similar levels of freedom, in terms of permission to go out during their free time, given to both. Amongst those who said they were not able to go out as often as they wished, the main restrictions were associated with lack of money, other obligations (studying, housework, babysitting for younger siblings) and tiredness/a lack of time more than any level of parental control. Some of the young people had extremely busy time schedules and found that they did not have the opportunity to go out socially very often:

> Respondent tells mother where he is going and if he is going to be late. (NB respondent's time fairly well accounted for: 2 nights at Tech, 2 nights at Youth Club, Saturday afternoon football, is accompanied by older brother when he goes ten pin bowling).

> I haven't the money – mother and father used to restrict me but now I take the responsibility for what I do. No, if I'm home late and can't get up in the morning that's my responsibility.

> Mother likes me to stop in sometimes. I have to clean my bedroom, help with the other housework, wash my hair.

> I have to look after my own clothes, washing, mending and that sort of thing. Unless I am going anywhere special I have to be home by 10.

In other cases, parental restrictions were imposed but these were mainly around the time that the young people were expected to come home and the frequency of nights out. It was here that a gender differential appeared too, with the young women seeming to be subject to more restrictions:

> I have to stay in some nights, mother says I have to. [Mother: She stays in 2 nights out of 7 that's all.] No but I'm always told off if I'm late. I'm always in by 11. [Mother: She comes home with her boyfriend. I always know she's alright

because she stands outside about 1/2 hr. He has to catch the last bus back to town.]

Well so long as mother and father know where I am when out, know where I've gone, I'm all right. In week never any later than 11pm because of buses from town, but if going anywhere special and say I'll be late it's all right.

I have to help my mum – because she goes to work like the rest of us. Friday and Tuesday stay in and most other evenings. Boyfriend has to be gone by about 10.45 pm. Father used to require respondent to be home by about 10.30 pm on most days – but he was less rigid about the weekends or if he knew she was going to a special dance. Respondent still uses this as a working basis.

Regardless of the young person's new status as a worker, most abided by the rules imposed by their parents, under whose roof they remained living. The respondents were asked how agreement on going out and returning home was reached. The majority explained that their parents decided:

Yes. Well in the week we don't have to be back by a certain time cos if we go out in the week we only go round here so we're always back by 11. Weekend on a Saturday about 12.30 sometimes we over run it a bit you know – mind you it's only been about 12.30 for a year – before it used to be about 12 but it's getting a bit higher. (Who settles these times?) Me mam.

My mother likes me to be in some nights. She doesn't want to see me get into trouble.

For the parents, the age of the young person seemed to be a significant factor and more independence was granted as they were perceived to have reached 'adulthood', usually around the age of 18:

I am allowed to be 1/2 hr later after this birthday. [Mother – We think 10.30 is late enough for any girl to be out unless they are going to a dance or somewhere special.]

When I was 18 and paid my board I could come in when I wanted. But before that I had to come in when they wanted me to. We keep the key behind the door.

My mother doesn't think I'm old enough to go out when I like. My mother tells me what time she wants me in.

What is evident from the data is that these young people were in the process of becoming adults by, in Eliasian terms, acquiring the 'appropriate behavioural standards of the time' (Goodwin and O'Connor 2009: 26) and this was something both they and their parents recognised. The process of becoming an adult and learning appropriate behaviours was mediated, in most cases, by parents, who gradually loosened their hold over their children by allowing them increasing freedoms and independence to manage their own behaviour, supported by them when necessary.

Becoming an Adult: Changing Relationships at Home and Beyond

A further section in the interview asked the young people to reflect on the experience of becoming an adult, specifically whether or not they felt that they were adults now their status had changed from schoolchild to worker. The temporal context of the research project is significant here, as this was a period during which there was considerable interest in young people's social position. The research was taking place at a time when 'there was a great deal of discussion ... about the age at which young people could be considered adults' (Dyhouse 2013: 169). In the early 1960s, young people aged under 21 were, in legal terms, defined as 'infants' and the change to legislation did not happen until the end of the decade (Dyhouse 2013: 169). The researchers' interest in the transition to adulthood may well have been influenced by the focus on legislative changes, but was also informed by Elias's approach to understanding this rite of passage (Goodwin and O'Connor 2009) as part of the process of 'changing relations with others throughout ... life' (Elias 2000: 377). We go on, below, to explore the impact of becoming workers on the relationships of the young people with their parents.

Although all of these young people had left school and started work, were paying part or all of their wages into the household budget and were enjoying increased independence, few felt that they had become adults at this stage of their lives. Only 28 per cent answered the question 'do you think of yourself as an adult?' positively. Some 55 per cent indicated that they did not consider themselves to be adults and a further 16 per cent felt that they had become adult in 'some way'. When pressed to explain what made a young person become an adult, their answers revealed the complexity of this issue as there was little common ground here. Although there was some agreement that leaving school and behaving in a 'different way' were signs of the transition to becoming an adult, most young people were unsure what would signify or mark this change in status. This uncertainty was perhaps more to do with the list of options offered during the interview which did not include what might now be considered symbols of adulthood – buying a house, relationship status, becoming a parent. The list used in the interview was more esoteric, including options such as 'independence', 'responsibility' and 'attitude' rather than more concrete and definite changes in status commonly associated with the transition to adulthood.

Another aspect of the transition to adulthood that was explored concerned roles at home and relationships with parents. Respondents were asked to reflect on whether life had changed at home now they had a job, in the question: 'Since you started work, are there any ways things have changed at home? Is it different at home now you are a worker?' More than half of the sample felt that their home lives had not changed sufficiently to warrant a positive answer to this question yet, when prompted, many came up with examples of how life had changed. Around a quarter believed that their lives at home had changed significantly and many commented that they felt they were treated more as an adult since starting work and earning their own money. Answers to this question focused on independence, responsibility, equality with parents and new freedoms:

> Treated more as grown up. Parents give respondent more responsibility – wouldn't before have been allowed to stay at home while they went on holiday.

For some young people this transition meant a decrease in their contribution to household jobs (presumably as they were now seen to be contributing financially instead):

> Don't have to do errands! Not picked on so much. Always used to be picking on you because you're the youngest, but when you go to work you become one of them.

> Don't get picked on half so much. Much better really.

Others explained that they were able to have more opinions of their own and they felt like they had more to contribute to adult conversations:

> Can talk with mother and father about things now I'm at work – can talk about general affairs, affairs with them and be more grown up.

> I buy my own clothes. The family talk to you about important things now.

> M thinks I'm more of a nuisance (P) I think because I talk more now. I didn't talk about school as much as I talk about what's happened at work. I'm always talking about what's happened at work.

Relationships and Marriage

Much of the literature around 1960s youth and transitions during the post-war period stresses that young people not only made smoother transitions into work but also that there pathways to adulthood were simpler and less protracted than they later became (Furlong and Cartmel 1997). Marriage in the 1960s tended to occur at an earlier age than in later decades but young people then largely lived at home until they married and had children. This meant that they married earlier and started families at a younger age than was to become the norm from the 1970s onwards. The respondents were not asked detailed questions about relationships with members of the opposite sex, although they were asked whether or not they had a boy or girlfriend (potential answers were yes, no or sometimes). Some 45 per cent said that they were in a relationship, 48 per cent were not and the remainder either did not respond or replied 'sometimes'. Many mentioned their relationships in response to other questions, for example, describing plans to marry, already being engaged to be married or describing their social lives with reference to 'courtship'. Few young people appeared to be married at the time of interview although, as the schedule did not include an explicit question on marriage, it proved difficult to identify young people who had already married (or become parents) as this was not recorded formally. Information on married respondents was gleaned from interviewer notes and comments in the margin of the interview schedule. From this we can establish that two of the sample were already married and both individuals still lived at home but had been joined by their spouse. The female respondent who was married had also become a mother just prior to the interview.

There was, however, considerable evidence of young people preparing for marriage although, again, this was not formally recorded as part of the interview. A number of the respondents were engaged to be married and mentioned this in answer to the question regarding savings:

> Hope to get married in 2–3 years' time so we are saving for later life.

> Saving for holidays, for when we get married at the moment.

> I'm engaged, saving up to be married.

> Saving up for a house to get married, looking ahead.

There were, then, few surprises in the data in terms of marriage and future family life. The trends identified amongst the majority of the sample mirror closely what has been identified by other studies of the time.

Leisure Time Activities

Teenage leisure activities have been well-documented since the post-war period when academic attention first turned to the study of teenage lifestyles. Roberts (1983) highlights the profusion of studies of teenage leisure published in this period as a consequence of the trends already identified in this chapter, namely increased spending power and the availability of free time as yet unfettered by marriage, children and associated domestic obligations. The role of leisure in the transition to adulthood is also well-documented and, as Roberts (1997a: 5) has indicated 'it is normally through leisure that young people first assert independence from adults, typically with the blessing of their elders, and learn to associate with equals without external supervision'.

Jephcott's (1967: 2) study of Scottish youth is perhaps one of the most comprehensive accounts of teenage leisure time of this period. She set out to investigate how young Scots, aged 15–19, spent their free time in the mid-1960s 'now that leisure is becoming less a footnote to work than important in its own right'. Her work is useful not only because it is a large-scale study of youth leisure but also because she categorised the types of leisure activities enjoyed by young people into four distinct groupings: 1) leisure time spent at home; 2) informal individual or small group activities such as swimming and snooker; 3) commercial organised activity, e.g. coffee bars, cinemas, dances, bowling; and 4) formal activities based on membership of groups and associations such as youth clubs, sports club membership and drama groups. She did not include evening classes and educational activities undertaken outside work as part of the leisure activities.

Our data broadly follows Jephcott's categories and her groupings are useful in helping to understand patterns of leisure time use in Leicester during this era. Respondents were asked about the use of their free-time but it is surprising, given the focus on teenage lifestyles by commentators of the time that the focus of the questions was around formal activities, namely evening classes and formal, membership-based club activities. The questions on formally structured leisure activities were far more detailed than the questions about unstructured or free time. We begin, then, by exploring the category of formal learning as a leisure pursuit. The findings here are of great interest as they reveal that almost half of the sample, some 47 per cent, was engaged in learning outside work. Some of this additional learning was undertaken as a compulsory part of the young person's employment, with around a third of those taking evening classes, doing so as part of their job. However, the other young people were attending such classes on a voluntary basis. The type of classes varied widely. Some were taking classes relating to hobbies such as woodwork but others were seeking to improve their qualifications and were studying for additional O-levels or other skills-based qualifications, such as typing and shorthand or, more broadly, office skills.

This level of personal commitment to what we would now see as continuing professional development or lifelong learning is fascinating. The motivation for these young people may have come from a range of different sources. First, many of these young people left school at the age of 15 without any qualifications, thus evening classes were a way of gaining certification at a later stage. Second, a number of young people explained that it was only after leaving school and entering work that they began to understand the value of education. The only way to address this would have been to attend such classes voluntarily, as it would not have been possible for most to return to education. Third, for a number of young people who did have the chance to stay on at school, those attending grammar school, for example, family finances often meant that, in reality, they faced considerable pressure to begin contributing to the household budget, therefore, staying on at school was a luxury that many could not afford. A final reason may well have been associated with the reality of the labour market. School leavers who did not possess qualifications were disadvantaged in some sectors of the labour market, therefore, gaining additional office based skills, for example, would have served to enhance their 'employability'. Further evidence of the young people's recognition of the value of learning only once they had left school is evidenced by their responses to an interview question which asked them to rank the status of a range of potential jobs/post-education outcomes. This list comprised: an apprentice, a shop worker, a semi-skilled worker, an office worker and someone still at school. The two options that were rated most highly were an apprentice and someone still at school. Those who ranked these roles highly frequently mentioned the value of qualifications and education in enhancing an individual's opportunities in the labour market:

[Interviewer]: Why did you rank 'someone still at school' as most successful?

I think you are better off, I wish I had stayed now. [Why?] It would have given me longer to make up my mind what I wanted to do, perhaps got a couple of A levels.

I don't think there is anything better than a good education, I should [have] liked to have stopped on to study certain subjects. You have a better chance of getting a much better job altogether. I wouldn't have got this job if I hadn't got [a] GCE.

A boy at school at my age should have his GCE and be going on to A levels. When he finishes school he'll have a good job to go to – better paid than the rest there.

You're at school to learn something – G.C.E or 'A' level, you're doing something – you've got a piece of paper to show a future employer.

A boy at school must want to be something and he is studying for it.

I don't think it [shop work] has really any future, you can be in a shop like Woolworths and still be at the same counter when you're 50.

[Interviewer]: Why did you rank 'an apprentice' as the most successful?

An apprentice is obviously learning a trade and something they'll never forget all through their lives. They'll always have a job at their fingertips. Somebody still at school is still learning and they will obviously have better opportunities because they will know as much.

They are about the best jobs (Why do you think they are the best jobs?) When they have finished training they are going to get the best paid jobs.

An apprentice is learning a trade, can always get a good job. A boy at school will go to the top and so will an office worker.

When he's finished his apprenticeship he's got a trade in his hands, he's pretty well sure of a job.

Learning outside work was then a significant part of the free time of many of the respondent's, whether this was voluntary or undertaken as part of their jobs. Another area of investigation was around what Jephcott (1967) classified as 'formal activities', such as membership of clubs and associations, for example, youth clubs, working men's clubs, sports associations and other 'special interest' groups, such as drama, religion and motorbike clubs. Membership of such groups was quite high with some 58 per cent claiming to belong to a club or association of some description. Youth clubs were the most popular type of group with around 28 per cent of the entire sample stating that they were formally members of such clubs. The range of other associations belonged to was wide, with young people mentioning groups as diverse as sporting clubs (football, judo, fishing, cycling), organised formal youth groups (army cadets, scouts, boys brigade, girl guides), religious groups, St John Ambulance, motorcycling and scooter clubs, and lastly work related groups (e.g. Society of Dyers). However, in many cases, as discussed in more detail below, club membership appeared to be an activity that respondents were losing interest in at this stage of their lives. Many had been active youth club members when still at school and although they remained as members, they were no longer attending on a regular basis.

What is, perhaps, most surprising about this survey of young people is that so little of the interview asked about free time or leisure time in terms of unstructured activities. Where other research of the period tends to include a focus on 'going out' or socialising, there was little emphasis on this aspect of the young workers' lives. This omission was commented on by an interviewer who found the lack of questions in this area frustrating:

Main interest appears to be motorbikes for their association 'with the lads'. I am convinced they do go around shops looking in windows at bikes and spare parts. I feel that it is a pity that this schedule in the leisure time section is so much orientated to formal activity which is directed more at the skilled and semi-skilled worker. This interview would have been much more fruitful if I had had opportunity to go into unorganised leisure pursuits of the girl and her friend.

Revisiting the study 50 years later, we have little sense of what the young people did in the evenings or at the weekends. We might expect, for example, to have seen far more mention of milk bars and coffee bars, dance halls, music events and parties. However, this facet of the teenagers' lives receives little attention here and the categories that Jephcott (1967) classified as leisure time spent at home, informal leisure and commercial organised activities, were not pursued as areas of research.

The glimpses we have of the social lives of these young people come, for the most part, in the interviewer reflections, from comments made by their parents during the interview and occasionally in response to the question about where and how money was spent. Questions about 'going out' were concerned with practicalities and gaining insight into how home relationships had or had not altered with increasing independence. Questions about friendships were concentrated on work relationships and friendships in the workplace. This is disappointing, as more emphasis on free time would have provided a greater sense of the extent to which teenage pastimes and youth subcultures were evident in Leicester during this period. The only section dedicated to free, unstructured leisure time was a short section that asked: 'Have you any friends that you see regularly' and concluded with the question 'What sort of things do you do together?' It is only here that we get a sense of the type of activities that this group were involved in when their time was their own. The interviewers did not probe this question in any depth and most respondents simply gave a short list of the type of activity they enjoyed with their friends:

> Meet in Coffee bar, play cards, go to youth club, nice nights just walk around.

> Ice-skating, bowling, follow the football. Pretty general things – dancing.

> Bowling, used to go dancing, don't now, used to go roller-skating, swimming things like that.

> Pictures, dancing, listen to radio, records.

> Down the cafe (Brunswick Bar), a coffee bar which is like a club as we call the owner by his first name. Standing about on the street or playing with a tape – recorder like that.

> Motorbike rides, bowling, pictures, dancing, drinking.

> Bowling alley, skittles or darts in a pub, occasional youth club with one of them but I am not a member. I go to the stock car races on Saturdays with my dad or on my own.

> Used to play football – generally go for drink now – see girlfriend.

As alluded to above, there was a sense that some of the activities previously enjoyed were no longer so attractive. The young people were in a period of transition in terms of leisure as well as in other aspects of life. For some this was because new relationships with a boy- or girlfriend had begun to take priority:

> Because I have a boyfriend. I go out with him instead.

I started courting and wasn't really interested anymore.

Or because working life had given them new interests and effectively begun to move them into an adult world of working men's clubs instead of youth clubs:

They lowered the age limit so there were loads of young boys around screaming and playing cowboys and Indians.

The club was dying, nobody went, I joined the WMC 2 weeks ago.

I lost interest, it wasn't a very good youth club, all there was to do was sit around listening to records.

I'd been at work a little while. It was all schoolgirls who went and the girls I knew stopped going.

Conclusion

In many respects, few surprises are encountered in the data on teenage leisure and youth culture found in this project. Teenagers' lives in the early 1960s were subject to a great deal of attention from the media and from academia both at the time and subsequently. This resulted in young people's lives being well documented. Patterns of youth culture during the period – the growing consumerism of the teenage generation and increasing marketisation of their free time, the increase in disposable incomes amongst young people and the corresponding interest in fashion, cosmetics, music and 'commercialised leisure' were all found in Leicester, as elsewhere. What is perhaps different in this case is that first the research was carried out at what can be described as the early stages of the birth of teenage culture and many of the young people who took part in this project were, to a great extent, still following traditional pathways. There was much talk of engagement and marriage and many of the young people seemed to be already moving away from what could be termed as teenage lifestyles before reaching their twenties. The period during which these young people were able to lead teenage life styles was short and, for many, there was not time enough to follow teenage pastimes before adult responsibilities took precedence.

We see in our data early glimpses of phenomenon such as Beatlemania and an interest in fashion and youth cultures (motorbikes, scooters, teenage-focused television programmes) arriving in Leicester but only at the tail-end of the teen years of this group. However, we also find young adults being given increasing freedom from family life and the independence, usually supported by parental intervention, to begin to make their own way in life. They talked of changed relationships at home, of becoming wage-earners and saving for their futures. Perhaps the most surprising finding here for those unfamiliar with the city was that the girls in the study were as likely to earn high wages as the boys and for those who trained in certain industries, the possibility of earning very good money was there. This was certainly unusual at the time when teenage girls tended to earn only around 80 per cent of the wages of teenage boys (Roberts 1983: 15).

Overall, then, the data illustrates the emergence of teenage lifestyle in Leicester and a certain shift in behaviours that differentiated the young workers from their parents. The changing experience of young people was closely linked to the economic prosperity of the time and the very buoyant local labour market, which gave young people access to potentially high earnings and to the independence this engendered.

Chapter 7

Whatever Happened to the Young Workers?

Introduction

> Well let us say that [with] any apprenticeship you've got a future. You've got 5 years for a start and then after that you can rely on a decent wage every week afterwards for the rest of your life.
>
> Apprentice Engineer, British United Shoe Machinery Company, 1964

> I worked in the British United Shoe Machinery Company in Leicester for 36 years. It went into receivership in October 2000 ... I knew for years that the shoe industry was going down, because everything was shifting to the Far East anyway, so we knew that the company was a little bit on the sticky side but that was for years and years.
>
> Duncan 2006: 2–3

When a cohort of young workers entered the Leicester labour market in the early 1960s, little could they have known or expected the economic turmoil that they would face throughout their working lives. They entered a labour market at 15 with expectations of a job for life in one of Leicester's three dominant industries – hosiery manufacture, boot and shoe manufacture and allied engineering industries. They could never have predicted that some 45 years later very little of these industries would remain or that they would have lived through the major recessions of the early 1970s, 1980s, 1990s and today. For this group of workers, as with many others in Western industrial nations, the smooth 'cradle to grave' career was not to be theirs. The young worker quoted above was a respondent of Elias's *Adjustment of Young Workers to Work Situations and Adult Roles* project and, when contrasted with the quote from Duncan (2006), it is clear to see that the optimism of many of those entering work in the early and mid-1960s was misplaced. But what actually become of the other young workers from this study? What we do know, as a starting point, is that around 100 of the respondents from the *Adjustment of Young Workers to Work Situations and Adult Roles* project were used as the basis for Ashton and Field's (1976) book *Young Workers: From School to Work* – a book that has proved to be one of the definitive accounts of young people's transitions from school to work and which is still cited in most contemporary works on school to work transitions (see Fergusson et al. 2000; Arrowsmith and Sission 2001; Worth 2003; Roberts 2004; MacDonald et al. 2005; and Furlong and Cartmel 2006). Using this data, they set out to 'understand the behaviour of certain types of young people and their problems of adjustment to work' (Ashton and Field 1976: 11), arguing that continuities in the young workers' experiences at home, school and their social class shaped the young workers' experiences of the transition to work and their subsequent careers. They argued that the typology of *careerless*, *short-term careers* and *extended careers* captured the different meanings attached to work by the young workers, reflecting their different experiences and self-image based on school, class and educational attainment. Using these categories, Ashton and Field (1976) then made predictions for the young people in terms of their subsequent careers (see below). Given the significance and impact of *Young Workers: From School to Work*, we feel it would indeed be of significant sociological interest to explore the veracity of these predictions within the context of the remaining *Adjustment of Young Workers to Work Situations and Adult Roles* data, re-discovered in the 2000s. In doing so we can explore questions such as what do we know about them? To what extent can their experiences be used as a lens through which to understand the transitional dilemmas faced by young people today? In this sense, like Laub and Sampson (2003), our focus here is on the 'within-individual' patterns of continuity and change – the continuities and changes within one group of young workers interviewed in the early to mid-1960s and re-interviewed in the early 2000s.

The remainder of this paper is organised into three main sections. After the introduction we will provide some background to Ashton and Field's (1976) approach. Moving on, and using data from the original respondents, we examine the young workers' experiences of transition from school to work and subsequent work and life histories. We have decided to present this data in two ways. First we will provide a broad overview of the data highlighting key trends, employment outcomes and work experiences, as described by the respondents themselves. We will then offer six qualitative vignettes to illustrate the broad themes we have found. In the concluding section we reflect on what can be learned from the experiences of this cohort of young workers, highlighting potential implications for those making the transition from school to work today. Here we also acknowledge the significance of what Gidden's (1991) labels *fateful moments* and what Thomson et al. (2002) refer to as *critical moments*; incidences that were highly significant for the young workers but which were not acknowledged in Ashton and Field's original analysis.

Three Categories of Young Worker: Careerless, Short-term Careers and Extended Careers

One of the most significant contributions of Ashton and Field's study is their model of the transition experience. This model was based on understanding transition outcomes through examining the impact of social class, family background and education on young people's movements into work. They aimed to illustrate 'the mutually reinforcing effects of experiences in the home, at school, and at work on the development and transmission of the different ways in which young people come to view themselves and their world' (143). In short, Ashton and Field (1976) suggested that we can understand what happens to young people and predict what will happen to them in the future by examining structural factors over which the young people have no control.

From this analysis they identified three groups central to understanding the transition process: the careerless, short-term careers and extended careers. They suggest that the three categories identify the different meanings attached to work by the young workers, reflecting their different experiences and self-images. For example, the careerless made the transition from the lower streams of state schools into semi-skilled and unskilled work without adjustment problems. Their concern, like their parents before them, was for the immediate present and little thought was given to the future (Ashton and Field 1976: 36). They were employed in jobs that provided good short-term economic rewards but with little chance of self-development. They frequently changed jobs, as both their boredom threshold and commitment to the job were low. This group learnt to believe that they had limited ability at school and, as such, did not consider themselves to be suited to jobs requiring lengthy training. Significantly, Ashton and Field (36) suggested that the majority of individuals in this group 'are from families in which the parents are in careerless jobs, i.e. jobs with low levels of income which do little more than cover the basic necessities of life … their parents will have had little formal education'.

In contrast, those with short-term careers were moderately successful at school, occupying a middle position between the careerless and those with extended careers. On leaving school they went on to seek jobs in the skilled manual trades, technical occupations and clerical work. These jobs offered the possibility of development through training and also a degree of security, illustrating their greater concern with the future. When they began work, they faced a lengthy period of training and/or further education, often paid for by their employer. This group learnt complex job-specific skills and tended to stay in the job until training was complete. They became 'locked into' the occupation and rarely envisaged a change in career once the skills were learnt. This group, according to Ashton and Field, believed themselves to be of moderate intelligence and capable of further development. They chose jobs that provided them with the opportunity to 'make something of themselves', often mirroring their own parents' career paths in similar jobs.

The third group identified as those with 'extended careers' generally had more middle-class backgrounds. At school they had been aware of the link between academic success and entry to a good career. Their focus was more on long-term rewards and their career paths, which offered continuous advancement and high and secure incomes, reflected this. Like those with short-term careers, their pay was low on entering work and promotion depended upon further education and training. This group saw continuity between education and work, and often had on-the-job training in addition to attending day release schemes. Their self-image was of intelligent individuals capable of considerable self-development. As such, they embarked upon careers that required a long period of learning in order to progress and develop their potential skills. The long-term rewards were considerably greater for this group.

In each case, Ashton and Field argue that the positive or negative image the young workers acquired of themselves within the family was then reinforced at school. Their entry into work and early experience of it further reinforced the self-image and orientation to work generated at home and in school. Findings from later studies reached similar conclusions to those of Ashton and Field, stressing the impact of social class background on the school to work transition (Brown 1987; Furlong 1992; Jenkins 1983; Roberts 1995; Willis 1977) and the ease with which young people managed the transition (Kiernan 1992; Bynner 1998). Indeed, as suggested above, Ashton and Field's work became an important text in the area of youth transitions. Their model, described above, formed the basis for many other analyses of youth transitions from the 1970s through to the early 1990s. These accounts of youth transitions tended to follow Ashton and Field's model of understanding transition by examining the structural factors that impacted on the young people's decisions about work and limited their 'choices' due to existing structures over which they had no control. It was not until the mid-1990s that research on transitions moved away from this model and began to consider the impact of individual agency on youth transitions. Whilst these later analyses have criticised the over-emphasis of Ashton and Field on opportunity structures at the expense of individual agency, without doubt, these subsequent analyses owe much to the early work of Ashton and Field (1976).

What Happened to the Young Workers: An Overview

By combining the data from the original 1960s interviews with the more recent follow up interviews we have full work histories for the respondents. The data offers a great deal of insight into what it was like to leave school in the 1960s and what work and employment was like for the young workers as they got older in the 1970s and 1980s. We can also clearly see how the recessions of the 1980s and 1990s impacted upon their careers. The data also offers insight into the respondents' experiences as they approach or enter retirement.

We have considered the young workers' experiences of leaving school in detail elsewhere (Goodwin and O'Connor 2005a). However, for the purposes of this paper, it is important to reflect again on these formative years in the labour market. A great deal has been written about school to work transitions in the 1950s and 1960s, but, as we have argued elsewhere, more contemporary commentators have left past accounts of school to work transitions largely unquestioned (see earlier). However, unlike the consensus view that transitions in the 1960s were smooth, linear, homogenised and unproblematic, the data from this study suggests a different pattern. When one considers the individual experiences of the school to work transition, the data suggests that the transitions were not linear in nature. Many respondents experienced breaks in employment, significant divergences from their predicted careers early on and reversals in their employment trajectories. The young workers also experienced unemployment and significant delays in starting work or commencing apprenticeships. The young workers themselves also perceived the transitional experience to be fraught with risks and uncertainties, unlike the smooth and uncomplex process predicted by others. The experiences of some were marked by being unprepared for work, reliant on the good will of teachers, schools, employment officers or older workers; good will that was often not forthcoming. There was also a heightened sense of anxiety and stress when apprenticeship papers were not signed. Ashton and Field's view that the young workers did not experience stress in the transitions from school to work, given that their previous experiences at home, school and peer group prepared them for the move, in hindsight now appears problematic.

The Middle Years

Following their initial experiences of work, the respondents subsequent work histories did not follow exactly the linear smooth trajectories predicted for them either. Instead, careers were characterised by greater levels of individual complexity and insecurity that could not be fully explained by family background, social class or education alone. Typically the respondents did not follow single career paths, but moved in and out of positions, occupations and employment based on the fluctuations of the local labour market and the fortunes of engineering, hosiery and shoe manufacture. There were many examples of individuals who had begun what Ashton and Field (1976) would have deemed to be middle-class careers, who shortly after being originally interviewed, moved into short-term careers in hosiery and textiles, often lured by high wages. Likewise, there were many who started out in low skilled positions in the footwear and hosiery industries who subsequently moved into salaried positions within the manufacturing and service sectors. If we consider job stability in more detail there is perhaps some, if not overwhelming, support for Ashton and Field's analysis. For example, those with predicted extended or middle-class careers showed slightly higher rates of job stability, with the majority having held five or fewer jobs in total. By contrast, more than two thirds of the careerless or short-term career groups had held six or more jobs, with 15 individuals from these groups holding between 10 and 50 jobs in 40 years of work. All of the respondents explained the high number of positions held by citing the decline of traditional industries in Leicester. As a consequence of this decline, many of the respondents, regardless of their social class of origin were happy to take *any* available work for financial reasons.

As we have seen above, Ashton and Field (1976) place a great deal of significance on attitudes to and experiences of education and training in the formation of the young workers' perspectives on work. For the short term group, not qualified for managerial positions, but at the same time not wanting dead end jobs, vocational education and training, often via apprenticeships, was the route for this group to 'make something of themselves'. The original data and follow up interviews support this to some extent but the actual individuals' experiences were somewhat more complex. For example, most in the short term group, clearly viewed their early occupational training and subsequent occupational socialisation (for example, as engineers or mechanics) as having real significance to them, with many respondents retaining a very strong sense of occupational identity formed in their very first jobs. Yet, within 10 years of leaving school, many were no longer working in the industry for which they had originally trained and found that their skills were no longer in demand. This led to skilled workers who had originally trained to work in hosiery, boot and shoe factories, moving into jobs in the newer service industries such as sandwich-making and snack preparation factories. Yet the experiences of those in the extended career group were not much better. Many of those who had trained as accountants, managers or for other professional roles, and those who had undergone lengthy periods of training and acquired higher levels of skills, also ultimately ended up working side-by-side with the careerless and those with short-term careers on the production lines of sandwich-making factories. The collapse of all three of Leicester's major industries meant there was as little demand for trained managers as there was for boot and shoe operatives.

Six Vignettes

In the following section we provide six vignettes to illustrate the way that for many of the young workers their work histories did not follow the linear and clear-cut paths predicted for them by Ashton and Field. Where possible we have identified respondents who were originally classified as being in particular employment pathways by Ashton and Field in 1976 and were re-interviewed by us 40 years later. We have selected two cases from each of the three groups, beginning with the extended careers group.

Geoff's Story

This respondent was identified by Ashton and Field as fitting with their 'extended career' group. He left school with five O-levels and secured a job as a trainee chartered accountant:

> The reason I went into accountancy was because mathematics was always my forté. I got grade A in GCEs and it was always felt that that was the right thing for me.

At the time of the original interview, he described himself as being 'on the road to becoming a professionally qualified man'. However, a short time after beginning his career, he was dismissed when his employers discovered that he had taken a part-time job at the local market. This was the first significant critical moment in Geoff's career biography and one that he left to fate rather than actively addressing. At this point his career path changed direction rather dramatically and from being categorised firmly in the extended career group, his path began to mirror the careerless route:

> I swapped and changed, because I didn't really know what I wanted. I couldn't find anything. I mean in those days, unlike today, you don't, you don't get a job unless you want to do it, but in those days you worked. And I drifted from job to job because I didn't really know, I mean I even ended up labouring at one point, but I just didn't know what I wanted to do.

In the following decade he had approximately 10 different jobs as diverse as being a knitter in a hosiery factory to a window cleaner. It was not until the birth of his first child that he began to reconsider his career path:

> I had a child during that time and, and I felt well, with my qualifications and, well I felt the skills I had, I was wasting my life. I decided then that I would have to change things and then from there I had three jobs between there and what I'm doing now.

He recognised the birth of his first child as critical moment that enabled him to take control of his career path and seek a career that more closely reflected his position on leaving school. At the time of the re-interview, Geoff was working as a national sales manager for a large company and he had been employed there for 30 years. After experiencing over a decade of following a careerless route, Geoff managed to return to his original predicted extended career pathway, by making this 'fateful moment' an 'empowering experience' (Thomson et al. 2002: 337).

Peter's Story

Peter secured his first job before leaving school. At the time of the original interview he had been working as a costing clerk in a large Leicester shoe factory for three years. He was identified as fitting the extended careers profile, with Ashton and Field suggesting that he would follow a clerical career path. During his interview he described his ambition to become a foreman and was very keen to explain that he did not work on the shop floor.

This respondent's career history illustrates very clearly the way that the peaks and troughs of the economic cycle, in particular periods of national and international economic recession, can impact on individual work/life biographies with both devastating and lasting effects. His career vignette below illustrates that although he did have two extended periods of employment, one lasting 16 years and the other for 17 years, these periods were punctuated by the effects of recession.

His first experience of redundancy occurred in 1978. Having worked in the same factory for 16 years and achieving a position as a departmental supervisor, he left the job when he was approached by another shoe company offering more money and better prospects. However, this was his first experience of the impact of economic downturn, as he was made redundant after only two years. At this point, Leicester's main industries of shoe, boot and textile manufacturing, whilst in decline, were still functioning and although the company he worked for went out of business, he found employment in the same industry as a supervisor. After seven years, Peter changed jobs again, motivated by an increase in salary and became a foreman in a factory making components for shoes rather than a shoe factory. He stayed there for 17 years leaving only when he was made redundant in 2002. This point represented Peter's first experience of unemployment and came at a time when the local shoe industry had completely collapsed and he was, at the same time, approaching retirement. He was out of work for one week and found his new job through the Job Centre – the first time that he had not been able to use his personal network to secure a new job. He took a job in another factory in the shoe industry but at a much lower level than he had been working. He became a shop floor factory worker on minimum wage, but was made redundant after only one month. This signalled the end of his career in the shoe trade and he accepted a job as a van driver working very long hours at a very low level of pay. This lasted only one month when he found work through a family contact as a warehouse manager, imputing information.

His career path, which until the recession of the 1970s had been on an upward trajectory, began to decline as a consequence of the demise of the shoe industry. The impact of this on Peter's well-being was immense. Redundancy hit him very hard:

> The fact that I'd been made redundant, and after, although I knew it was coming, I'd been made redundant after 17, 18 years at one company, and all me life in the shoe trade, so that was a problem. And the job where I was kicked out after a month hit me hard, but at the time, you know, you think 'Oh, OK, I've been made redundant, a few bob in the bank', it's not a lot but got a few bob in the bank, and we do alright, but the whole thing just got to me.

It is clear from this job history that recession and the decline of the manufacturing industry had a huge impact on individual work biographies. In this case, a skilled individual with industry-specific skills experienced, first hand, the deterioration and death of Leicester's key industry – shoe manufacture. Although he had gained many transferable skills over time, once he entered a new industry (electronics), he suffered a breakdown:

> I had no computer skills at all, and a keyboard didn't mean a thing to me, I didn't know where the A was, the B was, or anything. Never used one, never had a computer. I knew nothing about electric, or electricals ... I went in, and I found

it very, very difficult, on a learning curve, being, I'm what? Fifty-eight now, you know, I found it very difficult. I had a bit of a, depression, and stress. I went to the doc – what happened is, that I found it all getting too much for me, I couldn't cope … They give very little training. And I, sort of, kept breaking, well I did break down at work, crying and really upset, you know, I thought 'This isn't me, that's not me. I don't do that'. And, you know, generally the consensus was that it's a combination of not being in control, whereas all my career I've been the one, the manager, I've been the one who's telling guys what to do, sorting it out. Most of the language that people use in the shoe trade I know, and understand, but when people start talking about this 250 volt this, that and the other, I hadn't got a clue what they were talking about, so, and I wasn't in control of what was happening.

This case study shows the impact of broader changes on individual lives and that it is not possible for every individual to turn a critical moment to their advantage or into an empowering experience.

Mike's Story

Mike's profile fitted Ashton and Field's working-class short-term career profile. He left school at 15 with no qualifications and began his working life as a trainee dye operative in a large Leicester textile firm. He worked his way up in the company and became a training instructor, a shift manger and, lastly, a team leader. He stayed at this firm for 41 years leaving only when the factory finally closed down:

Well, all through the years in the textiles, we had, we had a lot of redundancies coming down from 7,000 people, right down to hundreds and hundreds of people, then we merged with another firm, which turned out to be a takeover in the end, a year later, and there were still redundancies and people were going, and … I made the decision, there was one stage where we could have got made redundant, but I was into, like, a tricky age, early forties, and I says, no I'm gonna stay, I'm gonna make this a career, I'm gonna stop, and I'm gonna be the last man out the gate. If we close I'll be putting the light out, and if not I'll be getting me retirement in the boardroom. None of them which worked out, as it turned out!

After being made redundant Mike found a new job almost immediately, starting work on the Monday after he was made redundant. He found work at a food preparation factory in Leicester, working as a team leader in a sandwich production factory. Although he was clearly relieved to find a new job so quickly he did not feel valued in his new role even though the new employers appeared to value the skills he brought with him from his previous role:

I think if you'd been walking past the gate they'd have had you! No, basically, me and me mate who went anyway, we were team leaders, and they grabbed us because we were team leaders. Yeah, they want supervisory or team-leading skills.

On first impressions this is a straightforward story – a long career history with single employer. However, Mike still experienced a number of critical moments at different life cycle stages. For example, with the benefit of hindsight he looked back on his first job choice with some regret:

I've only ever been for four job interviews, and I got them all, like, you know, so, couldn't be too bad! So I went to Smiths, to be a trainee manager there, worst thing I've ever done, not taking it, got that if I wanted it, went for another one at Corah's, got that and decided to go to Corah's, 'cause I didn't like the idea, one of the duties as trainee manager for Smiths, you had to get over to Loughborough for four o'clock every Thursday morning.

Another critical moment for Mike was the realisation and acceptance that the company he had worked for, for over 40 years was closing down. He began looking for another job immediately and took a very organised approach to this. When a colleague mentioned that he had secured a job at a food preparation factory, Mike had already begun the process of applying there himself:

And I'd already started a folder, which you do, get yourself organised, I said 'oh, I've got that one! I got that advert out the paper', and I'd already written for an application form. I said 'Oh, look, I've got this one'. He says 'It's alright'. And when I went up, I was very impressed with it.

Mike took control of the situation he found himself in and played an active role in ensuring that the consequences of events outside his control (closure of the factory and redundancy) were not left to fate. Instead he sought new opportunities as soon as the critical moment had occurred.

Mary's Story

Mary left school at the age of 15 with no qualifications. At the time of the original interview she was categorised by Ashton and Field as being in the short-term career group. She secured work on leaving school and began her working life as a dress machinist in a small textile factory. She received what she called a good training whilst working for her first employer and unlike other machinists she learnt how to do all aspects of her job:

Well, basically I were the only one who knew what I was doing. Sounds terrible don't it. But … they never, you know when we did things, we had to make a shirt up or something, now them girls would just sit there and think, they'd say I don't know where to start, don't know what to do. But 'cos I'd been trained in tailoring and that from the beginning, I knew what to do so it was always oh just go and ask Mary. She'll show yer and that was it. See they hadn't trained for anything else. They'd just been trained to do a couple of little bar tacks on a shoulder or putting tabs in, or putting straps on. It, it weren't skilled work at all.

However, her career history was dictated primarily by changes in the local labour market and she was forced to move from factory to factory due to redundancy as each successive one closed down. Eventually she decided to stop looking for work because she had been made redundant so many times and had reached a point where there were no longer any jobs available in the industry, as most manufacturers had closed down:

> But I didn't want to look for another job, I'd had enough by then. So I gave up. [laughs]. People will look at that [and say] for God's sake don't employ her, she keeps getting made redundant … But yeah, because look at all the times I've been made redundant. I've been lucky that I could fall into the same job that I was trained for. But now I wouldn't be able to. If I needed another job again I wouldn't be able to go back into that 'cos there's nothing left.

Ashton and Field predicted a short-term career path for Mary and, at the outset, this was the path that she followed in completing her training and becoming a skilled and well-paid dress machinist. However, due to structural changes in the local labour market, she found it increasingly difficult to secure employment where her skills were in demand. Numerous factory closures resulted in multiple redundancies and her career path began to resemble the careerless route of moving from job-to-job. Although she always sought new employment she was eventually defeated by events outside her control.

Mervyn's Story

Mervyn's profile at school leaving age fitted very neatly into Ashton and Field's careerless category. His original interview schedule reveals that he was identified as 'careerless'. He left school at 15 with no qualifications. His first job was as a storekeeper in a hosiery factory; a job he described as 'in the end it was the only job I could get'. He worked there for nine months and then started work for a builder. He left the builder to work as a maintenance worker. The reason for this move was financial:

> See, the money weren't very good, I were on £5 a week, not an hour, a week! So I left to go on the water works, which was paying something like £12 a week.

After three years he moved again for higher wages, although here he had far less job security:

> I went to be a bricklayer's labourer with a bricklaying gang, building houses, and me money doubled again, it made me self-employed. All it is, you pay your own stamp and pay your own tax basically.

After 10 years as a self-employed bricklayer, Mervyn took a job as a trainee scaffolder. This move was his first that was not financially induced. Indeed he took a cut in wages to become a trainee:

> I'd been doing it for 8–10 years, and like I was going nowhere and I'd got a young family by then, two children, although like I say the money was a dive, but the outcome would benefit me in the long run, which it has done. So I basically took it not for the money, but for the experience of scaffolding, cos that's what I wanted to be, a scaffolder.

Mervyn became an advanced scaffolder and worked in this field for almost 30 years, giving up only due to age and the associated dangers in such a physical job. Having retired from scaffolding he moved on to working as a hygiene employee in a food factory in Leicester:

> Yeh, it's hard to come down from a level where, how can I put it, I've always been in charge, well not always, but the majority of my life I've been in charge, when I'm in charge I'm the foreman so I made decisions, I decided what jobs had to be done and how they'd be done. To make a comedown from being that man to being just an ordinary, basic bloke is very hard, when you see things and see people telling you what to do, and you know full well they ain't got a bleedin' clue what they're talking about.

This case study is good example of an individual categorised as being at the bottom of the labour market and who began working life hoping for short-term rewards and little thought of the future. However, for him the critical moment was the realisation that he could make an active decision to turn his work trajectory around. His decision to take a reduction in pay in order to train for a new trade, mirrored the more middle-class behaviours predicted by Ashton and Field for the extended career group, who tended to delay immediate financial gratification for longer term rewards. This decision was primarily triggered by his own change in status when he became a father. The second critical moment came with the realisation that age meant he could no longer continue working as a scaffolder but he sought alternative work and took control of the situation in which he found himself.

Gary's Story

Gary's profile on being interviewed originally fitted closely to Ashton and Field's careerless profile and he was identified as being downwardly mobile. He left school without any qualifications and started work as a 'clicker', cutting out socks in a hosiery factory, moving up to become a warehouse manager. The factory closed down and he moved to a confectionary factory where he stayed for almost 25 years, again working his way through the ranks to become a warehouse manager and keeping his job through a number of takeovers by other companies. During the first part of his career history, he did not follow Ashton and Field's predicted careerless pathway. Instead, he remained with a single employer where he followed an upwardly mobile route through the company. For Gary, the critical moment came when this company closed down. He was made redundant at the beginning of the 1990s, which he described as a time when:

> ... the jobs were very, very scarce a very bad time. And there were no jobs in the paper, and I used to, I didn't use my car so I used to walk to the shop or to do the shopping and, er, anybody that was driving a van or, or posting letters, I thought he's got a job and I haven't. And I actually became quite depressed, I think.

At this point his career became far less stable and 25 years after leaving school, this critical moment had a significant impact on his career route as he began to follow a 'careerless' trajectory. He was unemployed for a period of five months and then, over the course of the next 10 years, his career history was made up of a series of short-term contracts in various jobs, interspersed with periods of unemployment. He went back to working for a food wholesaler as a driver, then lost his job when the company went bankrupt. He then found work with BT as an installation engineer but this was a short-term contract, which ended with another period of unemployment. He went back again to the company which had gone bust a few years earlier and worked as a van driver again, until the company folded again. After a brief period of unemployment, he was working, at the time of the re-interview, as a van driver for a paint firm.

Conclusions: Continuity, Change and the Implications for 'From School to Work'

The fortunate re-discovery of data from Elias's *Adjustment of Young Workers to Work Situations and Adult Roles* project has allowed us to re-examine the experiences of one group of young workers who left school in the 1960s and whose working lives have been dominated by the decline of manufacturing in the UK. A sample of the young workers from this study was used by Ashton and Field (1976) in their now classic text *Young Workers*. Whilst we did not set out to 'test', 'prove' or 'disprove' Ashton and Field's predictions, we have found great value in having the opportunity of going back to see what did happen to some of these young workers. What the data and each of the vignettes reveal is that Ashton and Field's predictions, whilst having some validity initially, are useful in the long term only as a theoretical model of what 'might have happened' to each of the young workers, based upon their social position on leaving school. The weakness of the Ashton and Field model, like any other models that make predictions, is that such models cannot account for unforeseeable events. Clearly it is impossible for anyone to predict the future – either their own individual future or the impact of future broader societal/economic changes on their own biographies. However, what emerges from the case studies presented here is that employment histories, like life histories, are rarely neat and easy to categorise in any sense, as there are numerous factors that lie outside the individual's control. Ashton and Field could not, for example, have predicted the impact of wider structural changes on the career paths of these young workers in the same way that contemporary youth researchers can do little more than guess at what might happen to young people leaving school in 2010. As Crow et al. (2009) suggest in their comparison of the recession of the 1970s and the current economic crisis:

> … we can note various similarities and differences in how we have come to be where we are. One similarity is that both have come as something of a surprise to those who grew accustomed to a prolonged period of rising prosperity. An obvious difference is that the intervening thirty years have seen the de-industrialization of the UK economy taken much further, and a corresponding rise in service sector employment'. (Crow et al. 2009: 2.2)

At the time that Ashton and Field made their predictions, the labour market was in a period of buoyancy and the seriousness of the looming economic crisis of the latter part of the 1970s was not yet evident. However, as we have seen, only a short time after the publication of the book, the local labour market was decimated by recession. Local industries disappeared and were, over time, replaced by jobs in the service sector, such as food and snack manufacturing. This unpredicted and unpredictable transformation of the labour market and associated job opportunities had a fundamental impact on the career progression of those who left school in the 1960s, regardless of their position on leaving school.

Second, Ashton and Field did not predict the significance of certain events on the life course of individuals. Yet we would argue that it is crucial to acknowledge and recognise the importance of what Giddens (1991) refers to as 'fateful moments' in determining the life course of individuals. For Giddens (1991: 113) a fateful moment is defined as a time 'when events come together in such a way that an individual stands at a crossroads in their existence or where a person learns of information with fateful consequences'. Like Thomson et al. (2002), who identified points of change in young people's biographies as 'critical moments', we can also clearly locate 'critical moments' in the narratives of these individuals based on an analysis of the interviews at the start of their lives and the re-interviews that took place over 40 years later. However, whilst Thomson et al. (2002: 351) are only able to reflect on the 'medium-term impact of critical moments' on the transition process, our dataset by contrast, places us in the privileged position of having access to a dataset of individual experiences across the life course and allows us to assess the long-term impact of critical moments on work, employment and careers. We were able to examine, not only the impact of critical moments at the point of transition, but also the moments that emerge later in adulthood. The passage of time also allows respondents to reflect on a lifetime of 'critical moments' and it may be that a recent event that is of huge significance to an 18-year-old talking about their own biography, may later in life prove to have been of little significance to their overall life history. The benefit of hindsight allowed our respondents to look back over a much longer period of time and, arguably, enabled us to pinpoint what really were the 'critical moments' that changed the direction of the individual's life course rather than just events that were fresh in the mind and therefore important.

As our research focus was on career and employment history, we can see that many of the critical moments that the respondents identify, related to their working lives. However, many also referred to more personal critical moments relating to categories similar to those identified by Thomson et al. (2002) for example, changes in family circumstances which had lasting significance. For example, certain life course events such as starting a family, well recognised as an important transitional stage in the life course (Furlong and Cartmel 1997), were important turning points for a number of individuals in this study. Certainly, the birth of children seemed to act as a trigger for some to change direction, as we saw in the cases of both Geoff and Mervyn. As Crow et al. (2009: 5.1) suggest:

> Uncertainty about what we know leads on to uncertainty about the future. Pahl's injunction to connect the sociological analysis of the private troubles of people's lives with the policy field of public issues was a deliberate echo of Mills' call in *The Sociological Imagination* (Mills 1970). This provides a useful reminder that sociology has an important role in exposing the traps into which many people may fall, and how their biographies turn out differently from how they were imagined.

Chapter 8

The Case of 10 Women from Leicester: Subsequent Careers

Introduction

Since the late 1950s, building upon the pioneering work of authors such as Jephcott et al.'s (1962) *Married Women Working*, there have been numerous considerations of the work, employment and career experiences of women from a variety of perspectives and using a variety of social sciences research methods. For example, there are the classic studies of the role of married women as workers (Jephcott 1962; Brown et al. 1964; Klein 1965) and those that explore the 'realities' of working life on the factory floor (Pollert 1981; Cavendish (Glucksmann) 1982; Westwood 1984). More recently, the careers of women professionals have been considered (Crompton and Le Feuvre 1996; Crompton and Harris 1998), alongside many formulations of work-life balance and gender-based discrimination have been problematized (Davey et al. 2005; Probert 2005; Wood and Newton 2006; Lovejoy and Stone 2011; Crompton and Lyonette 2010; 2011). Yet, the classic studies of young working-class women remain important, as they completely changed the landscape of transitions and gender and work research by fully recognising that work was fundamental in the lives of women as well as men. However, since this period, sociological attention appears to have turned away from these women and class-based studies appear to have fallen out of fashion (notable exceptions include Warren 2003 and James 2008). This has left something of a gap in our understanding of what did happen to the working-class young women who made the transition from school to work in the 1960s and 1970s and worked in industries that employed significant numbers of women, and now no longer exist. As Walters (2005: 194) has argued, there is a need for more 'in-depth qualitative research ... on the attitudes and work orientations in lower level occupations'.

Alongside the seemingly reduced interest in working-class women, there are very few accounts of women's careers in their entirety, using data collected on labour market entry and preparations for labour market exit for the same group of women. The closest we have in the UK are the *British Birth Cohort Studies*, although respondents to these surveys are not close to retirement (see Elliot 2008). Yet, data forms the *Adjustment of Young Workers to Work Situations and Adult Roles* (1962–1964) research, as Laub and Sampson (2003) highlight, affords us the opportunity to focus on the 'within-individual' patterns of continuity and change for a single group of women workers interviewed twice, but where the interviews are 40 or more years apart. As such, using this data, we can explore the extent to which this group of women followed linear and uncomplicated career paths and the extent to which other life events, such as marriage, children and grandchildren, impacted upon their careers in the context of a local labour market over a 40-year period.

Using Past Studies for Predicting the Careers of Working-Class Women?

There are three broad debates written about the women in our study that we would like to explore in this chapter. First, Elias, when writing about the adjustment of young workers, briefly considered the possible differing transitional experiences of young women and men. Building upon themes developed in *The Civilising Process* (2000) and *The Civilising of Parents* (1980), Elias wanted to understand how young workers acquired the behavioural standards of the workplace and internalised adult behaviours such as self-restraint and foresight. However, for Elias, school and family did not prepare young people for the realities of work, arguing that young people had to make a wider adjustment that was 'often imperfectly understood by them ... for which they are in many cases not too well prepared' (Young Worker Project 18 April 1962: 2), leading to transition as 'shock experiences'. Notwithstanding this apparent mismatch between existing experiences and the new demands of the workplace, Elias hypothesised that women would make the transition to work more smoothly, as they had more realistic expectations of work and their future roles.

> ... in spite of all the obvious answers still puzzles me – why, as it seems the shock-experience, is so much less strong in the case of girls than in that of boys, if it exists at all. Is it because the gap between childhood and adolescent dreams and their adult reality is in their sense less great? (Elias 1962b: 2)

Why would this be the case? As outlined earlier, for Elias there are eight specific problems in the experience of transition from school to work, including the prolonged separation of young people from adults and the indirect knowledge of the adult world. According to Elias, the prolonged separation of young people from adults (other than parents and relatives) and their indirect knowledge of the adult world are consequences of the increased separation of work from family life that occurred as part of the Industrial Revolution. This in turn means that the required behaviours of the workplace are further away from the behaviours exhibited at home and are behaviours that do not correspond to a high degree with adult 'reality'. Work roles take place outside the home and are largely unknown to young people. However, the exception to this, as Elias seems to be speculating, is that young women have less difficulty because they become habituated into the motherhood and wife role from the behaviours they learn within the home. For Elias, the young women's expectations and aspirations correspond significantly to the reality of female adult life in complex industrial societies. Their primary role as wife and mother means that work will inevitably be short-term until marriage and the birth of children. It is important to be clear here that Elias was not arguing that this is how it *should be* (unlike the politically conservative theories of, say, Parsons), more that this is how *it was/is*. Furthermore, Elias's views on the transitional experiences of women were, to some extent, reflected in the fieldwork/interviewer notes that accompanied the interview booklets. The following comments, written up after the interviews by those collecting data in the field, are not untypical:

> Respondent seemed very mature with her feet firmly on the ground. She seemed to enjoy her work ... but her real hopes were to be married in 10 years.

> ... well-organised young woman, very much concerned with earning as much money as possible towards her home. Marriage is clearly so important to her as a 'home making' activity that she does not want a career ...

As suggested earlier, Ashton and Field (1976) did use a number of cases from the study to examine school to work transitions in the 1960s. They developed a linear model for understanding career trajectories incorporating three distinct groups based on family and educational backgrounds: the 'careerless', who left school with few qualifications and entered unskilled work; the 'short-term careers', who entered skilled manual jobs with some security and higher salaries; and finally, the 'extended careers', who left school with qualifications and entered jobs with good prospects, high salaries and job security. Ashton and Field (1976) argued that it was possible to predict a future career or work path dependant on level of education, family background and the aspirations of each individual. However, this model was about men primarily, because marriage and family life were viewed as the 'escape route' for girls. So, for example, for the 'careerless', work was viewed as creating 'more problems for the men than for the women ... because the women can escape from work ... as they start a family' (102) or women in the short-term career group 'are able to accept and adjust to their work situation more easily and ... unlike the young men, they can opt out of the labour market for considerable periods in order to raise a family' (106). For women on the 'extended careers' path, the choice between work or home was more of a challenge, but 'lack of prospects at work may be the factor deciding them to subordinate their work to the more traditional female role of housewife and mother' (89).

Finally, other aspects of Elias's work on young workers that have broader applications are his notions of fantasy and reality (see Elias 1962a). Elias hypothesised that, due to the increased separation between family and work in industrialised societies, young people would tend to have 'idealised' notions of what their new life phase would be like. Fantasy and reality elements are important as 'coping mechanisms' for dealing with uncertainty – the idealised view of the future helps individuals to cope in making the adjustment to the unknown world of work. This idea can be applied to other aspects of life as they underpin many 'transitional' experiences. For example, just as Elias argued that young people

' ... perceive more the wider choices of adulthood than its restraints and frustration' (Elias 1962: 2), it is not inconceivable that older women workers have highly selective, unrealistic perceptions of work in later life (or even life after work), with them perceiving the wider choices and freedoms (such as a period of reduced work, increased leisure time, holidays and enjoyment), rather any of its constraints and frustrations (the need to continue working, reduced finances, the increased likelihood of ill health or any other restrictions that older age and/or retirement may bring). Of particular interest here is the women's need to continue working in later life and their continued roles as carers. Indeed, Yeandle (2005: 10) describes how individuals aged from 50 to 75 are experiencing a period of great change and uncertainty in their lives.

> ... a period in which they are just as able to be active as they were previously, but in which family roles, household composition, leisure pursuits and other unpaid roles such as volunteering or learning are subject to change. Gender continues to be a key factor mediating experience and attitudes in this life phase'. (Yeandle 2005: 10)

For those women with grandchildren, the role of carer is likely to be far from over once their own children become adults and leave home. Indeed grandparents and grandmothers, in particular, are well recognised as being significant providers of childcare, enabling their own adult children to be active in the labour market (Wheelock and Jones 2002; Crompton and Lyonette 2010). However, research on working-class women approaching retirement suggests that whilst grandmothers are very keen to spend time with their grandchildren, this is only on their own terms, particularly where free time is limited due to their own employment commitments (O'Connor, 2006). Those at the bottom end of the labour market, with few skills and qualifications, may have limited options (few of which are attractive) and their experiences of later life working may differ considerably to the idealised notion of being a grandmother.

Ten Working-class Women: Forty Years in One Local Labour Market

The industrial history of Leicester in the East Midlands, UK, was, as we have noted elsewhere in this book, dominated by three main industries: engineering, hosiery, and boot and shoe manufacture. These industries employed 140,000 people at their peak, ensuring the city was characterized by low unemployment, relative prosperity and good opportunities for work in the 1960s. These factories employed a sizeable number of women and offered a wealth of employment opportunities for unqualified school leavers seeking low-skilled or unskilled work. In Tables 8.1 and 8.2 we have attempted to provide a visual representation of the key work and life events, as well as the type of work undertaken by the women in the study over the 40-year period in this one local market.

Table 8.1   Employment and key life events

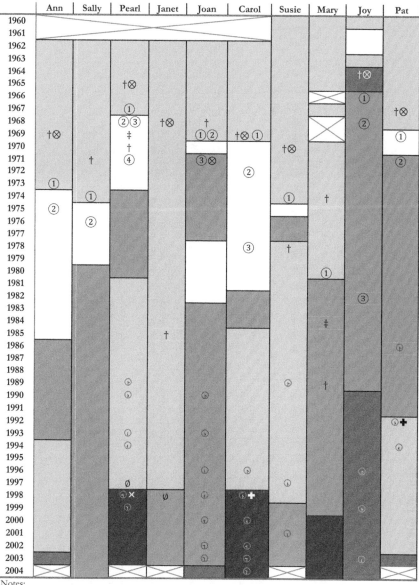

Notes:

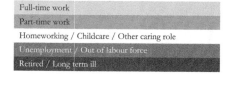

Full-time work	⊗ Left home
Part-time work	† Married
Homeworking / Childcare / Other caring role	‡ Divorced/separated
Unemployment / Out of labour force	①②③ Number of children
Retired / Long term ill	⊙☻◑ ✚ Number of grandchildren
	∅ Illness

Table 8.2 Job moves and job titles

Name	Job Types						
Ann	Clerical Worker	Boot and Shoe	Factory Worker	Clerical Worker			
Sally	Clerical Worker Clerical Worker	Clerical Worker	Clerical Worker	Clerical Worker			
Pearl	Shop Worker	Cashier	Shop Worker	Receptionist	Auxiliary Nurse	Careworker	
Janet	Clerical Manager Telephonist Shop Manager	Worker Publican Shop Owner	Cashier Bar Worker Bookkeeper	Clerical Worker Telephonist	Receptionist	Publican Shop Owner	Hotel
Joan	Hosiery Worker Hosiery Worker	Boot and Shoe School Meals Asst.	Cleaner Hosiery Worker	Hosiery Worker	Hosiery Worker		
Carol	Shop Worker Receptionist	Holiday Home Manger Receptionist	Receptionist	Clerical Worker Receptionist	Receptionist	Clerical Worker	
Susie	Shop Worker Receptionist Clerical Worker	Boot and Shoe Receptionist Clerical Worker	Boot and Shoe Secretary Clerical Worker	Petrol Attendant Secretary	Telephonist Personal Assistant	Telephonist Office Manager	
Mary	Factory Worker Midwife Midwife	Shop Worker Hosiery Worker	Hosiery Worker Hosiery Worker	Hosiery Worker Trainee Nurse	Hosiery Trainee Midwife	Worker Midwife	Factory Worker Midwife
Joy	Boot and Shoe Hosiery Worker	Carer Hosiery Worker	Shop Worker Cleaner	Brewery Worker	Factory Worker	Factory Worker	
Pat	Hosiery Worker Hosiery Worker	Hosiery Worker	Hosiery Worker	Hosiery Worker	Hosiery Worker		

Note: * Boot and Shoe and Hosiery has been summarised here as it could involve a number of different functions including cutting, overlocking, stitching, etc. All other jobs are recorded according respondent's definition.

These tables were constructed using the event history data collected in both phases of the research and from the interviews with the women more generally. As we did not collect employment data by month, we have presented the data in years to give a broadly accurate overview of the women's activities during a period of around 45 years. Embedded within Table 8.1 are symbols to represent key life and work events such as marriage, birth of children and birth of grandchildren, where these were recorded in the event histories or interviews. To explore some of the themes raised in the tables in detail, we have separated the careers into three sections – early careers, middle careers and later careers – for ease of analysis and discussion. However, this is only an analytical device and we do not want to give the impression that these periods are separate, hermetically sealed periods of time that are always fully distinct.

Early Careers

> I definitely would look for a hairdressing job, but the apprenticeship makes it a long time before you can earn good money. I just think it is an interesting job and one you could do after you were married. (Ann)

We have broadly categorised this period as the time between leaving school, getting married and having the first child. Obviously this period varies for the women in our study somewhat – starting either in 1960 or in 1962 on leaving school and continuing until the mid-1960s or early 1970s. During this period, the local labour market was very buoyant with significant numbers of jobs in all three of Leicester's major industries. As discussed above, this is a key period in the lives of this group of women, with Elias arguing that they would have less difficulty in their transitions from school to work and in their early careers, due to their more 'realistic' perceptions of the labour market. These views are echoed in the work of Ashton and Field (1976) and their assertions that work and employment would be a secondary priority to marriage and motherhood for some of the women studied. So did these young women make smooth transitions to work? Did they feel prepared for the labour market and their new working roles? How did their expectations differ or reflect the reality of the workplace?

> I wanted to leave [school], I couldn't wait to leave at the end. I wanted to get a job, I wanted to work, I wanted to be able to buy clothes. I can remember feeling that. (Pearl)

> Looking back now I should have maybe learnt more you know but at the time I couldn't wait to leave school. (Joy)

As Tables 8.1 and 8.2 illustrate, given the labour market conditions, it is perhaps not surprising that all of the women in the study commenced full-time work in clerical jobs, hosiery, boot and shoe manufacturing or shop work, and found work relatively easily after or just before leaving school. These jobs were primarily obtained through the youth employment officer at their school, through advertisements in the local press or via contacts that the young women already had in the organisations they went to work for. At the time of the interviews in the early 1960s, the majority of those young women were on their first or second job and the majority were relatively content with their early employers. However, some of the young women had worked at as many as six jobs since leaving school – a characteristic of non-linear transitions (see Chapter 4). For example, Mary was in her sixth job role in three years, having started her career working in shops, where she worked for two different employers for a total of six months, before trying her hand at hosiery work as a trainee machinist, with a further three employers over a two year period. Her reasons for moving between jobs were variously recorded as 'I was absolutely bored and I didn't like the people I worked with'; 'I was fed up with tabbing. I wanted to go on a machine'; or 'I found the work far too difficult. I wasn't very happy'. Joy also appears to have had a more unusual start to her career – she was sacked from her first position as a boot and shoe worker for taking time off without permission, but rather than find alternative employment, she stayed at home as a full-time carer to look after her mother. Joy also left her second job before the shop she worked for could sack her. Mary was also unusual, but for different reasons, as despite having worked full time in the hosiery industry and as a shop worker, she spent a total of three years between 1966 and 1969 training to be a midwife. She is unusual in our group, as the only woman to significantly divert from the 'standard' jobs available in the local labour market and return to an extended period of vocationally oriented training.

Alongside their work experiences, from Table 8.1, we can see that all of the women had married in this initial period of their lives (and two of the women would go on to be married twice). With the exception of one respondent, who had adopted children, all of the women had given birth to children. The majority of the births were concentrated in the 10-year period between 1964 and 1974, when the women were aged between 19 and 20 and 29 and 30.

Middle Careers

We have located this period as starting in the early to mid-1970s and continuing for the 10 years, or so, up to 1985. In this period the majority of women have returned to either part-time or full-time working, with their children having started school. From Table 8.1 we can see that for the majority of women, the birth of their first child resulted in a shift away from full-time employment. Most women spent some time offering full-time childcare following the birth of their first child. For two of the women it meant a move to part-time work to allow for childcare responsibilities. There are two main exceptions to this. First, Janet did not have children, although she later adopted children from her second marriage and as such, stayed in continuous full time employment. Second, Joy's career varies slightly from the pattern as she gave up working completely following her first marriage. She returned to the labour market following the birth of her first child in 1966, working part-time until she was made redundant in 1990. Overall, marriage and the birth of the first child signalled a number of changes in the women's lives, leaving the family home, having children shortly after and varying working patterns or leaving the labour market fully for a period of time. As such, the women in the study do conform in many respects to the predictions made by Ashton and Field (1976):

> ... but at that time you tended not to go back when you had babies, you became a housewife and you didn't have the maternity leave or you weren't even offered maternity leave at that time ... It was just accepted, I think most people left work, had babies and stayed at home until the children went to school. (Sally)

> ... and then I got married and left to have my first baby so ... that's why I left there. (Carol)

However, the assumptions in the literature of the time that marriage and motherhood would permanently exclude women from the labour market and, while the majority did expect to give up work at some point, nearly all of them also anticipated the resumption of waged work once their children started school. It is clear from the data presented in Table 8.1 that the women returned to work, sometimes as little as one year after the birth of their first child. There are a number of reasons for this and the women in the study cite economic necessity, a desire to move away from only undertaking domestic labour or a perceived need they had to be doing something useful and constructive. Indeed, although many authors have viewed working-class women's participation in the labour market as temporary, short-term and secondary to domestic responsibilities, Warren (2000: 5.3) has argued that, in fact, for working-class women in low paid jobs, regardless of the low wages received, this money undoubtedly represented 'a key source of household income'. Yet, as we have suggested, money was not the only reason for returning to work:

> I had three children and stayed at home to look after them um ... which was more the done thing then. It was becoming the thing to do to go out to work but nothing like it has become. I can remember feeling when my son went to school 'I've got to do something else'. I'm getting a little bored of all the ritual of housework and cooking, and cleaning and all the general things, and I decided to look for something part-time. (Carol)

The returning women were greatly aided in re-entering the local labour market given the characterises of the local labour market itself and that employment in the Leicester factories was, in part, designed around the needs of women. Brown et al. (1964: 34) illustrated how in one major hosiery factory in Leicester that employed a large number of women, 'some 65% of them in fact had "concessions" to allow them to work less than the normal working hours each day or work part-time'. In the Brown et al. (1964) study, 80 per cent of the respondents said that they regarded this reduction in their hours of work as virtually essential to enable them to combine the two roles of worker and housewife. In our study, part-time work also becomes a favourable working pattern following the birth of the first child. However, the length of time spent working part-time does vary from as little as three years to as much as 25 years. The average amount of time spent working part-time for the women in the study was 14 years.

> I was able to get a part-time job in one of the local shops. The three children were at school yes, yeah. I did that for quite a number of months and then I thought no I'm not really ... this is not what I want to do working in a shop, though it was quite good because it built up my confidence again, because I did lose a certain amount of confidence. I think you do when you're just at home and just ... talking ... seeing other mums and children and what have we. So I decided I was going to look for something part-time ... but office, in the office. (Carol)

> I did three nights a week. I went from, it was about eight o'clock at night until seven in the morning. Because I had to fit it in with me husband you know, so that I was out at night and he was at work all day. (Pearl)

> I didn't go back full time work not till they [children] all went to school. 'Cos a year and a quarter later I had [child three] as well, so I had three children altogether – under two.

> But I did do a night time job at, cleaning after I had [child three], she were born '71 and I went cleaning at night time at ... the Gas Board in De Montfort Street ... till [child three] went to school and then I went back into normal work. (Joan)

Other women have reported working in factories during school hours and only in term-time, and bringing children into work if necessary. These arrangements appeared to suit the employers of female-dominated workforces who were seen to be largely sympathetic to the other, more domestic demands placed on their female employees (O'Connor 2006). These industries also offered opportunity for 'outwork' or home working and many women in the city used the skills they had learnt in factories to carry out work tasks at home. Machinery was installed in their homes and garments were delivered to the women to make up from home, enabling them to continue earning money whilst simultaneously carrying out their domestic responsibilities (Phizacklea and Wolkowitz 1995).

> ... it was sportswear and such like, shorts and socks, tops and that. Examine 'em and pack 'em, yeah. [I: Was that a full time job?] No, I did school hours like 9.30 till three o'clock. (Joan)

> Well we'd got a friend at the time who just started up a chemical company and he asked me if I'd look after his books for him, so I did that at home, with the children riding bikes round the kitchen table ... he turned up with this carrier bag with these you know these bits and pieces in and sort of said would I keep his accounts? And I used, he used to drop in little letters for me to type and I used to type his statements and those sort of things. And really I did that until my youngest went to playschool ... I was with him until 1988. (Sally)

Some women, like Joan, also used a combination of working arrangements to suit her changing needs and growing family. As Joan suggests:

> I did school hours for a few years and then I did 30 hours after that, so a bit longer later on like ... [then] I did a little bit at home. I did hand flat knitting for a couple of years at home. A few years actually. [I: What does that involve?] It's a big DVA machine on, swing back, that's all these big heavy knits like fisherman jumpers, kind of thing. Heavy work in the summer. (Joan)

Yet as Joan describes, combining caring and domestic roles with homeworking was not an easy option. The work was always there, she was paid on a piece rate, making the demands on the job particularly challenging and, given the garments she was making, the work was also very physically demanding. Alongside the conditions of such work, Crompton (2003: 544) has argued it is frequently the jobs at the lowest levels that are the most flexible, enabling women to participate in the labour market and still perform their caring and domestic roles. Yet it is exactly this flexibility and the associated job insecurity that hinders the smooth development of women's careers over time, as breaks in employment for childbearing and rearing, and periods of part-time work are not conducive to the development of linear, 'successful' careers. In addition, during this period, the traditional industries of the city began to decline and by the early 1980s, jobs that had previously been widely available to a largely low-skilled and feminized workforce began to disappear. Women employees found themselves facing job losses through factory closures and redundancies in much the same way as their male colleagues during the recession of the late 1970s and early 1980s. As Pollert (1981: 228) describes, women were often not entitled to the same redundancy payments and they were often on short-term contracts or had gaps in their employment history due to time out of the labour market. Yet the women in our study seem to have fared better than Pollert (1981), Crompton (2003) or even Ashton and Field (1976) could have predicted. Despite having time out of the labour market to look after children and despite having to work flexibly in their return to the labour market once the children were at school, none of the women had any gaps in their employment and seemed to be able to return to work as and when they wished and on their own terms. A good illustration of this is Pat. Pat spent all her early and middle working life working as a hosiery worker and became a very skilled machinist quite early in her career. Despite the closure of many of the larger textiles companies, Pat never had difficulty in obtaining work and, despite experiencing a number of redundancies, could find work relatively easily with different smaller employers.

> ... you know when we did things, we had to make a shirt up or something, now them girls would just sit there and think, they'd say I don't know where to start, don't know what to do. But 'cos I'd been trained in tailoring and that from the beginning, I knew what to do so it was always oh just go and ask Pat. She'll show yer and that was it ... See they hadn't trained for anything else. They'd just been trained to doing a couple of little bar tacks on a shoulder or putting tabs in, or putting straps on. It, it weren't skilled work at all ... [I] look at all the times I have been made redundant I've been lucky that I could fall into the same job that I was trained for. (Pat)

Although whilst economically active, Pat was able to find work easily after each redundancy and did not appear to suffer adversely the effects of unemployment, the full impact of her 'flexible career path' is likely to be felt only in retirement. The hidden costs of such a frayed career path only fully emerge as retirement begins and the working-class women find their choices restricted due to a lack of financial security – largely brought about by the low status and lack of employment rights in the type of jobs they had held during their working lives.

Later Careers

Based on our data we have used the term 'later careers' to identify the period post-1986 up until the time of the re-interviews in the mid-2000s. This period was a complex and difficult time for workers in the Leicester labour market and by 1987, employment prospects had begun to change beyond all recognition for the majority. The larger manufacturing companies in hosiery, textiles and boot and shoe manufacture had begun to close, with traditional roles in these industries being replaced by lower skilled, lower paid jobs in the service sector. Indeed, between 1991 and 2002, the number of full-time women's jobs in manufacturing continued to decline, falling by 7,000 in this period (Buckner et al. 2004). During this time, employment prospects in Leicester became concentrated in administrative and secretarial roles, sales and service jobs such as snack and sandwich preparation. However, despite significant labour market restructuring, the majority of the women in this study, like many working-class women, remained active in the labour market right up until their late 50s. Regardless of the changed landscape of employment prospects, our data illustrates that this group of women were remarkably tenacious in ensuring that they remained economically active for the majority of their careers and continued to contribute to the household income. Table 8.1 reveals that 4 out of the 10 women re-interviewed were still working in their late 50s. Of the others, Pearl had left work due to ill health, Carol and Mary had retired and four others were out of work. Of those out of work, Joy had not worked for 15 years but had not actively sought work during that time;

whereas Ann, Joan and Pat had only recently left their employers. Sally, as she had throughout her career, was still working as a clerical worker and had taken this up full-time since 1994. Janet had moved into part-time work in 1998 due to ill-health and was working as a bookkeeper and Susie was working part-time in clerical work. Regardless of their current employment status, we asked all of the respondents about their perceptions or experiences of retirement:

> I keep saying I'm going retire at 60 and my husband keeps saying no you carry on, and I must admit I don't know as I'd be ready at 60. (Sally)

> Well I'd like to preferably retire on you know when I do become pension age rather than having to carry on for years and years. But there again, my husband don't retire until after me 'cos he's two and a half years younger so I possibly might do and retire a bit further on. (Joan)

> I mean I'd love to go back to work but I can't yet, at least a year, but when, I'd love to go back to work, it drives me mad. It drives me mad being at home. I've got to be so careful because I can't do things like lift, I mean I'd like to go back to old people but I can't lift now so, that's really out the window because you've got to be able to lift them. (Pearl)

In the follow-up interviews we asked the women how they would spend their time once retired:

> Go abroad ... not just Turkey, I mean my plan is to go to all sorts of places, but yeah to go abroad, travel. I mean that's what we're in all these pensions for, well [husband] is, all these pensions. (Pearl)

> In the summer I can think of a 101 things I'd like to do, but then I think what do you do on a wet November morning, what are you going to do with yourself? I think we'd probably have to have a project to keep us busy. (Sally)

> Going out and about and holidays yeah. Hopefully. (Joan)

> If I'm without a book I'm miserable to live with if I'm without a book. I'm like that actually, always seem to be reading ... I'm a terrible bookworm. What do I do, well I read, I make my own clothes, I do as I like now [laughs]. And it's wonderful, sheer heaven. (Carol)

However, as we have suggested above, although many have idealised notions of the freedoms that retirement may bring, few expected that they would have had to resume child care roles and look after the their grandchildren while their children go out to work.

For Carol, retired after her redundancy in 1998, it was very difficult to be doing 'nothing' and she was desperate to go back to work. However, her daughter was finding childcare with a newborn baby very difficult and so Carol stepped in to help. This meant looking after the children, doing the school run and collecting the youngest child from nursery.

> I help quite a lot. I do the school run. I went over this morning and when I got there, there was only two of them going to school. There's one that goes to play group and the baby goes to nursery twice a week … so there's a lot of to-ing and fro-ing and I help her as much as I can with that … When I was made redundant in the June I had a whole six weeks of just being here to try and cope with the whole family. And during that time she had her third child so … it was … it was really hectic, it was really hectic and I was desperate to get out, to get out to work! I mean she knows that I was, I found it very difficult, it was good and they were very good but it was quite stressful at times. (Carol)

Pat also explains that she undertakes caring duties for her grandchildren as she feels that it is something worthwhile and productive even though she cannot work due to ill-health.

> Even though I think, 'right what am I going to do today?', I've got to do something. Because I've always been on you know with 4 children, you know what it's like with children, you're on the go like all the while, I spend a lot of time with the grandchildren, I take me grandchildren out. I have to be doing something, I can't just sit here. (Pat)

In many respects, the caring functions offered by these women in later life echoes the care they offered their own children in the late 1960s and early 1970s and it is interesting looking back on what these women saw their primary role to be. We asked the respondents to reflect back on their careers and outline what they felt to be the two of three main successes or highpoints to date. The majority of women re-interviewed cited marriage and children as their main highpoints and only one woman mentioned work at all. For example:

> Having the children I suppose, having the Grandchildren, married. (Joan)

> Well I think I'd have to put my kiddies first, yeah. (Pearl)

> I don't seem to have had any real success, what [you?] would say high points …
> Yeah children, grandchildren then. (Joy)

Women, Work and the Life Course

Having presented the stories of the 10 women based on different phases of their career histories, we end this chapter by providing an overview of the women's lives across the individual life course. In the following section we look first at the patterns that emerge across all the women's lives, highlighting intersections of career and childbirth. We then go on to explore the lives of four of the women in more detail illustrating how marriage, childbirth and later the birth of grandchildren intersected with and impacted on labour market participation.

Table 8.1 depicts the employment and key life events of all 10 women over a period of almost 45 years, from 1960 to 2004. This timespan begins when the women left school and ends as they approach retirement and labour market exit. What is most striking is the dominance of work in this depiction of the life course. Full- and part-time work were key parts of these women's lives interrupted only relatively briefly by periods out of the labour market to care for children full-time. Most of the women had been economically active consistently across the life course with the exception of periods of motherhood and periods of ill health. The longest period of economic inactivity due to domestic responsibilities was 11 years. Two women had taken 11 years out of the labour market to care for their children. Most of the women worked full-time on leaving school and part-time on returning to the labour market after childrearing.

Table 8.2 adds more detail to the women's stories by listing their job moves by role and showing the number of jobs they had held. This table is illuminating as it reveals the complexity of some of the women's job histories in terms of sheer number of jobs and in the range of roles they had worked. Susie, Mary and Janet had each held multiple jobs. Reading the table from left to right, we see that Susie had moved from early jobs, first as a shop worker then into factory work to eventually working in an office role. Mary had retrained as a midwife and had been employed in a number of different places since qualifying. Janet had moved between employed and self-employed roles across her career. Other women had held very few jobs and had remained within industries to a greater extent; for example, Pat had always worked in hosiery and Sally had been a clerical worker throughout her career.

Below we go on to explore these trends across the life course, by highlighting the cases of four of the women. Taking Figure 8.1a first, the straightforwardness of Ann's career history is evident from the diagram. Her 'life events' depicted on the bottom part of the graph were concentrated in a relatively short space of time, a trend compounded by the absence of grandchildren. She married and continued to work full-time until the birth of her first child. This birth triggered her exit from the labour market and she remained economically inactive until her children were of secondary school age. She then commenced part-time work until her children were adults and, at that stage, she returned to full-time work. At the time of the interview she was unemployed. In contrast, Mary's graph (Figure 8.1b) shows a more complicated picture, particularly at the start of her working life, when she moved in and out of the labour market due to retraining. Somewhat unusually, her life events fall into the middle section of her biography and, as yet, she does not have grandchildren to populate the later part of the graph. Once settled into a full-time job, some years after initially leaving school, she worked full-time until the birth of her only child. At this point she reduced her working hours to part-time and continued to work part-time until retirement.

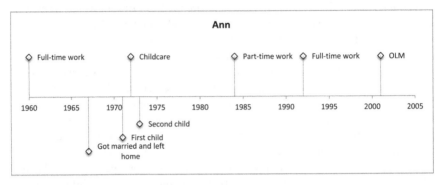

Figure 8.1a   Ann's labour market positions and life events

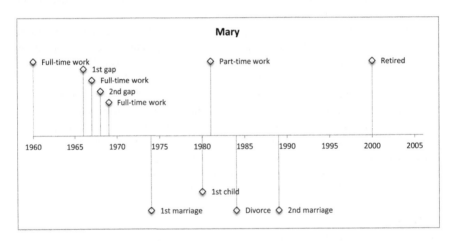

Figure 8.1b   Mary's labour market positions and life events

Figures 8.1c and 8.1d depict Joy and Carol's career and life event biographies. These diagrams contrast markedly with the previous two in terms of life events. For both Joy and Carol, the life events part of the graph is far more crowded with activity, as both have three children each and both have grandchildren. Their life events are, therefore, spread across the life span. Joy's working life began with a disjointed and non-linear transition from school to employment, where she experienced periods of time in and out of the labour market. After the birth of her first child, she worked part-time and continued to do so after her second and third child were born. She did not return to full-time work and, at the time of interview, had been out of the labour market for almost 15 years. Carol's school to work trajectory was more linear and she entered full-time work straight from school and continued to work part-time until her first child was born. She then exited the labour market, had two more children and did not return to being economically active until her youngest child was at primary school. She then returned to employment, initially part-time, but increasing to full-time soon afterwards. She continued to work full-time until retirement, which coincided with the birth of the second and third of her seven grandchildren.

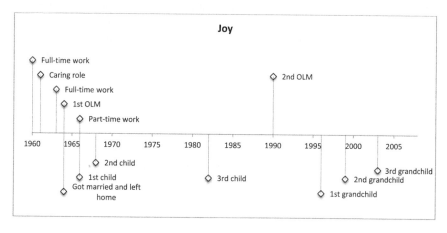

Figure 8.1c   Joys's labour market positions and life events

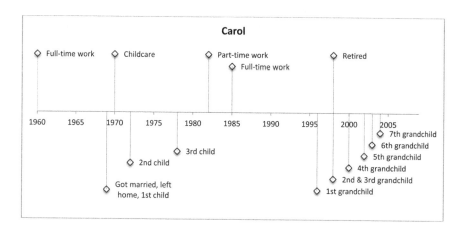

Figure 8.1d   Carol's labour market positions and life events

Conclusions

The women all entered the labour market in the early 1960s and their careers have been tied to one of the dominant local industries – hosiery, boot and shoe or related engineering. From the careers of these women, we can see that they did make relatively straightforward transitions to work at ages 15 and 16 and, despite their initial lack of experience or qualifications, succeeded in the labour market. However, such linearity does not automatically suggest that the careers of the women in the study were, in any way, uncomplex or unproblematic. These women, in their early careers, had to deal with the social norms that meant that women would only work full-time until marriage and/or the birth of their first child. To a large extent these women did conform to these expectations, but did so on their own terms and reflective of their own desire and the need to continue working. Despite the predictions of authors such as Ashton and Field (1976), while motherhood may have provided an alternative route for these women, it did not provide the complete escape route suggested. The view that work would inevitably be a short-term experience did not materialise for these women. These women, especially in their middle careers, combined careers with the demands of childcare and a very rapidly changing local labour market. Working flexibly, through part-time work, school hours, shifts and even homeworking, the women succeeded in maintaining a career and the role of carer in the home. In middle and later careers, the women combined working lives with other life events, such as remarriage, the birth of more children and, later, the births of their grandchildren, without significant breaks in employment until their late fifties. However, despite many of the 10 women of Leicester working for over 45 years, often in very demanding circumstances, they still perceived marriage and the birth of children and grandchildren as their 'highpoints' or most significant moments. Indeed, despite their demanding working lives, it is to carer roles that many of these women have returned in later life, combining care for grandchildren in order that their own children may develop their own careers. The careers and lives of working-class women still have much to tell us and should continue to be the focus for academic and policy research for some time to come.

Afterword
Thoughts, Reflections and Future Possibilities

Some way through putting this book together we realised that we needed a mechanism for finishing the book and this chapter of the *Adjustment of Young Workers to Work Situations and Adult Roles* project story. However, given the history of the project, and the fact that the research work is on-going, a formal 'solid' set of conclusions seemed too definite, too 'end like' and would not represent fully our own reflections on what we have achieved over the past few years nor speak to the possibilities of what is still to come – opportunities and prospects. We therefore hit upon the idea of ending this text with an 'afterword' – not a 'fixed ending' but a reflection on both process and content. This will also provide something of a moving on point for us, a metaphorical 'line in the sand' from which we can move forward to consider the *Adjustment of Young Workers to Work Situations and Adult Roles* anew. This is also in keeping with the process-oriented approach advocated by Elias himself. Our research is an on-going process that will continue – put crudely, it has no beginning, no end point, it is just an enduring process. Or as Goudsblom (1977) suggests:

> Sociology is a process; it has no definite beginning, and, one hopes, no end. Goudsblom (1977: 201)

Reflections: 'Never Ending Story'

As stated earlier in the book, we have been working on this restudy of Elias's *Adjustment of Young Workers to Work Situations and Adult Roles* project since 2000 and, despite the material presented in this volume, the research is still a 'live' project with much more to do. What we have presented here is something of a snapshot of the data and some of the background detail to the *Adjustment of Young Workers* research; yet, despite this, there is still more work to do with the data collected from the original research, with us only having scratched the surface of the 1960s data and with significantly more analysis to undertake with the follow-up interviews. The sheer scale of the data has been both a blessing (provided years of work, opened up another area in Eliasian scholarship, reignited interest in restudies and so forth) and also a curse, in that it has presented a series of problems, not least the amount of time required to analyse all of the data fully. When we started the project we were very much like the fabled 'children in a sweet shop' not knowing where to start, where to look first or where to begin our analysis. The veritable array of interesting data, life stories captured and the vignettes that transported us back some 40 years to the time of the Beatles, the Cuban missile crisis and Khrushchev, Castro, Kennedy, Che Guevara, Harold Macmillan and so forth, made it hard to choose what to consider first. Rather than interviewer notes, gender, youth culture or education and training we could equally have explored work histories, consumption, union membership, parental and sibling occupations, household relationships and friendships networks. We could easily have mapped the rise and fall of many of Leicester's main factories through the young worker narratives and plotted that against the decline of UK manufacturing more generally. As such the volume of data has meant that, almost inevitably, even after 15 years of considering and exploring this data there are areas in the *Adjustment of Young Workers* project that remain of interest to us but which we simply have not had the time or capacity to investigate in any detail. We are pleased that others have understood the potential this data has to offer and, to that end, we would recommend reading Williams and Quinn (2014). Yet, still, this means there remains considerable scope, and seemingly endless analytical possibilities, left within the *Adjustment of Young Workers* data to fill numerous future volumes.

Given the opportunities that this data has presented us (and continues to do so) one cannot help but also reflect on the concerns of the original research team and fieldworkers. The *Adjustment of Young Workers* project contained a volume, level and complexity of data that would have meant that those working on the research would have been able to produce multiple books and articles beyond Elias's concerns with the shock hypothesis. If this had been done, the *Adjustment of Young Workers* research would have taken its rightful place alongside other classic studies undertaken in what one might term the heyday of sociological studies that vividly documented work, family, education and community in the UK. The *Adjustment of Young Workers* easily ranks alongside past studies such as: *Village on the Border* (Frankenberg 1957), *The Family Life of Old People* (Townsend 1957), *Family and Class in a London Suburb* (Willmott and Young 1960), *Tradition and Change* (Stacey 1960), *Married Women Working* (Jephcott et al. 1962), *Home, School and Work* (Carter, 1962), *The Family and Social Change* (Rosser and Harris, 1965) and *The Affluent Worker in the Class Structure* (Goldthorpe and Lockwood 1969), all of which added significantly to our understanding of work and employment at that time and are a major source of understanding of labour and work history in the UK. One cannot help but reflect again on the consequences of the disputes that surrounded the research and the implications that those disagreements had for both Elias and for the other researchers involved as well as for British sociology more generally. The other researchers were denied, perhaps, career changing publications (or at least career 'enhancing'), Elias was unable to present a unique (for the time) approach to studying youth that focused on youth concerns as opposed to adults' concerns about youth, and British sociology lost what would have become a classic study of one of the UK's main centres of manufacturing.

So What Have We Achieved in the Volume?

We have told the story of the research to date. In the early chapters of this book we introduced the Young Worker Project and its troubled history. What we have come to learn is that in the past, just as now, few research projects ran smoothly from commencement to completion. Empirical research is messy and it is rare for plans to unfold as envisaged. Yet this project seems to us to have had a very complicated evolution full of intrigue, mystery and upset. That the original project was led by a leading sociologist of the twentieth century and represented his only engagement with empirical research on this scale simply provides another source of fascination for contemporary social science. In many ways, knowing now how controversial certain aspects of the project were, it is surprising that any of the findings were published. However, the difficult history of the project was perhaps the reason that the data were retained despite many attempts at disposal of this large archive. The retention of the data created an opportunity to create a rich longitudinal data set from what was once purely cross-section data on school leavers.

We would suggest that another remarkable feature of this project lies in the extensive surviving ephemera. Along with the dataset itself we were able to create a substantial project archive formed by correspondence between various associated project team members, the original research proposal and funding arrangements, project meeting minutes, draft publications, letters of appointment and resignation and so on. Such papers proved to be of great value as these led us to be able to trace members of the original research team and re-interview them about their time on the project. Taken together this documentation equipped us with sufficient information to be able to trace the evolution and disintegration of the project based on evidence gathered at the time. From a social research perspective we were also fortunate to find that the fieldnotes made by the interviewers who were encouraged to reflect on their research encounters had survived intact. Thus we had unparalleled access to rich descriptions of respondents, their families and their surroundings giving a detailed snapshot of life in 1960s provincial England.

This book has focused on two key aspects of this project: an analysis of the original data and a focus on a previously unknown aspect of the work of the renowned sociologist Norbert Elias. Revisiting data from the 1960s has allowed us to question current views on historical transitions. We have explored the original dataset, the majority of which was never analysed at the time, in great depth. The passing of time between the data collection phase and the analysis some 40 years later has placed us in a privileged position – able to access raw data from an earlier time with the benefit of considerable hindsight. The data reveal that the widely accepted belief that transitions in the post-war period were largely smooth and linear is something of a simplification of the lived reality for many of the young workers. It was common for them to experience disrupted transitions with multiple job moves, difficulties securing employment, periods of unemployment and a lack of choice in the local labour market. Indeed from this data it is possible to trace the emergence of what is now termed the 'precariat' and we see the beginnings here of what was to be the devastating impact of industrial decline on the youth labour market for the next generation of school leavers. There was, for example, evidence of young people working in temporary and insecure employment the terms of which were often dictated by market forces in the declining textile industry. Experiences of 'short-work', which at the time were seen as simply quiet periods can, with the benefit of hindsight be linked to the beginnings of the industrial decline that impacted the Leicester and wider UK economy in the following decade.

The data also reveals a great deal about the gendered nature of transitions in the 1960s. This provides a valuable perspective on past transitions because as we have argued the gender dimension was rarely explored by researchers at that time. The inclusion of girls as well as boys in the original study has enabled us to consider how the experience of transition has changed over time and, again, to question many accepted assumptions about the past. The original research team were enlightened in comparison to many other contemporaneous academics and the inclusion of a sample of female school leavers has revealed a number of trends. Few of the girls imagined futures outside of the labour market as stay at home housewives and equally few had experienced this with their own mothers, the majority of whom had worked outside the home. As Sharpe (1984: 22) argued, such a lifestyle was never realistic for working-class women who 'either worked outside the home or took in work' and it was the 'emerging middle class that conformed most closely to the idealised model of mothering at home set within the romantic cameo of happy family life'. Certainly these school leavers were ambitious in career terms and few intended or envisaged staying at home once married with children. What we see instead are young women pursuing the best-paid jobs with the most comprehensive training programmes in order to maximise their earning potential and the acquisition of skills that they knew were valued in the local labour market.

While the data on girls is valuable because so little attention was given to the female experience in the post-war decades, the data on boys is of interest in other ways. We can now look back at their experience of the transition and also question assumptions made about young men in the labour market during this period of economic boom.

The study of 1960s youth culture is an area that has been far from neglected in the academic literature. This was a decade that witnessed the birth of the teenager, of youth leisure and of mass consumption by young people for the first time. The fashions, musical tastes and leisure pursuits of young people in the 1960s are well known and frequently appear in the media as a method of characterising a period and a generation of young people known as baby boomers. Yet again what the data reveal is that while the decadent 1960s may have been the reality in big cities such as London the concept of the teenager was far slower to reach the provinces. What we see is the emergence of some elements of what later came to represent 1960s youth culture but this was relatively rare in Leicester in the early 1960s.

A unique and defining feature of this research has been the opportunity to create a longitudinal study from what was originally a 'one-off' survey of school leavers. The discovery of the data some 40 years after it was collected enabled us to revisit some of the respondents as they approached retirement. Interviewed originally as teenagers, this cohort were, when we re-contacted them, in their mid- to late 50s and were, therefore, focused on the opposite end of the transition experience: the move from employment to retirement. This provided us with an unparalleled opportunity to trace and re-interview respondents and to reflect on their careers over the life course with the benefit of access to their own accounts of starting working life as teenagers. This unique view of the life course enabled us to understand the juxtaposition of personal and professional lives over time and the impacts of each at different points. At some stages in the individual story it was the macro level events that impacted on career pathways so we see the devastating effect of recession and industrial decline on individual lives and career paths. This cohort of school leavers witnessed first-hand the disappearance of the once secure and sought after jobs in thriving industries. The promise of jobs for life for those who secured apprenticeships in well-established industries proved to be relatively short-lived. Many of the young workers found that the specialised skills they had developed in the hosiery, textile and boot and shoe industries became increasingly irrelevant as local factories ceased production. Redundancy, with little prospect of another job in the same sector, became a reality for the young workers as they approached their mid-careers.

The data allowed us, then, the opportunity to explore the impact of what we can term more micro-level or personal events on individual lives such as the impact of redundancy at the mid-career point. This is perhaps most evident in the life course histories of the 10 women we successfully traced. In their stories the coming together of the personal and professional is very marked and we see the impact of events such as marriage and, more specifically, childbirth and childrearing on career paths very clearly. The importance of this chapter is that it seeks to understand the lived experience of working-class women on their approach to retirement after decades of working life. Most made relatively simple transitions from education to work as teenagers and entered the local labour market. Although marriage and the birth of children interrupted working lives what is revealed are patterns of complex childcare arrangements coupled with messy or non-linear work histories. These jigsaws of work and family enabled the women to combine the competing demands on their time when their own children were growing up. What is perhaps more interesting and less studied is the impact of later life events on career histories. So, for example, remarriage, bereavement, the birth of grandchildren and ill health all impacted in different ways on the middle and late career periods of this group.

Endnotes

In summary, what we have achieved has gone some way towards realising the exceptional, and perhaps unprecedented, opportunity the data offered us in reflecting on 50 years of work and employment across individual life courses with an empirical 'anchor' at each end consisting of detailed entry and exit interviews in one locality. These interviews are narratives of work through the life course. As Laub and Sampson (2003: 10) have argued, such 'narratives help us unpack mechanisms that connect salient life events across the life course, especially regarding personal choice and situational context'. These narratives from this group of once young workers have allowed us to reflect on the evolution of the individual life course, to identify significant turning points and to explore the consequences of global change on individual lives. The life histories we have reconstructed cover a 40-year period from the early 1960s to the early 2000s and take us up to the retirement of the young workers. Now, more than 10 years on from the first re-interviews, we have the possibility of considering further interviews as our respondents celebrate their seventieth birthdays and continue their post-employment lives. This would provide an insight in to how more recent changes to the world economy have impacted on the lives of this group, many of whom 10 years earlier were already facing precarious and uncertain futures.

Appendices

Appendix 1   The interview schedule

D.S.I.R. YOUNG WORKER PROJECT

DEPARTMENT OF SOCIOLOGY

UNIVERSITY OF LEICESTER

Sample No. ....

Appendix 2 A note on the sample

YOUNG WORKER PROJECT.
_____

A NOTE ON THE SAMPLE

The sample for the Young Worker Project has been
drawn in the following manner. From the card index of all
school leavers at the Youth Employment Office, which is
ordered according to sex, year of birth, and within that,
alphabetically, the years of birth 1944-1948 were selected.
All names were checked, and information was collected about
all those who left school in summer and Christmas 1960, and
summer and Christmas 1962.

For each young person the following information
was collected:- name, address, date of birth, school(s)
attended, date of leaving, name of firm for first job, and
the nature of the job obtained. The Youth Employment Office
lists contained the names of some people resident outside
Leicester and working in the City; these were not collected.
All girls with more than one year's further education, and
all boys with more than one year's further education and
leaving in summer or Christmas 1960 (as well as all who had
attended schools for handicapped children, and those who had
entered the Armed Forces) were then eliminated. This left
a total of 4160 names and addresses.

Bibliography

Abrams, M. (1959) *The Teenage Consumer*. London: London Press Exchange.

Afshar, H. (2009) Sheila Allen Trailblazing Professor of Sociology at Bradford University. *The Guardian*, Tuesday 27 January 2009. http://www.theguardian.com/education/2009/jan/27/sheila-allen [Accessed 15 April 2012].

Ahier, J., Chaplain, R., Lindfield, R., Moore, R., Williams, J. (2000) School Work Experience: Young People and the Labour Market. *Journal of Education and Work*, 13 (3): pp. 273–88.

Ashton, D.N. (1973) The Transition from School to Work: Notes on the Development of Different Frames of Reference Among Young Male Workers. *The Sociological Review*, 21: pp. 101–25.

———. (1974) Careers and Commitment: The Movement from School to Work. In Field, D. (ed.) *Social Psychology for Sociologists*. London: Nelson.

Ashton, D.N. and Field, D. (1976) *Young Workers: From School to Work*. London: Hutchinson.

Ashton, D.N. and Green. F. (1996) *Education, Training and the Global Economy*. London: Edward Elgar.

Ashton, D.N. and Lowe, G. (eds) (1991) *Making Their Way: Education, Training and the Labour Market in Canada and Britain*. Milton Keynes: Open University Press.

Ashton, D.N. and Maguire, M. (1980) Young women in the labour market: Stability and Change. In Deem, R. (ed.) *Schooling for Women's Work*. London: Routledge and Kegan Paul, pp. 112–25.

Ashton, D.N., Maguire, M. and Spilsbury, M. (1988) Local Labour Markets and Their Impact on the Life Chances of Youths. In Coles, B. (ed.) *Young Careers: The Search for Jobs and the New Vocationalism*. Milton Keynes: Open University Press.

Backhouse, G. and Thompson, P. (2000) On the Hunt for Research Data from 'Classic Social Studies'. *Newsletter of the British Sociological Association Network*, October 2000.

Banks, J. (1989) From Universal History to Historical Sociology. *The British Journal of Sociology*, 40 (4): pp. 521–43.

Banks, M., Bates, I., Breakwell, G., Bynner, J., Emler, N., Jamieson, L. and Roberts K. (1992) *Careers and Identities*. Milton Keynes: Open University Press.

Bates, I. (1993) A job which is 'Right for me'? Social Class, Gender and Individualisation. In Bates, I. and Riseborough, G. (eds) (1991) *Youth and Inequality*. Buckingham: Open University Press.

Bazalgette, J. (1975) *School and Work Life: A Study of Transition in the Inner City*. London: Hutchinson.

Beck, U. (1992) *Risk Society*. Beverly Hills: Sage.

Beynon, H. (2007) Richard Brown: Sociologist Whose Research Looked at the Wartime Experience of Women Workers. *The Guardian*, Thursday 14 June 2007. http://www.theguardian.com/news/2007/jun/14/guardianobituaries.obituaries.

Blackler, R. (1970) *Fifteen Plus: School Leavers and the Outside World*. London: Allen and Unwin.

Blackman, S. (2007) 'Hidden Ethnography': crossing Emotional Borders in Qualitative Accounts of Young People's Lives. *Sociology*, 41 (4): pp. 699–716.

Bowles, S. and Gintis, H. (1976) *Schooling in Capitalist America: Educational Reform and the Contradictions of Economic Life*. London: Routledge and Kegan Paul.

Brod, H. (1987) A Case for Men's Studies. In Kimmel, M. (ed.) *Changing Men: New Directions in Research on Men and Masculinity*. Sage: London.

Brooks, D. and Singh, K. (1978) *Aspirations Versus Opportunities: Asian and White School Leavers in the Midlands*. Leicester: Commission for Racial Equality.

Brown. P. (1987) *Schooling Ordinary Kids: Inequality in Unemployment and the New Vocationalism*. London: Tavistock.

Brown, R. (1987) Norbert Elias in Leicester: Some Recollections. *Theory, Culture and Society*, 4: pp. 533–9.

———. (2001) Correspondence with the authors, 6 February 2001. Leicester: University of Leicester.

Brown, R., Keil, T. and Riddell, D.S.R. (1963) *Young Worker Project: Composition of Sample*. Unpublished memorandum, University of Leicester/Marbach, Deutsches Literaturarchiv.

Brown, R.K., Kirkby. J.M. and Taylor, K.F. (1964) The Employment of Married Women and the Supervisory Role. *British Journal of Industrial Relations*, 2: pp. 23–41.

Buckner, L., Tang, N. and Yeandle, S. (2004) *Gender Profile of Leicester's Local Labour Market*. Sheffield: Sheffield Hallam University. http://www.shu.ac.uk/_assets/pdf/ceir-LeicesterwebAcrobat204.pdf.

Bynner, J. (1998) Education for what? *Education and Training*, 40 (1): pp. 4–5.

Bynner, J., Chisholm, L. and Furlong, A. (eds) (1997) *Youth, Citizenship and Social Change in a European Context*. Aldershot: Ashgate Publishing.

Canny, A. (2001) The Transition from School to Work: An Irish and English Comparison. *Journal of Youth Studies*, 4 (2): pp. 133–54.

Carter, M.P. (1962) *Home School and Work*. London: Pergamon Press Ltd.

———. (1963) *Education, Employment and Leisure: A Study of Ordinary Young People*. London: Pergamon Press Ltd.

———. (1969) *Into Work*. Harmondsworth: Penguin.

Cartmel, F., Furlong, A., Biggart, A., Sweeting, H. and West, P. (2002) *Managing Transitions: A Biographical Approach*. Paper Presented to the British

Sociological Association Annual Conference, University of Leicester, March 2002.

Cavendish, R. (aka Glucksmann, M.) (1982) *Women on the Line*. London: Routledge.

Chisolm, L. (1987) *Gender and Vocation*. PSEC Working Paper No. 1, University of London, Institute of Education.

Clarke, J., Hall, S., Jefferson, T. and Roberts, B. (1976) Subcultures, Cultures and Class. Theory 1. In Hall, S. and Jefferson, T. (eds) *Resistance Through Rituals: Youth Subcultures in Post-War Britain*. London: Hutchinson.

Cohen, P. and Ainley, P. (2000) In the Country of the Blind?: Youth Studies and Cultural Studies in Britain. *Journal of Youth Studies*, 3 (1): pp. 79–95.

Cohen, S. (1972) *Folk Devils and Moral Panics*. London: MacGibbon and Kee.

Coles, B. (1995) *Youth and Social Policy*. London: University College London.

Collinson, D. and Hearn, J. (1996) Men at Work: Multiple Masculinities/Multiple Workplaces. In Mac An Ghaill, M. (ed) *Understanding Masculinity: Social Relations and Cultural Arenas*. Buckingham: Open University Press.

Connell, R.W. (1995) *Masculinities*. Cambridge: Polity Press.

———. (2000) *The Men and the Boys*. London: Polity Press.

Corti, L., Day, A. and Backhouse, G. (2000) Confidentiality and Informed Consent: Issues for Consideration in the Preservation of and Provision of Access to Qualitative Data Archives. *Forum Qualitative Sozialforschung / Forum: Qualitative Social Research*, 1 (3). http://www.qualitative-research.net/fqs-texte/3-00/3-00cortietal-e.htm.

Corti, L., Foster, J. and Thompson, P. (1995) Archiving qualitative research. *Social Research Update*, 10. Guildford: University of Surrey.

Crompton, R. (2003) Employment, Flexible Working and the Family. *British Journal of Sociology*, 53 (4): pp. 537–58.

Crompton, R. and Harris, F. (1998) Explaining Women's Employment Patterns: 'Orientations to Work' revisited. *British Journal of Sociology*, 49 (1): pp. 118–36.

Crompton, R. and Le Feuvre, N. (1996) Paid Employment and the Changing System of Gender Relations: a Cross-National Comparison. *Sociology*, 30 (3): pp. 427–45.

Crompton, R. and Lyonette, C. (2010) Family, class and gender 'strategies' in mothers' employment and childcare. In Scott, J., Crompton, R. and Lyonette, C. (eds) *Gender Inequalities in the 21st Century: New Barriers and Continuing Constraints*. Cheltenham: Edward Elgar.

———. (2011) Women's Career Success and Work–life Adaptations in the Accountancy and Medical Professions in Britain. *Gender, Work and Organization*, 18 (2): pp. 231–54.

Crow, G., Hatton, P., Lyon, D. and Strangleman, T. (2009) New Divisions of Labour?: Comparative Thoughts on the Current Recession. *Sociological Research Online*, 14 (2) http://www.socresonline.org.uk/14/2/10.html.

Dale, A., Arber, S. and Proctor, M. (1988) *Doing Secondary Analysis*. London: Unwin Hyman.

Dart, B. and Clarke, J. (1988) Sexism in Schools: A New Look. *Educational Review*, 40(1): pp. 41–9.

Davey, B., Murrells, T. and Robinson, S. (2005) Returning to Work After Maternity Leave. *Work, Employment and Society*, 19 (2): pp. 327–48.

Deem, R. (1994) Feminist Educator's Peregrination through Sociology: An Inaugural Lecture. Delivered at Lancaster University, 4 May 1994.

Delamont, S. (2003) *Feminist Sociology*. London: Sage.

Dennehy, K. and Mortimer, J. (1993) Work and Family Orientations of Contemporary Adolescent Boys and Girls. In Hood, J.C. (ed.) *Men, Work and Family*. London: Sage.

Department for Scientific and Industrial Research (1960) Human Sciences Committee, 22 March 1960, Agenda and Minutes. London: DSIR (National Archives DSIR 17/691).

Douglas, J.B. (1964) *Home and School*. London: MacGibbon Kee.

Dunning, E. (1971) The Development of Modern Football. In Dunning, E. (ed.) *The Sociology of Sport: A Selection of Readings*. London: Frank Cass.

———. (2006) *Working with Elias: Reminiscences of Elias's View of the Sociology – Anthropology Interface*. Paper presented at the Elias in the Twenty-First Century conference, University of Leicester, 10 April 2006.

Dunning, E. and Hughes, J. (2013) *Norbert Elias and Modern Sociology: Knowledge, Interdependence, Power, Process*. London: Bloomsbury.

Dyhouse, C. (2013) *Girl Trouble: Panic and Progress in the History of Young Women*. London: Zed Books.

Edley, N. and Wetherell, M. (1995) *Men in Perspective: Practice, Power and Identity*. London: Prentice Hall.

Elias, N. ([1939] 2000) *The Civilising Process*. London: Blackwell.

———. (1961) *Application for a Grant for Special Research to DSIR*. Unpublished. University of Leicester (Teresa Keil Collection).

———. (1962a) *Notes in Reply to the Staff Meeting from 16th October 1962*, 22 October 1962. Marbach: Deutsches Literaturarchiv.

———. (1962b) *Third Memorandum*. Unpublished. Marbach, Deutsches Literaturarchiv.

———. (1962c) *Second Memorandum*. Unpublished. Marbach, Deutsches Literaturarchiv.

———. (1962d) Unpublished letter to Conor Cruise O'Brien, 10 December 1962. Accra: University of Ghana.

———. (1963) Young Worker Project. Unpublished Letter to Illya Neustadt, 24 February 1963. Marbach: Deutsches Literaturarchiv.

———. (1964a) Unpublished Letter to Teresa Keil and David Riddell, 4 June 1964. Marbach: Deutsches Literaturarchiv.

———. (1964b) *A Note On the Problem of Typing the Questionnaires*. Unpublished, 21 October 1964. Marbach: Deutsches Literaturarchiv.

———. (1965) Unpublished Letter to A.B. Cherns, 9 November 1965. Marbach: Deutsches Literaturarchiv.

————. (1970) *What is Sociology?* New York: Columbia University Press.

————. (1972) Unpublished Letter to Jennifer Platt, 4 March 1972. Marbach: Deutsches Literaturarchiv.

————. (1980) The Civilising of Parents. In Goudsblom, J. and Mennell, S. (eds) (1998) *The Norbert Elias Reader*. Blackwell: London.

————. (1987) Retreat of the Sociologists. *Theory, Culture and Society*, 4: pp. 223–47.

————. (1994) *Reflections on a Life*. London, Polity.

————. (1998) The Changing Balance of Power between the Sexes in Ancient Rome. In Mennell, S. and Goudsblom, J. (eds) *Norbert Elias: On Civilization, Power and Knowledge*. Chicago: The University of Chicago Press.

Elliott, J. (2008) The Narrative Potential of the British Birth Cohort Studies. *Qualitative Research*, 8 (3): 411–21.

Evans, K. and Furlong, A. (1997) Metaphors of Youth Transitions: Niches, Pathways, Trajectories or Navigations. In Bynner, J., Chisholm, L. and Furlong, A. (eds) *Youth, Citizenship and Social Change in a European Context*. Aldershot: Ashgate Publishing.

Evans, T. and Thane, P. (2006) Secondary analysis of Dennis Marsden's *Mothers Alone. Methodological Innovations Online*, 1 (2). http://erdt.plymouth.ac.uk/ mionline/public_html/viewarticle.php?id=31 [Accessed 23 June 2012].

Field, D. (ed.) (1974) *Social Psychology for Sociologists*. London: Nelson.

Fielding, N. (2000) The Shared Fate of Two Innovations in Qualitative Methodology: The Relationship of Qualitative Software and Secondary Analysis of Archived Qualitative Data. *Forum Qualitative Sozialforschung / Forum: Qualitative Social Research*, 1 (3), http://www.qualitative-research.net /fqs-texte/3–00/3–00fielding-e.htm [Accessed 7 February 2013].

Fletcher, J. (1997) *Violence and Civilisation: An Introduction to the Work of Norbert Elias*. Cambridge: Polity Press.

Francis, B. (2002) Is the Future Really Female? The Impact and Implications of Gender for 14–16 Year Olds' Career Choices. *Journal of Education and Work*, 15 (1): pp. 75–88.

Frith, S. (1984) *The Sociology of Youth*. Lancashire: Causeway Press.

Fuller, A. and Unwin, L. (1998) Reconceptualising Apprenticeship: Exploring the Relationship between Work and Learning. *Journal of Vocational Education and Training*, 50 (2): pp. 153–71.

————. (2001) *From Skill Formation to Social Inclusion: The Changing Meaning of Apprenticeship and its Relationship to Communities and Workplaces in England*. Paper presented to the Work, Employment and Society Conference, University of Nottingham, 11–13 September 2001.

————. (2003) Creating a 'Modern Apprenticeship': A Critique of the UK's Multi-Sector, Social Inclusion Approach. *Journal of Education and Work*, 16 (1): 5–25.

Furlong, A. (1986) Schools and the Structure of Female Occupational Aspirations. *British Journal of Sociology of Education*, 7 (4): pp. 367–77.

————. (1992) *Growing Up in a Classless Society?* Edinburgh: Edinburgh University Press.

————. (1993) *Schooling for Jobs*. Aldershot: Avebury.

Furlong, A. and Biggart, A. (1999) Framing Choices: A Longitudinal Study of Occupational Aspirations Among 13 to 16 Year Olds. *Journal of Education and Work*, 12 (1): pp. 21–35.

Furlong, A. and Cartmel, F. (1997) *Young People and Social Change: Individualization and Risk in Late Modernity*. Buckingham: Open University Press.

Furlong, A. Cartmel, F., Biggart, A., Sweeting, H. and West, P. (2002) *Complex Transitions: Linearity in Youth Transitions as a Predictor of 'Success'*. Paper presented to the British Sociological Association Annual Conference, University of Leicester, March 2002.

Gaskell, J. (1983) The Reproduction of Family Life: Perspectives of Male and Female Adolescents. *British Journal of the Sociology of Education*, 4 (1): pp. 19–38.

Geiger, T., Moore, N. and Savage, M. (2010) *The Archive in Question*. CRESC Working Paper Series, WP 81.

Gillies, V. and Edwards, R. (2012) Working with Archived Classic Family and Community Studies: Illuminating Past and Present Conventions around Acceptable Research Practice. *International Journal of Social Research Methodology*, 15 (4): pp. 321–30.

Glasser, S. (1999) Percy Cohen: Sociologist Who Served LSE and Fought Racism. *The Guardian*, Wednesday 13 October 1999. http://www.theguardian.com/news/1999/oct/13/guardianobituaries4.

Glueck, S. and Glueck, E. (1930) *500 Criminal Careers*. New York: A.A. Knopf.

————. (1950) *Unravelling Juvenile Delinquency*. New York: The Commonwealth Fund.

Goodwin, J. (1997) The Republic of Ireland and Effective Vocational Education and Training: Moving on From Finlay and Niven. *International Journal of Vocational Education and Training*, 5 (2): pp. 33–56.

————. (1999) *Men's Work and Male Lives: Men and Work in Britain*. Aldershot: Ashgate Publishing.

————. (2001) *The Influence of Family and School on Dublin Men's Working Lives: Preliminary Findings*. The Centre for Labour Market Studies, University of Leicester Working Paper No. 30.

————. (2002) Irish Men and Work in North-County Dublin. *Journal of Gender Studies*, 11: pp. 151–66.

Goodwin, J., Hills, K. and Ashton, D. (1999) Training and Development in the United Kingdom. *International Journal of Training and Development*, 3 (2): pp. 167–79.

Goodwin, J. and Hughes, J. (2011) Ilya Neustadt, Norbert Elias, and the Leicester Department: Personal Correspondence and the History of Sociology in Britain. *British Journal of Sociology*, 26 (4): pp. 677–95.

Goodwin, J. and O'Connor, H. (2001) *'I couldn't wait for the day': Young workers' reflections on education during the transition to work in the 1960s*. The Centre for Labour Market Studies, University of Leicester Working Paper No. 33.

———. (2002) *Forty Years On: Norbert Elias and the Young Worker Project*. The Centre for Labour Market Studies, University of Leicester Working Paper No. 35.

———. (2003) *Exploring Complex Transitions: Looking Back At the 'Golden Age' of Youth Transitions*. ESRC Young Worker Project (Research Paper No. 5). Leicester: University of Leicester, The Centre for Labour Market Studies.

———. (2004) *Boys' Gendered Transitions for School to Work*. ESRC Young Worker Project (Research Paper No. 7). Leicester: University of Leicester, The Centre for Labour Market Studies.

———. (2009) Through the Interviewer's Lens: Representations of 1960s Households and Families in a Lost Sociological Study. *Sociological Research Online*, 14 (4).

Goody, J. (2006) *The Theft of History*. Cambridge: Cambridge University Press.

Grieco, M. (1987) *Keeping it in the Family: Social Networks and Employment Chance*. London: Tavistock.

Griffin, C. (1984) Young Women and Work: the Transition from School to the Labour Market for Young Working Class Women. Stencilled paper, CCCS, Birmingham University.

———. (1985) *Typical Girls?* London: Routledge.

Halsey, A.H. (2004) *A History of Sociology in Britain*. Oxford: Oxford University Press.

Hammersley, M. (1997) Qualitative Data Archiving: Some Reflections On Its Prospects and Its Problems. *Sociology*, 13 (1): pp. 131–42.

Harris, I. (1995) *Messages Men Hear: Constructing Masculinity*. London: Taylor and Francis.

Haywood, C. and Mac an Ghaill, M. (2003) *Men and Masculinities*. Buckingham: Open University Press.

Heaton, J. (1998) Secondary Analysis of Qualitative Data. *Social Research Update*, 22. Guildford, UK: University of Surrey.

Hebdige, D. (1974) *The Style of the Mods*. Birmingham, UK: Centre for Contemporary Cultural Studies.

———. (1979) *Sub-Culture: The Meaning of Style*. London: Methuen.

Hinds, P., Vogel, R. and Clarke-Steffen, L. (1997) The Possibilities and Pitfalls of Doing Secondary Analysis of a Qualitative Data Set. *Qualitative Health Research*, 7: pp. 408–24.

Hodkinson, P. (2009) Young People's Fashion and Style. In Furlong, A. (ed.) *Handbook of Youth and Young Adulthood: New Perspectives and Agendas*. London: Routledge.

Hubbard, G. (2000) The Usefulness of Indepth Life History Interviews for Exploring the role of Social Structure and Human Agency in Youth Transitions. *Sociological Research Online*, 4 (4). http://www.socresonline.org.uk/4/4/hubbard.html.

Hughes, J. (1998) Norbert Elias and Process Sociology. In Stones, R. (ed.) *Key Sociological Thinkers*. London: Macmillan.

Irwin, S. and Winterton, M. (2011) *Qualitative Secondary Analysis in Practice: an extended guide*. Timescapes Working Paper. http://www.timescapes.leeds.ac.uk/assets/files/secondary_analysis/working%20papers/WP7-Nov-2011.pdf [Accessed 12 January 2013].

James, L. (2008) United by Gender or Divided by Class? *Gender, Work and Organization*, 15 (4): pp. 394–412.

Jenkins, R. (1983) *Lads, Citizens, and Ordinary Kids: Working-Class Youth Life-Styles in Belfast*. London: Routledge and Kegan Paul.

Jephcott, P. (1942) *Girls Growing Up*. London: Faber and Faber.

———. (1943) *Clubs for Girls. Notes for New Helpers at Clubs*. London: Faber and Faber.

———. (1948) *Rising Twenty. Notes on Ordinary Girls*. London: Faber and Faber.

———. (1954) *Some Young People*. London: George Allen and Unwin.

———. (1967) *Time of One's Own: Leisure and Young People*. Edinburgh: Oliver & Boyd.

Jephcott, P., Seear, N. and Smith, J.H. (1962) *Married Women Working*. London: Allen and Unwin.

Johnston, L., MacDonald, R., Mason, P., Ridley, L. and Webster, C. (2000) *Snakes and Ladders: Young People, Transitions and Social Exclusion*. Bristol: The Policy Press.

Joly, M. (2011) Norbert Elias's Networks in the British Intellectual Field Before His Appointment in Leicester (1945–54). Paper presented at the BSA Conference, London, 6–8 April 2011, pp. 1–9.

Jones, G. (1995) *Leaving Home*. Buckingham: Open University Press.

Keil, E.T. (1964) Unpublished letter to Norbert Elias, 26 June 1964. Marbach: Deutsches Literaturarchiv.

———. (2000) Correspondence with the authors, 28 June 2000. Leicester: University of Leicester.

Keil, E.T. and Riddell, D.S. (1964) Unpublished letter to Norbert Elias, 22 May 1964. Marbach: Deutsches Literaturarchiv.

Keil, E.T., Riddell, D.S. and Green, B.S. (1974) Youth and Work: Problems and Perspectives. In Williams, W.M. (ed.) *Occupational Choice*. London: Allen and Unwin.

Keil, E.T., Riddell, D.S. and Tipton, C.B. (1963a) Unpublished letter to Norbert Elias, 1 March 1963. Marbach: Deutsches Literaturarchiv.

———. (1963b) A Research Note: The Entry of School Leavers into Employment. *British Journal of Industrial Relations*, 1(3): pp. 408–11.

Kelley, J. and Kenway, J. (2001) Managing Youth Transitions in the Network Society. *British Journal of Sociology of Education*, 22 (1): pp. 19–33.

Kettler, D., Loader, C. and Meja, V. (2008) *Karl Mannheim and the Legacy of Max Weber*. Aldershot: Ashgate.

Kiernan, K. (1992) The Impact of Family Disruption in Childhood on Transitions Made in Young Adult Life. *Population Studies*, 46: pp. 213–34.

Kilminster, R. (1987) Introduction to Elias. *Theory, Culture and Society*, 4: pp. 213–22.

King, R. and O'Connor, H. (1996) Migration and Gender: Irish Women in Leicester. *Geography*, 81(4): 311–25.

Klein, V. (1965) *Britain's Married Women Workers*. London: Routledge.

Korte, H. (2001) Perspectives on a Long Life: Norbert Elias and the Process of Civilization. In Salumets, T. (ed.) *Norbert Elias and Human Interdependencies*. Montreal: McGill-Queen's University Press.

———. (2013) Norbert Elias at the University of Leicester. *Cambio. Rivista sulle trasformazioni sociali*, 5 June 2013. http://www.cambio.unifi.it/upload/sub/ Numero%205/12_Korte.pdf.

Laub, J.H. and Sampson, R.J. (2003) *Shared Beginnings, Divergent Lives: Delinquent Boys to Age 70*. Harvard: Harvard University Press.

Laurie, P. (1965) *Teenage Revolution*. London: Anthony Blond.

Lawy, R. (2002) Transition and Transformation: The Experiences of Two Young People. *Journal of Education and Work*, 15 (2): pp. 201–8.

Lawy, R. and Bloomer, M. (2003) Identity and Learning as a Lifelong Project: Situating Vocational Education and Work. *International Journal of Lifelong Education*, 22 (1): pp. 24–42.

Layder, D., Ashton, D. and Sung, J. (1991) The Empirical Correlates of Action and Structure: The Transition from School to Work. *Sociology*, 25 (3): pp. 447–64.

Leicester Mercury. (2013) 50 Years Ago Beatles Made Their Low-Key Debut in Leicester. http://www.leicestermercury.co.uk/50-years-ago-Beatles-low-key-d ebut-Leicester/story-18563919-detail/story.html [Accessed 1 March 2014].

Liston, K. and Mennell, S. (2009) Ill Met in Ghana Jack Goody and Norbert Elias on Process and Progress in Africa. *Theory, Culture & Society*, 26 (7–8): pp. 52–70.

Lloyd, T. (1999) *Young Men, the Job Market and Gendered Work*. York: Joseph Rowntree Foundation.

London School of Economics (1960) *Women, Wife and Worker*. Problems of Progress in Industry, 10. DSIR. London: HMSO.

Lovejoy, M. and Stone, P (2011) Opting Back In: The Influence of Time at Home on Professional Women's Career Redirection after Opting Out. *Gender, Work and Organization*, 19 (6): pp. 631–53.

Maizels, J. (1970) *Adolescent Needs and the Transition from School to Work*. London: Athlone Press.

Marshall, T.H. (1982) Foreword. In Giddens, T. and Mackenzie, G. (1982) *Social Class and the Division of Labour: Essays in Honour of Ilya Neustadt*. Cambridge: Cambridge University Press.

McDowell, L. (2001) *Young Men Leaving School: White Working Class Masculinity*. Leicester: Youth Work Press.

McKinklay, A. and Hampton, J. (1991) Making Ships, Making Men: Working for John Brown's Between the Wars. *Oral History*, Spring: pp. 21–8.

McRobbie, A. and Garber, J. (1976) Girls and Subcultures: An Exploration. In Hall, S. and Jefferson, T. (eds) *Resistance through Rituals: Youth Subcultures in Post-war Britain*. London: Hutchinson.

Mennell, S. (1992) *Norbert Elias: An Introduction*. London: Blackwell.

Mennell, S. and Goudsblom, J. (1998) Introduction. In Elias, N. (1998) *On Civilization, Power and Knowledge*. Chicago: University of Chicago Press.

Mills, C.W. (1959) *The Sociological Imagination*. New York: Oxford University Press.

Morrison, A. and MacIntyre, D. (1971) *Schools and Socialisation*. Harmondsworth: Penguin.

Myrdal, A. and Klein, V. (1956) *Women's Two Roles: Home and Work*. London: Routledge and Kegan Paul.

Nagel, U. and Wallace, C. (1997) Participation and Identification in Risk Societies: European Perspectives. In Bynner, J., Chisholm, L. and Furlong, A. (eds) *Youth, Citizenship and Social Change in a European Context*. Aldershot: Ashgate Publishing.

Nayak, A. and Kehily, M.J. (2008) *Gender, Youth and Culture: Young Masculinities and Femininities*. Basingstoke: Palgrave Macmillan.

Neustadt, I. (1959a) *Employment of Married Women in a Leicester Hosiery Factory: Brief Statement of Progress of the Research*. Department of Sociology, University of Leicester. Unpublished.

———. (1959b) Research into *Employment of Married Women in a Leicester Hosiery Factory*. Memorandum, 20 October 1959. Department of Sociology, University of Leicester. Unpublished.

———. (1962) Unpublished letter to Norbert Elias, 22 October 1962. Marbach: Deutsches Literaturarchiv.

———. (1964a) Unpublished letter to Norbert Elias, 8 June 1964. Marbach: Deutsches Literaturarchiv.

———. (1964b) Unpublished letter to Norbert Elias, 20 July 1964. Marbach: Deutsches Literaturarchiv.

Nilan, P. (2000) 'You're Hopeless I Swear to God': Shifting Masculinities in Classroom Talk. *Gender and Education*, 12: pp. 53–68.

O'Brien, C.C. (1963) Unpublished letter to Professor Norbert Elias, May 28 1963. Accra: University of Ghana.

O'Connor, H. (2006) *Women, Work and Childcare: An Intergenerational Study of Two Generations of Women*. Unpublished PhD thesis, University of Leicester.

O'Connor, H. and Goodwin, J. (2004) She Wants to Be Like Her Mum. *Journal of Education and Work*, 17 (1): pp. 95–118.

O'Connor, H. and Madge, C. (2001) Cybermothers: Online Synchronous Interviewing Using Conferencing Software. *Sociological Research Online*, 5 (4).

Paechter, C. (2003) Masculinities and Femininities as Communities of Practice. *Women's Studies International Forum*, 26: pp. 69–77.

Penn, R. (1985) *Skilled Workers in the Class Structure*. Cambridge: Cambridge University Press.

Phizacklea, A. and Wolkowitz, C. (1995) *Homeworking Women*. London: Sage.

Pilcher, J. (1995) *Age and Generation in Modern Britain*. Oxford: Oxford University Press.

———. (1996) Transitions to and from the Labour Market: Younger and Older People and Employment. *Work, Employment and Society*, 10 (1): pp. 161–73.

Platt, J. (1976) *Realities of Social Research*. London: Catto Windus.

———. (2003) *The British Sociological Association: A Sociological History*. Durham: Sociology Press.

———. (2004) Epilogue Essay: Jennifer Platt. In Halsey, A.H. (2004) *A History of Sociology in Britain*. Oxford: Oxford University Press.

Pollard, S. (1983) *The Development of the British Economy, 1914–1980*. London: Edward Arnold.

Pollert, A. (1981) *Girls, Wives, Factory Lives*. London: Macmillan.

Probert, B. (2005) 'I Just Couldn't Fit It In': Gender and Unequal Outcomes in Academic Careers. *Gender, Work and Organization*, 12 (1): pp. 50–72.

Public Record Office. (2001) *The Public Records System*, 28 August 2006. http://www.nationalarchives.gov.uk/foi/?source=ddmenu_about2.

Pye, N. (1972) *Leicester and Its Region*. Leicester: Leicester University Press.

Rauta, I. and Hunt, A. (1972) *Fifth Form Girls: Their Hopes for the Future*. London: HMSO.

Reisz, M. (2009) Sheila Allen, 1930–2009. *Times Higher Education*, 19 February 2009. http://www.timeshighereducation.co.uk/news/people/obituaries/sheila-allen-1930-2009/405398.article.

Riddell, D.S. and Keil, E.T. (1963) *Young Worker Project: Note on Sample*. Unpublished. University of Leicester (Teresa Keil Collection).

Riddell, D.S., Keil, E.T. and Green, B. (1963) Letter to Norbert Elias, 2 December 1963. Marbach: Deutsches Literaturarchiv.

Roberts, K. (1975) The Developmental Theory of Occupational Choice: A Critique and an Alternative. In Esland, G. et al. (eds) *People and Work*. Edinburgh: Holme McDougal.

———. (1977) The Social Conditions, Consequences and Limitations of Careers Guidance. *British Journal of Guidance and Counselling*, 5: pp. 1–9.

———. (1983) *Youth and Leisure*. London: Allen and Unwin.

———. (1984) *School Leavers and their Prospects. Youth and Labour Markets in the 1980s*. Milton Keynes: Open University Press.

————. (1995) *Youth and Unemployment in Modern Britain*. Oxford: Oxford University Press.

————. (1997a) Same Activities, Different Meanings: British Youth Cultures in the 1990s. *Leisure Studies*, 16: pp. 1–15.

————. (1997b) Structure and Agency: The New Youth Research Agenda. In Bynner, J., Chisholm, L. and Furlong, A. (eds) *Youth, Citizenship and Social Change in a European Context*. Aldershot: Ashgate Publishing.

Rojek, C. (2004) An Anatomy of the Leicester School of Sociology: An Interview with Eric Dunning. *The Journal of Classical Sociology*, 4 (3): pp. 337–59.

Ryan. P. (2001) The School to Work Transition: A Cross National Perspective. *Journal of Economic Literature*, XXXIX: pp. 34–92.

Ryrie, A.C. and Weir, A.D. (1978) *Getting a Trade. A Study of Apprentices' Experience of Apprenticeship*. London: Hodder and Stoughton.

Savage, M. (2005) Revisiting Classic Qualitative Studies. *Forum Qualitative Sozialforschung / Forum: Qualitative Social Research*, 6 (3), (Art. 31). http://qualitative-research.net/fqs/fqs-eng.htm.

Sharpe. S. (1976) *Just Like a Girl: How Girls Learn to Be Women*. Harmondsworth: Penguin.

————. (1984) *Double Identity: The Lives of Working Mothers*. Harmondsworth: Penguin.

Smith, D. (2000) *Norbert Elias and Modern Social Theory*. London: Sage.

Strathdee. R. (2001) Changes in Social Capital and School to Work Transitions. *Work Employment and Society*, 15(2): pp. 311–26.

Szakolczai, A. (2000) Norbert Elias and Franz Borkenau: Intertwined Life-Works. *Theory, Culture and Society*, 17 (2): pp. 45–69.

Thompson, P. (2000) Re-Using Qualitative Research Data: A Personal Account. *Forum Qualitative Sozialforschung / Forum: Qualitative Social Research*, 1 (3). http://www.qualitative-research.net/fqs-texte/3-00/3-00thompson-e.htm.

Thomson, R., Bell, R., Holland, J., Henderson, McGrellis, S. and Sharpe, S. (2002) Critical moments: choice, chance and opportunity in young people's narratives of transition. *Sociology*, 36(2) pp. 335–54.

Times Educational Supplement (1971) *Lost Property*. London: Times Educational Supplement 29 January 1971.

Tolson, A. (1987) *The Limits of Masculinity*. London: Routledge.

Turner, B. 2006 British Sociology and Public Intellectuals: Consumer Society and Imperial Decline. *The British Journal of Sociology*, 57 (2): pp. 169–88.

Unwin, L. and Wellington, J. (2001) *Young People's Perspectives on Education, Training and Employment*. London: Kogan Page.

Van Krieken, R. (1989) Violence, Self-Discipline and Morality: Beyond the Civilizing Process. *Sociological Review*, 37 (2): pp. 193–218.

————. (1998) *Norbert Elias*. London: Routledge.

Veness, T. (1962) *School Leavers: Their Aspirations and Expectations*. London: Methuen.

Vickerstaff, S. (2001) *Learning for Life? The Post-war Experience of Apprenticeship.* Paper presented to the Work, Employment and Society Conference, University of Nottingham, 11–13 September 2001.

———. (2003) Apprenticeship in the 'Golden Age': Were Youth Transitions Really Smooth and Unproblematic Back Then? *Work, Employment and Society,* 17 (2): pp. 269–87.

Wallace, C. (1986) From Girls and Boys to Women and Men: The Social Reproduction of Gender Roles in the Transition from School to Work. In Walker, S. and Barton, L. (eds) *Youth, Unemployment and Schooling.* Milton Keynes: Open University Press.

———. (1987) *For Richer, For Poorer. Growing Up in and Out of Work.* London: Tavistock.

Walters, S. (2005) Making the Best of a Bad Job? Female Part-Timers' Orientations and Attitudes to Work. *Gender, Work and Organisation,* 12 (3): pp. 193–216.

Warren, T. (2000) Women in Low Status Part-Time Jobs: A Class and Gender Analysis. *Sociological Research Online,* 4 (4). http://www.socresonline.org.uk /4/4/warren.html.

———. (2003) A Privileged Pole?: On Women's Diverse Economic Positions in Britain. *Gender, Work and Organization,* 10 (4): pp. 605–28.

Watts, A.G. (1967) Counselling and the Organisation of Careers Work in Schools. *Aspects of Education,* 5 pp. 44–53.

Westwood, S. (1984) *All Day, Every Day. Factory and Family in the Making of Women's Lives.* London: Pluto Press.

Wheelock, J. and Jones, K. (2002) Grandparents Are the Next Best Thing': Informal Childcare for Working Parents in Urban Britain. *Journal of Social Policy,* 31 (3): pp. 441–63.

Wight, D. (1993) *Workers Not Wasters.* Edinburgh: Edinburgh University Press.

Williams, G. and Quinn, M. (2014) MacMillan's Children: A Long View of Young Workers and Trade Unions, *Industrial Relations Journal,* 45 (2) pp. 137–52.

Williams. J., Murphy, P. and Dunning, E. (1984) *Hooligans Abroad: The Behaviour and Control of English Fans in Continental Europe.* London: Routledge.

Willis, P. (1977) *Learning to Labour: How Working Class Kids Get Working Class Jobs.* Farnborough: Saxon House.

Wilson, M.P. (1957) Vocational Preferences of Secondary Modern School Children. *British Journal of Educational Psychology,* 23.

Wolfinger, W.H. (2002) On Writing Field Notes: Collection Strategies and Background Expectancies. *Qualitative Research,* 2 (1): pp. 85–95.

Wood, G.J. and Newton, J. (2006) Childlessness and Women Managers: 'Choice', Context and Discourses. *Gender, Work and Organization,* 13 (4): pp. 339–58.

Yeandle, S. (2005) *Older Workers and Work-Life Balance.* York: Joseph Rowntree Foundation. http://www.shu.ac.uk/research/csi.

Young Worker Project (1962a) Minutes of Second Meeting, 7 March 1962. Unpublished. Marbach: Deutsches Literaturarchiv.

————. (1962b) Minutes of Fifth Meeting, 18 April 1962. Unpublished. Marbach: Deutsches Literaturarchiv.

————. (1962c) Minutes of Sixth Meeting, 9 May 1962. Unpublished. Marbach: Deutsches Literaturarchiv.

————. (1962d) Minutes of Sixth Meeting, 9 May 1962. Unpublished. Marbach: Deutsches Literaturarchiv.

————. (1962e) Minutes of Tenth Meeting, 6–7 June 1962. Unpublished. University of Leicester (Teresa Keil Collection).

————. (1962f) Minutes of Eleventh Meeting, 9 May 1962. Unpublished. Marbach: Deutsches Literaturarchiv.

Index

For Product Safety Concerns and Information please contact our EU
representative GPSR@taylorandfrancis.com Taylor & Francis Verlag GmbH,
Kaufingerstraße 24, 80331 München, Germany

Printed and bound by CPI Group (UK) Ltd, Croydon, CR0 4YY
01/05/2025
01858357-0001